Springtown Camp

from the inside

Willie Deery

GUILDHALL PRESS

Published in May 2010

GUILDHALL PRESS
Unit 15, Ráth Mór Business Park
Bligh's Lane
Derry BT48 0LZ
Ireland
T: (00 44 28) 7136 4413
E: info@ghpress.com • W: www.ghpress.com

The author/photographers assert their moral rights in this work in accordance with the Copyright, Designs and Patents Act 1998.

Cover and inside design by Kevin Hippsley
Copyright © Willie Deery/Guildhall Press
www.springtowncamp.com

ISBN: 978 1 906271 30 5

A CIP record for this book is available from the British Library.

 Guildhall Press is grateful to Derry City Council for Service Level Agreement support under the remit of the Heritage and Museum Service.

 *Proceeds from this book will be donated to Derry-based charity Action With Effect (www.actionwitheffect.org) and towards maintenance of the non-profit Springtown Camp website (www.springtowncamp.com).*

All rights reserved. No part of this publication may be reproduced or transmitted in any form or by any means, electronic or mechanical, including photocopy, recording, or any information storage or retrieval system, without permission in writing from the publisher. This book is sold subject to the condition that it shall not, by way of trade or otherwise, be lent, resold or otherwise circulated without the publisher's prior consent in any form of binding or cover other than that in which it is originally published and without a similar condition to this condition being imposed on the subsequent purchaser.

Acknowledgements

I wish to express my sincere appreciation to the many individuals, groups and organisations in Derry and across the world who helped me research, write and produce this very personal account of life in Springtown Camp.

To Paddy McCourt and Gareth Flanagan for their patience in teaching me basic computer skills which enabled me to capture the words and images necessary to tell the story.

To the following for sharing their memories, images, thoughts and experiences: Jim Sullivan, Leo 'Moose' Sangiolo, Robert L Reiss, Bill Marschner, Sandy McDermott, Marvin L Hoffrichter, Mary Poshydaew, Jimmy Jennings, Kathleen Kelly, Tommy Cooke, Katie Campbell, Maureen Fox, Mary McMonagle, George Lynch, Brendan Wilkinson, Stevie Wilkinson, Erin Hutcheon, Lornie McMonagle, Hugo McConnell, Seamus McConnell, Hugo Lewis, Lily Stanley, Liam and Bernie Quigley, John McLaughlin, Rory Quigley, Sadie Campbell, Philomena Doherty, John Doherty, John Bryson, Patrick Durnin, Peter Divin and Phil Cunningham.

Thanks to all those organisations who supplied, or permitted access to, articles, photographs or other research material: Derry Navcommsta Alumni Association, Getty Images, *Derry Journal*, *Londonderry Sentinel*, *Irish Independent*, *Mirrorpix*, *New York Times*, *Irish News*, British Library, Creggan 60th Exhibition, Derry Heritage and Museum Service, Bloody Sunday Trust, Libraries NI, Bigger and McDonald Collection, Derry Central Library and their very helpful staff.

To Kevin, Declan, Joe, Jenni and Paul at Guildhall Press for their professional assistance and advice.

If I have omitted anyone, please accept my apologies.

To all of you, my heartfelt thanks for your time, input and assistance. I hope I have done you all justice.

Any omissions or errors are mine and hopefully will be overlooked in the reading.

Dedicated to all those women, men and children who shared their lives, endured the hardships, and created lasting friendships in Springtown Camp over many years. The fondest of memories will always dwell with me.

INTRODUCTION

Writing and researching this book has given me great pleasure. I travelled extensively to uncover as much detail about Springtown Camp as I possibly could. In the USA, I met former American Naval personnel who served in the camp during World War II and many others with a connection to the camp.

I have been privileged to receive hand-written accounts from those US residents I couldn't speak to personally of their time in the camp. Jim Sullivan, co-founder of the Derry Navcommsta Alumni Association, assisted greatly in making many of these valuable contacts.

I have also talked to numerous former Springtown Camp residents who are now domiciled throughout the rest of the globe – in Australia and New Zealand, sun-drenched Port Elizabeth in South Africa and the rainy streets of Bradford in west Yorkshire. I also visited London, Manchester, Glasgow and North Wales, as well, of course, as talking to countless ex-campers still resident in Derry.

To my delight, I found everyone only too willing to talk about their time and experiences in the camp.

I have always believed that the story of Springtown Camp should be told. I thought it was important that today's generation could discover the harsh conditions their parents, grandparents and great-grandparents had endured in relatively recent times gone by. And equally important, appreciate how they coped and survived, how they reared good families and fought for their dignity in the face of adversity.

It is what everyone who lived in the camp from that very first day on Thursday 22 August 1946, until the very last day on Wednesday 11 October 1967, truly deserved.

The camp residents were defenceless people who had to suffer injustice, prejudice and a denial of their basic human rights, simply because they were poor, mostly unemployed and mainly Catholic. Their choices were stark – emigrate from the city of their birth, stay and tolerate the grinding reality, or stand up and confront the powers-that-be.

I tell this story through my own eyes as a young boy growing up in the camp, happy and contented, but oblivious to the unrelenting everyday pressures which our parents lived under. Until finally realising the true effect it had on them.

Everyone who lived there has a story to tell of Springtown Camp . . .

This is mine.

Willie Deery

Contents

Chapter 1	The US Navy Set Up Camp	7
Chapter 2	Housing Conditions and the Struggle for a Home	25
Chapter 3	Early Battles with the Corporation and Rural Council	36
Chapter 4	Getting Acquainted	61
Chapter 5	Jane Russell Adoption	68
Chapter 6	Early Childhood Days	79
Chapter 7	Setting Up Shop	90
Chapter 8	New School and Making Do	94
Chapter 9	Changing Seasons	122
Chapter 10	Exodus	138
Chapter 11	Tip, TV and Teens	144
Chapter 12	Doherty Fire and Women's Protest	156
Chapter 13	New Houses and Men's Retreat	164
Chapter 14	Big Boys and Girls	168
Chapter 15	The 10.40 to Springtown	175
Chapter 16	Women's Protest Continues	185
Chapter 17	First Job and Great Characters	194
Chapter 18	Protests Intensify	214
Chapter 19	Mothers of the Camp	234
Chapter 20	End of the Camp	247
Chapter 21	After the Camp	252
Appendix A	Springtown Camp Milestones	269
Appendix B	Tenant Listings 1947–66	292

Chapter 1
The US Navy Set Up Camp

As people throughout the world gladly said goodbye to 1940, they lived in hope the New Year would bring an improvement on the previous one. That looked a forlorn aspiration as World War II raged between the nations of the world with one notable exception – America. It was after high-powered, secret meetings between American and British leaders in early 1941 that Colonel Julian C Smith and Major Jack P Juhan from the United States arrived in London for several top-level briefings. Two days later, they visited the British amphibious warfare base at Rosneath in Scotland, where they had a meeting with British Prime Minister Winston Churchill.

Having viewed Rosneath's facilities and surrounding areas, they returned with their findings to the United States. Soon afterwards, in May of the same year, the American Government sent two high-ranking officers, Major George F Good and Captain Bruce T Hemphill, to England on a secret mission. This time, they were accompanied by several top naval civil engineers and they were to look at four possible base sites, two in Scotland and two in Northern Ireland.

Their itinerary included a five-day stay in Derry in which they surveyed the city and other outlying areas, one of which was the port at Lisahally. The visit spurred a rapid succession of decisions and events, and on 12 June 1941, the British Government signed a contract with American firm GA Fuller-Merritt Chapman Corporation to construct bases in Northern Ireland and Scotland, using £35m of lend-lease funds.

The geographic focal point of the plan, known as Base 1, entailed the construction of naval bases and camps in Derry designed for the refuelling and repair of destroyers and submarines.

On Monday 30 June 1941, 362 'civilian' technicians and twenty-five supervisory officers from the US Navy's Civil Engineer Corps sailed into Derry and

Above: A view of Northland Road approaching the camp gate before the US Navy built the huts, 1940.
Below: The road leading to the Branch Road past Jackson's big house. Picture taken just before the US Navy built Springtown Camp, 1940.

were stationed at Ebrington Barracks. A further 900 American civilian contractors were later to arrive and begin construction of several naval bases. The foothold in Derry was crucial to American operations, because the US fleet could not operate efficiently more than 2,000 miles from a naval base.

The local Derry people looked on in amazement as large building equipment, including mobile cranes, bulldozers, road graders, ditch diggers and mobile welding plants, rolled off American ships and onto the streets of Derry. This was the first time such equipment had ever been seen in the city and was used to great effect in rapid construction work at Lisahally, Springtown Camp, Creevagh and other important installations. Upwards of 2,000 local workers were employed as tradesmen, labourers and drivers. For the first time in living memory, Derry had almost full employment.

US Navy's Creevagh Camp Hospital, 1942.

Springtown Camp was built in lightning-fast time, and to local people living in close proximity, it seemed that the huts went up practically overnight. In what was previously a green field covered with buttercups and daisies, military-style accommodation sprang up before our very eyes.

'It was as if you went to bed at night and woke up in the morning and the field was full of green corrugated-tin huts,' said one local woman.

Springtown was to be one of the main bases in Derry for the billeting of US personnel. It was certainly the biggest and best equipped. By the end of that year, American civilian workers in Derry had doubled to over 700. At this stage, the US had a massive array of facilities, including radio installations, a ship- and submarine-repair base, storage facilities already constructed in Derry and major works at Lisahally.

World War II was in progress, although the United States was not in the war at this point. That was soon to change, because on the now-infamous date of Sunday 7 December 1941, the Japanese Navy attacked the US Naval base at Pearl Harbour, Hawaii. The attack occurred before the Japanese declared war on America, provoking a global outrage. Now the world's most powerful nation was at war. The battle of the oceans was, of course, of the utmost importance, as it would have a significant influence on the outcome of the war itself.

The first 'official' US servicemen to arrive in the British Isles after the attack on Pearl Harbour arrived in Derry on 18 January 1942 on the trawler *Albatross* and were duly quartered in barracks at their plush, newly built headquarters in Springtown Camp. They consisted of the Headquarters and Service Company under Major James J Dugan from Boston, Massachusetts, and B Company under Captain Frank A Martincheck. All were suitably assigned to their respective billets/huts. A further and larger contingent was to arrive on the destroyers *Wilkies*, *Roper*, *Madison* and *Sturtevant*. The story of Springtown Camp had begun.

Springtown Camp commanders Captain Frank Martincheck and Major James Dugan, 1942.

By that time, a substantial amount of work had already been carried out, which included a large administrative complex, underground bombproof rooms at Magee College, a jetty at Lisahally, the accommodation at Springtown Camp and at Beech Hill, Ardmore, and a 200-bed hospital at Creevagh.

On Thursday 5 February 1942, Derry City was officially commissioned as a naval operation base, thus becoming the US Navy's first shore establishment in Europe; by 22 February 1942, ship-repair facilities and shops were ready for use. Derry City then became the main port for the refuelling, repairs and servicing of the US fleet of destroyers and submarines that were used for the invasion of Europe.

The camp, which was surrounded with green fields, was ringed with an 8ft-high chain-link fence with three lines of barbed wire on top. The two entrances to the camp were heavily guarded around the clock by US Marines: the main one was the top gate with entry from the Northland Road, and the other was the bottom gate with entry from the Buncrana Road.

It was clear that the Americans spared no expense in making life comfortable for their personnel at the camp. Springtown consisted of 302 huts, a chapel, gym, laundry, canteen, barbershop, theatre and a jail. Also installed were soda fountains and ice-cream machines. By all accounts, this was a splendid camp.

A sailor hard at work in the camp's laundry room making sure everything is spic-and-span.

There was always pressing work to be done to keep the camp's supply of uniforms in good order.

The soda fountain in the camp where many young Derry children tasted Coca-Cola for the very first time courtesy of the American Navy.

Navy personnel had their own newspaper called *Derry NOB News*, NOB being short for Naval Operations Base. It carried news of happenings in and around the camps in Derry and informed Navy personnel of films and shows scheduled each night. Regular contributors to this paper were Helmar Schaich from Hut 113 Springtown Camp and Jim Schwartzberg from Hut 17 Springtown. A full entertainment programme was available to fill leisure time, with something different in the camp every night, including films, a show or a boxing bill. With world-class stars like Bob Hope and Al Jolson appearing live on stage at the Springtown theatre, they certainly had a home from home.

But what do we know about the young US Navy personnel who first occupied the camp? Who were they? What were their thoughts about life in Springtown Camp, and this place called Derry, 3,000 miles from their homeland?

It was important, I felt, that I should try to track down some of the US personnel who actually served in the camp and put to pen and paper the personal stories and memories of their stay. I contacted Jim Sullivan, co-founder of the US Navcommsta Londonderry Alumni Association, who displayed an interest in this book. Jim was of great assistance and he kindly furnished me with the names of twenty of his members who had served in Springtown Camp. I went about the task of locating some of them and, bearing in mind these former US Navy men would be in their mid-eighties, I wondered what response I would receive. To my delight, I found them very willing to talk to me and give their experience of life in the camp. Even better, some sent me on handwritten personal letters and included photographs as well as giving me their phone numbers. Some were torpedo men, gunners, gunners' mates, machinists, radio communications men and intelligence officers. Their duties were repairing, refuelling, and re-arming destroyers and submarines for the forthcoming invasion of Europe. All mentioned the hard work that went into doing their respective jobs. These young Navy men and Marines, now stationed in Springtown Camp, came from every state in the Union, from New York to California, from Montana to Alabama, but they were united in one aim: to bring this vicious war to an end as quickly as possible.

Sero Startoni, a young eighteen-year-old gunner's mate from Pennsylvania, left New York pier No 92 on 15 November 1943 on his way to Springtown Camp. He remembers it took his ship seven long days sailing unescorted across the Atlantic to reach its destination at Glasgow. From there, they boarded a train that took them to a boat which sailed to Derry. On arriving at the camp, Sero was issued with a Springfield rifle and 100 rounds of ammunition and assigned to a hut occupied by gunners, gunners' mates, seamen, torpedo men and torpedo men's mates.

DERRY-NOB NEWS

The Only Paper Published Exclusively For U. S. Naval Personnel in the ETO

Vol. II   Saturday, December 11, 1943   No. 51

FOURTEEN NEW CPOs INCLUDED IN 236 BASE ADVANCEMENTS

THE 1943 NAVY

Learning the use of a stereocomparagraph, which contours from aerial photographs, is all in a day's work for

WAVES Betty Protzeller, Fairmont, Minn., left and Patricia Phillips, Jackson, Mich., right. Know how to typewrite, Betty?

PORTRUSH RED CROSS CLUBS OPEN

The Eglinton Hotel, famous, Portrush landmark, has been taken over by the American Red Cross and has been converted into a U. S. Servicemen's Club.

Club Director Torres A. Lyche, LaGrange, Ill., ably assisted by Miss Virginia Sutton, Storm Lake, Iowa; and Miss Hazel Kingsbury, Manhattan, N. Y., announced that the new club has facilities for one hundred and fifty enlisted personnel.

Mr. Lyche also announced the opening of the ARC Officers' Club which was converted from the Bay View Hotel.

Cafeteria style meals will be served at the Savoy Restaurant, under ARC supervision with the aid of the volunteer staff directed by Lady Babington, wife of Sir Anthony Babington, Lord Justice of Ulster.

Dancing at the Orange Hall, largest dance hall in Portrush, will be sponsored certain nights each week by the ARC with the first affair scheduled for December 1.

BILLY GILBERT TO DO FOUR SHOWS

Comedian Billy Gilbert and his stage company will make four appearances before Navy and Marine audiences Monday and Tuesday. Exact times at each camp are listed under camp columns.

LT. CMDR. R. W. WALLING ANNOUNCES THE SECOND LARGEST LIST THIS YEAR

More than half the enlisted men who were recently recommended for competitive examinations, received passing grades and were promoted to the next higher rating, according to an announcement issued through Lt. Cmdr. R. W. Walling, NOB Personnel Officer.

Fourteen chief petty officers were listed; fifty-one first class petty officers; ninety-seven second class petty officers; sixty-five third class petty officers; three seamen first class and six hospital apprentices first class were included in the announcement. Following is the complete list:

Chief Radioman, (Acting Appointment)
Jack D. Godwin-Austin, Oildale, Cal.

Chief Shipfitters (Acting Appointment)
John F. Curran, Monogahela, Pa.; Casine F. Falco, Philadelphia, Pa.; Steve Livchak, Jr., Lorain, O.; Victor R. Otto, N. Tonawando, N.Y.; Oscar B. Pender, Vienna, Ill.

Chief Machinist's Mates (Acting Appointment)
Walter H. Jewell, Rollingsford, N. Hamp.; Jesse B. Stone, Conway, Ark.

Chief Storekeeper (Acting Appointment)
Charles J. Bierau, Brooklyn, N.Y.; George M. Greenleaf, Guma, Ariz.; Lloyd James, San Diego, Cal.; Hermit T. Moore, Adamsville, Tenn.

Electrician's Mate, First Class
Thomas S. Riddle, Frankfort, Ky.

Radioman, First Class
John E. Lindholm, Minnetouka, Minn.; Joseph Marrah, Jr., Owasso, Mich.

Radio Technician, First Class
Charles K. Chrismon, Greensboro, N. Car.; William W. Lawson, Cave City, Ky.

Shipfitter, First Class
Morris Borders, Omaha, Neb.; Carl R. Brown, Coffyville, Kan.; Milton G. Carrier, New Bedford, Mass.; Ralph F. Huss, Rawson, O.; Francis D. Henson, Valier, Ill.; John V. Kieffer, Linden, N. J.; Edgar A. F. Langis, New Bedford, Mass.; Richard R. Reinsch, Marion, Ind.; Bennie J. Mostrog, Farrell, Pa.; Jack E. Smith, Oakland, Cal.; Hilaire F. St. Marie, Grand Forks, N. Dak.; Robert E. Taylor, Springfield, Mass.

Printer, First Class
Lawrence J. Dopita, Plainville, Kansas.

Machinist's Mate, First Class
Louis Bucknot, Jr., Euclid, O.; Charles M. Carter, Worcester, Mass.; Herman L. Crow, Phoenix, Ariz.; Peter A. DiDonoto, Schnectady, N. Y.; John L. Jacobson, N. Richmond, Wisc.; Paul Krustchinsky, Houston, Tex.; Raymond G. McKibben, Yorktown, Ill.; Stuart L. Rice, Elgin, Ill.; Bernard J. Schreibner, Elkhard, Md.; Rocco Silvestri,

US Naval newspaper for all the Derry bases. This paper brought news to US personnel of all events and promotions taking place locally, Saturday 11 December 1943.

Sero recalls: 'I remember it was around March 1944 when work intensified. We were working twelve-hour shifts round the clock, loading ship after ship with 20mm, 40mm, and .50 calibre machine guns. With so much happening we knew D-Day wasn't far off.

'A normal day in Springtown Camp was up at dawn, chow [breakfast], bussed to the shipyard, loading trucks with ammunition and artillery pieces taken from the arms dumps that were in bunkers at the side of the huts underground. Dinner, then back to work again till late, before being bussed back to camp.

'We did have great entertaining shows and many movies in the theatre in Springtown Camp, so at nights we would take in a show or movie or maybe just read a book, write a letter home or play cards. One thing, for sure, is we were never bored in the camp, as there was always plenty going on around us.

'We always looked forward to visiting town, where we would enjoy the locals' company in some nice friendly bar. I must say, we were always made very welcome wherever we went in Derry. Before returning to the camp, I remember we always had to bring fresh loaves of bread back with us for our buddies. Everyone loved the fresh bread baked in Derry.

'The Derry girls were very attractive and always friendly, but any notion you had of bringing one to the camp with you was a non-starter, as the Marines patrolled the camp gates and the ammunition dumps, and a spider wouldn't get past them,' he recalls with a laugh.

US Navy personnel Frank Rose and Paul Bray with children from a local orphanage who attended a party at the camp, Christmas 1943.

US Navy personnel with children from a local orphanage attending a camp party.   *Bob Reiss's US Navy bed in Hut 214 Springtown Camp, 1943.*

'Springtown Camp holds fond memories for me and I'm sure for all who were stationed there. The scenery surrounding the camp itself was breathtaking, with views of the close-by mountains of Scalp and Eskaheen. The local people were always very friendly and hospitable towards us. We had a wonderful camp commander, and the officer personnel were always respectful and courteous towards all of us. The cooks and bakers in the camp always put on a great spread of food for us, and we always looked forward to chow time there. The camaraderie in the camp was always wonderful, with each hut having men from every state in America: Carl L Bauer from Dubois County, Indiana, James E Barrett, Weaverville, North Carolina, Oliver F Size, San Pedro, California, and Fred H Budd, Geneva, Illinois, to name but a few.

'It was a bittersweet day when I and most of the men at the camp were transferred to different ships on 18 August 1944, leaving only the radiomen behind in Springtown. As we boarded our ship at Lisahally, we didn't know what the future had in store for us, or indeed for our former camp.'

Another young American teenage lad, Leo Sangiolo, or 'Moose', as he was known to his mates, arrived in Springtown in April 1943 from his native Hanson, Massachusetts, for his tour of duty. Moose, a nineteen-year-old torpedo man attached to the Ordnance Department, remembers with fondness the many parties they had for children from the locality.

'The parties would be on Thanksgiving, Independence Day on the Fourth of July or at Christmas time, and it was great just to see the smile on their wee faces as they were introduced to the delicacies of Hershey chocolate, candy and

US Navy torpedo man Leo 'Moose' Sangiolo with his mate at Springtown Camp, 1943.

ice cream, and their first taste of Coca-Cola.' Moose went on to say how hard they had to work during their twelve-hour shifts, and what an important role the men in Springtown played in World War II. They ensured the destroyers and submarines were armed to the hilt and in perfect condition throughout in preparation for the impending invasion of Europe.

'We wanted to make absolutely certain,' he went on, 'that the destroyers and submarines were in tip-top shape for the battles that lay ahead of them in the Atlantic, and that our mates on board them had every chance of achieving victory and returning home safe and sound. That was our aim and I think we were successful in doing just that.'

While talking to him, I could grasp the contentment he felt about this. He also relayed to me the excitement that swept the camp when the news filtered through about the many world-famous entertainers who would be performing for the Navy personnel in the camp theatre.

Moose's tour of duty in the camp ended in August 1944 when his unit was transferred to the heat of battle in the Pacific. He continues to live a happy and contented life in Hanson, Massachusetts, and says he still remembers his old buddies from his days in Derry, and, at times, still lets his mind wander back to his time in Springtown Camp.

Bob Reiss with Derry orphans at Christmas dinner, Springtown Camp, 1943.

The Navy men, as they were known here, became very popular with the local Derry children because of the kindness they had shown them. At different times like Thanksgiving or Christmas, they brought children from local orphanages and other children from different streets in Derry out to Springtown in their trucks and treated them to a slap-up party. Afterwards, they would take the children to their homes again in the large Navy trucks, which in itself was an additional treat.

Of course, they were not only popular with the children of Derry, but also with the young ladies – much to the annoyance of the local lads, who were plainly jealous of these young, good-looking fellows in their smart uniforms and cultured accents from far-off romantic places like California, New York, South Carolina, Boston and Philadelphia.

Robert L Reiss, known as Bob to his mates, will always remember his nineteenth birthday, for on that day, 4 April 1943, he arrived in Derry's Springtown Camp and was assigned to Hut 214.

Bob recalls he was glad to see his bunk bed, tired after a long journey from New York across the Atlantic Ocean on the merchant ship *Henry S Lykes*.

Sparks and riggers of the US Navy posing for Navy photographer in Springtown Camp, 1943.

His ship had come as part of a convoy guarded by a naval armed guard carrying anti-aircraft guns. He remembers a lot of his old mates who were with him that day: Darryl Ramsey, John Ramsey, Charlie Breslin, Al Ricard, AJ Richards, Herb Rhode and Henry Rigali, who was later killed in France.

Bob also fondly remembers John Gaulden, who was in the camp with him, who fell in love and married a local Derry girl. He was not the only one: thirty-five newly married women known as the War Brides left on board the *Marine Haven*, which sailed from Derry to America in September 1944, one month after their husbands left.

'I often think back all those years to the many stars who entertained us in the theatre in the camp: Bob Hope, Jerry Colonna, Frances Langford and Billy Gilbert to name but a few,' says Bob. 'In my spare time, which we hadn't much of, I made a small truck which had wheelbarrow wheels and an engine from a motorcycle, and I used to drive around

Bob Hope and Frances Langford appearing in Derry's Springtown Camp in 1943.

Springtown Camp in it, much to the amusement of my mates. In the summer of 1944, I was transferred to Falmouth, England, where I remained until May 1945. I left for home from Southampton, England, on the *General William S Black* on VE Day, returning to Boston. I am now eighty-five years old and living in Connecticut, but my mind often slips back to my old buddies and my days in Springtown Camp, Derry, with its beautiful, scenic surroundings, and memories of the hospitality of the Derry people.'

John Gaulden, who married a Derry girl while stationed in Springtown, pictured with Bob Reiss.

Bob Hope and Jerry Colonna signing autographs for US personnel in the camp, 1943.

One of the first US Navy men in Springtown Camp was Marvin L Hoffricter, who was stationed there from February 1942, and three friends, Florien Bednarski, Theodore Dannecker and Howard Dodds. The latter three were there right until the end of Springtown Camp's time as a base.

Another buddy of theirs, Bill Marschner, relayed to me that he loved his time in the camp, working in the personnel office and the captain's office. His pride was evident as he talked of his duties, and he also recalls doing a stint in the code room, as he was connected to operations, communications and intelligence.

'During our time off, we used to have great fun at the movies in the camp. They were shown most nights, while other nights we would have a show with some big stars on stage, or a night of boxing with our own boxers taking on the cream of local boxers.'

He also looked forward to going into the town and enjoying the company of the Derry people, as the banter was super. Bill had a high regard for the local people, whom he describes as always friendly and considerate towards their US friends. He also remembers the 'in' craze that swept through the camp with a lot of Navy men getting 'crew hair cuts' and 'bee bobs'. Bill recalls that world-famous comedian Billy Gilbert was the star attraction at a gala concert held in the Springtown Camp theatre on Tuesday 14 December 1943.

On Monday 6 December 1943, a packed Springtown gym hall was the scene of a very competitive basketball match between Creevagh Eagles and Springtown Cooks and Bakers, with the Creevagh team running out winners by 33 to 28. The Springtown team manager, Helmar S Schaich from Hut 113, immediately issued a return challenge to the Creevagh team. The very next night, the Springtown gym was bursting at the seams again as the Americans staged a major six-fight boxing tournament between the camp's elite boxing team and a team of Irish boxers.

The Americans fancied their chances in all contests, and with some of the Navy boxers members of the world-famous Golden Gloves, it was no wonder.

The first match was between Freddy 'Doc' Cappola from Stanford, Connecticut, and 'Shifty' McGowan from Derry. Cappola gave a good account of himself in the first two rounds, but in the third round, McGowan threw a combination of punches and had Cappola in trouble and the fight was stopped with McGowan winning on a TKO (technical knockout).

The second bout was a thrilling affair between George 'Pal' Boukas from Chicago, Illinois, and Jim 'Battling' Harkin from Derry, with each boxer giving their all. At the end of the fight, the referee thought it too close to call and awarded a draw.

The third bout was an exhibition between Jerome 'Young' Cline from Detroit, Michigan, and Jim 'Spider' Kelly. The skills of Kelly drew sustained applause from the packed hall throughout the bout.

Up next was the camp favourite, Cherry Schlumbrecke from New Orleans, who faced John 'Frosty' Rodgers from Belfast. Schlumbrecke opened with a flurry of punches, much to the delight of the big, partisan crowd. Rodgers sidestepped him, bobbing and weaving until Schlumbrecke ran out of steam and, boxing cleverly, took the decision on points.

George 'Happy' Hunt from Steubenville, Ohio, matched punches with Paddy Harkin from Derry, and was thought to be in front when he received a bad gash over his right eye. The referee had no option but to stop the fight in favour of Harkin.

The only winner among the US Navy men was Albert 'Powerhouse' Panica from New York, who outpointed P McMenamin from Omagh in a close-fought contest. This was to be one of many future boxing tournaments to be held in Springtown gym.

The following night had a much slower pace for the Navy men, as they headed to the picture house in the camp to watch the film *Lady of Burlesque*, starring Barbara Stanwyck and Michael O'Shea.

The legendary Jim 'Spider' Kelly.

Joe White, US Navy, talking to a Marine guard at the entrance to the camp, 1943.

Above: Security pass of James Patton, a lorry driver for the US Navy. Strict security was in operation and everyone entering or leaving the camps had to show their pass. Below: James Patton's stamped pass book to all the camps, 1943.

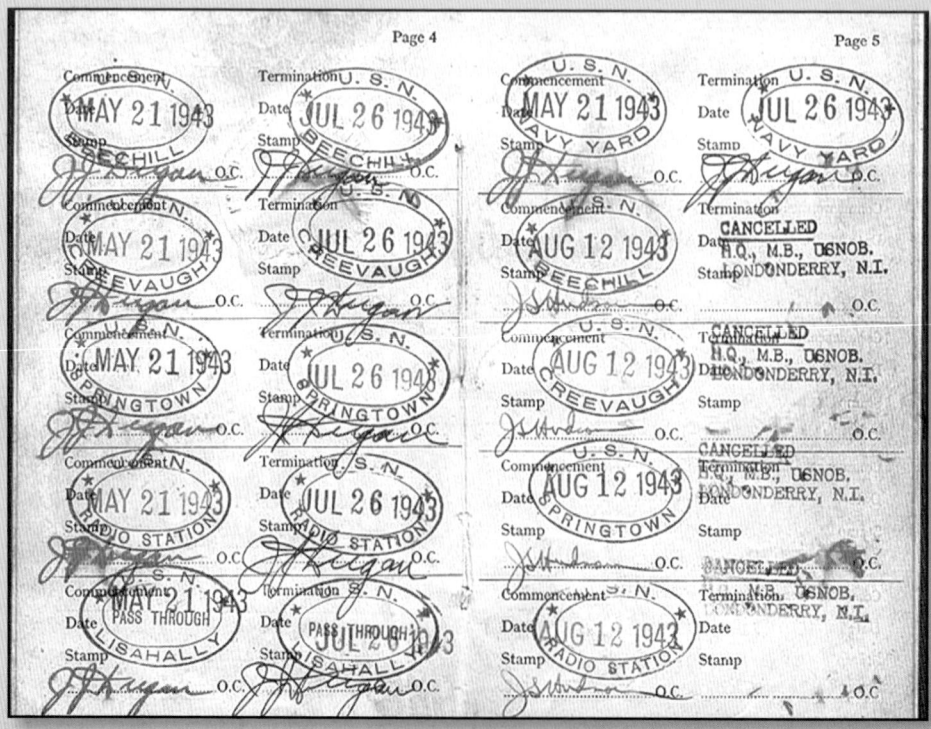

US Naval bases were guarded by US Marines and security was watertight. Everybody and everything was checked and double-checked before it was allowed inside any of the camps.

Local man James Patton from Gloucester Avenue was a lorry driver employed by the US Navy. His duties were to transport materials and other items to the different bases in Derry. Despite James being well known to most of the Marine guards, he still had to present his photographic war pass each and every time he entered each camp. James often told his family about the many boxing matches that had taken place in Springtown gym between the US Navy boxers and local boxers.

He recalled to them one night in particular, when the Americans matched their champion, a Golden Gloves contestant, with a local boxer, who they'd heard had a bit of a reputation locally. The sailors of the American forces turned up in their droves to support their hero, fully expecting to see an annihilation of the Derry boxer. However, little did they know that the local boxer was none other than Jim 'Spider' Kelly. Much to their surprise, Kelly went on to give the US boxer a lesson in the finer arts of the sport that he wouldn't forget in a hurry. The massive crowd could do nothing but sit back and admire Kelly's silky skills.

Elkie Clarke shows he has lost none of his skill as he throws a right hand to the face of his opponent in a veteran exhibition bout in Derry.

Left: Fond memories of snow time in the camp for the US Navy stationed there, 1943.

Below: The radio men from the US Navy were the last Americans to leave Springtown Camp in August 1945.

On 18 August 1944, the Marine Barracks in Derry was disbanded, and with that, most of the naval personnel in Springtown Camp also departed. They were transferred to a ship docked at Lisahally, which sailed from there on its journey across the Atlantic.

Derry played such a crucial role in the Battle of the Atlantic that, at the conclusion of the war, Lisahally was the designated port for the surrender of the German U Boats; the first eight submarines surrendered at the port on 14 May 1945.

However, some personnel still remained in Springtown Camp. These were the radiomen, who continued to play a major role in the war, and were a key communications facility for all naval operations in this theatre. They, of course, would remain guarded by the Marines. The radiomen would stay in the camp until it was disbanded on Monday 12 November 1945, thus ending the US Navy's association with Springtown Camp.

Chapter 2
Housing Conditions and the Struggle for a Home

With the war over, the military bases in the city and outlying areas were vacated by late November 1945. The Northern Ireland Government contacted Derry Corporation, asking them to inform the Ministry of Health and Local Government of any temporary hutments in their area which, if converted to temporary housing at government expense, they would be prepared to manage on the government's behalf.

With an acute housing shortage in Derry and district, the Corporation apparently proceeded to take an interest in the proposed government scheme. They did this with the full knowledge of the Derry Rural District Council, in whose area Springtown Camp was situated.

On 31 December 1945, the then town clerk signed, on behalf of Derry Corporation, an undertaking to manage Springtown Camp within the proposed government scheme. The Corporation's town clerk sent the following letter to the Minister of Health and Local Government at Stormont.

'My Council have considered the terms of the Ministry's circular and undertake to manage such temporary housing as may be provided by the conversions, at government expense, of any or all of the huts described above. We will accept responsibility for the re-housing of the occupants of the accommodation so provided, on the termination of the period of the user. It is not proposed to acquire the land for permanent housing because the land is not within the area of the Corporation.'

This clearly shows as far back as 1945 the Corporation on record as accepting full responsibility for re-housing the residents of such camps. They, of course, later changed their minds on this issue and denied responsibility for the re-housing of the tenants. This very issue was to become a major stumbling block between them and the Rural District Council with the residents stuck in the middle. However, as time passed by, it was clear that both the government's and the Corporation's deeds did not match their words, and the camps still lay empty some nine months later.

Derry was experiencing the worst housing shortage in living memory. With many a small two-up, two-down terraced house serving as home to two and sometimes three families, people living in these appalling conditions couldn't take much more. The city had many badly run-down, poorly maintained tenement buildings. Serious overcrowding made life a living hell for many, and tuberculosis (TB) was prevalent as a direct result of too many people living so close together. With no houses being built by the old Derry Corporation, these families had no prospect of finding a home, and with a serious shortage of rented accommodation, the future for many parents with young children was bleak, to say the least.

One tenement building in William Street was home to forty-nine people, and one dwelling in Limewood Street was home to twenty-three. Under such pressure, something had to give. At times, as many as twelve people cooked, ate and slept in one shared room. The only means of cooking was on a small Primus stove burning paraffin oil, which emitted damaging fumes and led to serious health problems for the residents.

Squatters Take Over Vacant Huts

Several camps in the city, previously occupied by US and British personnel, were now left vacant as the war was over. They may have been tin huts, but they were spacious and would provide much better living conditions than those the beleaguered people were currently enduring. It was only a matter of time before someone took the decision to squat in them, to give themselves more space, to give their children somewhere to play, and to allow their family to breathe clean air as opposed to breathing oil fumes from a paraffin stove. That time arrived minutes before midnight on Wednesday 21 August 1946 when the initiative was taken by four families living in Limewood Street, led by Adam Smith.

Pioneer squatter Adam Smith.

Group of children at Bligh's Lane Camp, 22 August 1946.

Smith and his co-residents transferred whatever furniture and bits and pieces they possessed into four huts at Bligh's Lane Camp, and even though the huts had neither electricity nor running water, they were still a vast improvement to the conditions they had been living in. Soon, others followed suit, and it was a common sight to see heads of families staking their claim to a hut by leaving a piece of furniture inside it and writing their name on the door. Within hours, the Bligh's Lane Camp was full.

'We have endured squalor for too long,' said Adam Smith. 'It stops here, it stops now, we are here to stay. For eight long years, my wife, myself and our five children – four boys and one girl aged between seven and eighteen – have had to live in one room at thirty-seven Limewood Street. Can you imagine what that was like, all of us eating and sleeping in one small room? Desperation drove me to this; I just couldn't take it anymore.'

Two of the other families lived at 27 Limewood Street. The worst case of them all was that of Joe Doherty: Joe, his wife and nine children shared one small room in a three-bedroom terraced house in which, altogether, there were twenty-three people. The primary tenant of the house, George Doyle, had eight of a family himself. The Doherty family had recently suffered the death of one of their six-week-old twins, and to quote the words of the mother, 'Is it any wonder?' Mrs Doherty went on to say, 'Some of us had to sleep on the scullery floor, and every night we had to lift the baby's cradle up onto the table to leave room on the floor for others to lie down. At least the children will have fresh air up here in the hut.'

The menfolk set about the task of making the huts habitable, and the next day, the silence of the camp was replaced by children's laughter as they played in the open spaces of lush green grass. That day, the RUC visited the squatters, but apart from asking a few questions, they didn't interfere. By now, the news of this initiative taken by Adam Smith and others had swept the city like wildfire. Within hours, four families took control of four huts at the bottom of Bishop Street, and other families moved into the camp at Clooney in the Waterside.

The first squatters arrived in Springtown Camp on Thursday 22 August 1946. Among the first occupiers were Philip Killen, Hugh McMonagle, Bernard Sheerin, Billy Cassidy, Johnny Doherty and James McCloskey along with their families. All the squatters said they would pay any reasonable rent requested by the powers-that-be, and that it was their intention to approach the Corporation to have the mains water and electricity turned on.

The next day, Mayor Sir Basil McFarland, accompanied by Paddy Maxwell MP, EH Babington, city solicitor, and RS Sidebottom, assistant town clerk, met with a deputation from the squatters. The squatters were represented by Adam Smith, Charlie McIntyre and H Doherty from Bligh's Lane Camp, H Smith and H Brown, Bishop Street, and Matt Mulhern from Clooney Camp, together with their spokesman, Paddy Fox, chairman of the Derry Labour Party.

The Corporation agreed to turn on the water and electricity to the huts when the arrangements for payment of the electricity were made. They also agreed to begin refuse collection from the camps. However, the mayor stated that the matter of Springtown Camp, which he believed 'people are already moving into as we speak', had nothing to do with his Corporation, as it was in the Rural Council area. Nevertheless, Paddy Maxwell MP had agreed to take that matter up with the minister responsible at Stormont after consultation with the Rural Council.

Other families who had arrived at Bishop Street hoping to move into a hut were disappointed at finding all the huts occupied; twelve families, totalling over 100 people, decided to move into the former US camp at Creevagh. Once again, no attempt was made to stop them squatting in the huts by the camp's caretakers. In fact, after they consulted with the police, they willingly handed over the keys to the squatters. Even though, like Bligh's Lane Camp, there was neither water nor electricity in the huts, they were still viewed as a huge improvement on their previous homes. Clooney Camp was filled to capacity within hours as eighteen families took possession of the huts there. At Belmont Camp, the story was the same: there were forty-seven huts in Belmont, and by Friday 23 August, thirty-seven families, made up of eighty adults and 150 children, had moved in, and the remaining ten huts were earmarked by families who chalked their names on a hut and put a curtain on one of the windows to stake their claim.

By 5.00 pm on Friday 23 August 1946, which was less than two days after the first squatters made their move, the approximate numbers of squatters in the camps were reported as follows:

- Bligh's Lane Camp – 9 families with a total 48 people
- Bishop Street Camp – 4 families with a total of 23 people
- Creevagh Camp – 4 families with a total of 22 people
- Belmont Camp – 40 families with a total of 242 people
- Clooney Camp – 16 families with a total of 90 people
- Springtown Camp – 10 families with a total of 62 people.

The next day, desolate families squatted in other camps at Corrody, Beech Hill, Eglinton and Mabuoy. The roads were full of horse-drawn carts loaded with furniture and other belongings of families leaving the squalor of rat-infested slum tenements for large, open, spacious huts. The owners of horses and carts were busy over the next few days, working all hours flitting families to the camps. Some families who rented furnished rooms in tenement buildings had no furniture or beds of their own to bring to the camps. They were seen walking to different camps carrying just a bag of belongings. One of the worst cases of this abject poverty was in the Belmont Camp.

A mother and her seven young children had been in the workhouse for the previous two years while her husband tried without success to rent a room. He, himself, was sleeping anywhere and everywhere, so when the opportunity presented itself to reunite his family, he lost no time, moving his family out of the workhouse and into one of the huts at Belmont Camp. With no possessions of their own, on their first night they had to sleep on the concrete floor, huddled together to keep warm. The next day, the children could be seen bringing straw into the hut to make makeshift beds for the night. The unemployed father was an ex-soldier of two wars and had two young sons still serving with the British forces. In contrast, other huts had some fine furniture and were as spic-and-span as any modern home. The poor family was soon to see the kindness of their new neighbours, who very quickly made sure the family had food and some bedding to tide them over until they got on their feet.

This kindness was to become a feature of the community spirit that was to prevail in the camps. That weekend, John McCool, who was one of the first squatters in Belmont Camp, decided to have a housewarming party; the whole of the camp decided they, too, would join in the party mood, making it one big happy camp.

The movement to Springtown Camp by the long-suffering people was so swift that by 26 August 1946, a mere four days after the squatters' action began, nearly 100 huts were occupied. Housing approximately 450 people, Springtown now accommodated more people than the combined total of the other camps. They came from all areas of Derry: Fox's Corner, Walker's Square, Lecky Road, Wellington Street and as far away as Ardmore in search of a new beginning in Springtown Camp. A complete new community had emerged overnight, a few known to each other, but most complete strangers to one another, thrust together by deplorable living conditions and circumstances over which they had no control.

The Springtown Camp people had arrived.

Clooney Camp, from where many families were evicted and moved to Springtown Camp to live, June 1947.

How would these people get on with each other? Most were complete strangers to each other. They did, however, have one thing in common: they were all in the same predicament and were driven by despair to take this action. They simply couldn't endure any longer the deplorable conditions they were living in. During the next few days, the families were busy making the huts more comfortable. Even though there was neither electricity nor heating, they made the best of it with Tilley lamps lighting up the huts at night. The important thing was they had space, and plenty of it, as the huts were massive.

At first, the families moved from hut to hut, before finally deciding on the hut of their choice. Families separated the huts by placing sheets on a line across the middle, with a family occupying half of a hut. The entrance to the huts was from the front gable, through half-doors, just like a horse's stable. The bottom half could be bolted and the top half could swing open.

At night, families visited each other in their huts and relayed their family history to their new neighbours. Slowly but surely, everyone got to know each other. The children soon mingled in their new-found freedom of spacious play areas, which had both hard-stand (concrete) areas and many grassed areas; it was like a dream park for them. What a difference from the narrow streets to this massive open area which was completely surrounded by green fields and trees. The quality of life for the children was certainly improved no end, as was their health.

Life was surreal that weekend for the people of the camps; however, life in Derry went on as normal. The Carnival Queen dance was being held in the Guildhall with music by the Carlton Swingtette: crowds were queuing outside the Palace Cinema where *Whispering Ghost* was showing; *Waterloo Road* was being screened at the Strand Cinema; the Rialto was showing *The Courage of Lassie* while *That Night With You* was on at the Midland Cinema.

On the football field, a young Eddie Crossan was scoring for Derry City at the Brandywell, earning Derry a 1–1 draw with Distillery.

One of the first photographs taken of the camp, January 1942.

From Saturday night onwards, families were streaming towards Springtown Camp in increasing numbers. By Sunday, there were nearly 1,000 people living in the corrugated-tin huts. Springtown Camp from its inception was a place of enormous interest to the people of Derry – for more reasons than one. On the second day of the squatters moving into the huts, there were scenes which the local press reported as 'amazing'. In Northland Road and Buncrana Road, many hundreds of sightseers came from all over the city in pouring rain to watch the mass exodus of people from the city to the camp. They were not only there to watch, but to lend support and encouragement to the squatters. The numbers of sightseers swelled to such an extent that they completely blocked the roads and traffic was brought to a complete standstill as they watched families ferrying bits of furniture in prams, donkey- and horse-drawn carts, and every other possible means of conveyance.

Police were quickly on the scene but were totally powerless to do anything because of the sheer numbers of sightseers. With no alternative but to let everyone sort themselves out, they just stayed and observed the scenes themselves.

A shore patrol of the Royal Navy and a guard of Admiralty Civil Police were on duty near the camp; they, too, chose to take no active part in the proceedings and were content to do as the police did and just looked on in amazement at the crowds.

That weekend certainly highlighted the chronic shortage of houses in Derry as mothers and fathers of young children, some as young as three months, chose to live in a tin hut with neither electricity nor running water, with few toilet or washing facilities, rather than the living conditions they had previously endured.

It was indeed a momentous week in the city. Coupled with the massive squatters' initiative, the first brick was laid in a new housing estate called Creggan.

Finally, the building of Creggan houses begins in August 1946.

Settling Into The Camps

In the next few days, the people of the camps improvised as best they could to make life more bearable in the huts.

The huts were large, open units with no internal partitioning or internal doors, no sanitary facilities, no running water, no heating facilities. In fact, they were just like big barns; water, heating and sanitation were the most urgent problems facing the squatters.

Although Springtown Camp was regarded as a big improvement on previous living conditions, the huts were still not considered habitable; much still needed to be done to make them suitable to live in. With regards to water, there were only two water taps in the camp: one situated at the bottom of the camp and one in the middle, supplying several hundred people. The toilet facilities were confined to just one hut, which housed all the toilets.

With huts being very big, keeping them warm was an immediate problem for the people. They came up with a novel idea to light braziers – tin barrels with holes in the sides to facilitate the flow of air through them. This enabled the residents to burn sticks and coke. They lit the braziers outside the huts, and when the coke reddened to such a degree that the smoke disappeared, they transferred them inside. This was the only source of heating the people had in the early days of Springtown Camp.

Cooking was carried out on a little paraffin-fired Primus stove, with lighting provided by several Tilley lamps strategically placed throughout the hut. The younger people fetched kettles, buckets and basins full of water from the two water taps that served the whole camp. This entailed carrying the water a distance of about 100 yards for a lot of the residents.

***

The squatters' takeover of the camps was causing considerable consternation with the powers-that-be in Derry's Guildhall. At a meeting on Tuesday 13 September 1946, the Corporation discussed a letter they received from the Ministry of Health and Local Government on 3 September. The Health Minister in his letter offered ownership of Belmont Camp to the Corporation. Unionist councillors didn't want anything to do with any of the camps while nationalist councillors supported the squatters' actions.

A vote was taken. The six nationalists, Aldermen Fox and McCarroll, along with councillors Deeney, Doherty, Downey and Mullan, voted to accept the offer, with unionist mayor Basil McFarland, Aldermen Little, Cooke and Kennedy, with councillors Orr, Dowds, Glover, Graham, McGowan,

Hamilton, Hill, and McLaughlin voting against. The proposal to decline the offer was carried by twelve unionist votes to six on the nationalist side.

Paddy Fox, chairman of the Derry Labour Party, who became a champion of the squatters, wrote in support of the people. 'I support these homeless citizens of this disgraceful city of ours, who have had the courage to take over the disused huts. I do hope the action taken is indicative of a new spirit amongst the long-suffering common people, and will result in bringing to book our landlord Corporation and their "yes men". Today, I have seen little children playing on green grass, who yesterday were playing in the gutter or were confined in overcrowded, undersized, unhealthy and fabulously rented caricatures of homes. Today I have seen young mothers breathe God's clean fresh air in green surroundings. Tomorrow – what? Will the common people decide? I call on all sections of the general public to support our fellow citizens in their fight. I call on every section of every branch of the trade union movement in this forgotten, neglected dead-end city to stand in support of these the homeless people of our city.'

***

Springtown Camp was situated about 200 yards outside the city boundary on the outskirts of Derry. This fact was to be used to great effect by the Corporation in later years. The camp at Springtown was easily the best equipped of all the camps in Derry, comprising 302 huts, a chapel, cinema, theatre and a gym, among other amenities. However, when the US Navy personnel left Springtown Camp, they stripped the huts bare, including removing all the electricity cables. Still, the huts were in good condition, being only four years old, and they were very spacious. The Corporation turned on the water supply and up-stand water taps were installed in the middle and bottom of the camp. The sanitation used was the same as the US Navy had used during their tenure.

The unionist Corporation was furious at the development of the squatter situation. On 27 August 1946 at a Corporation meeting in the Guildhall, Mayor Sir Basil McFarland, in answer to a question from unionist councillor CD Milligan, said, 'Some of the camps occupied are being overrun by people who are not being controlled.' He went on, 'So far as the Rural District Council is concerned, with regard to Springtown Camp in particular, I am in touch with the Ministry in Belfast.'

He was proposing to travel to discuss the matter with his officials the next day. To the annoyance of the unionist-controlled Corporation and Rural Council, the squatting into huts continued unabated for the next few weeks.

The town clerk, in his report to a meeting of the Corporation on Tuesday 20 September 1946 on the squatting issue, reported:

'As you are aware, a number of families from the city have taken over, without permission, possession of War Department camps. The huts are situated mostly outside the city boundary.

'The latest information in my possession on the number of squatters is as follows:

- Springtown Camp; families 101, persons 454
- Clooney Camp; families 24, persons 102
- Belmont Camp; families 40, persons 191
- Bishop Street Camp; families 3, persons 17
- Bligh's Lane Camp; families 6, persons 29
- Total; families 174, persons 793.

'In addition to these, other camps in more outlying districts have also been taken over. With the knowledge of the Ministry of Health and Local Government, the Corporation has taken action in regards to the camps as follows.

'Springtown: turned water supply on, requested the naval officer-in-charge to permit the electricity supply to continue. Arrangements have been made to clear, at intervals, the sewerage.

'Clooney: water turned on, refuse bins supplied; occupants have lodged a deposit for electricity supply and it has been connected.

'Belmont: water turned on and there is a sewer which occupants are using; application has been made for electricity, but no supply has as yet been granted.

'Bishop Street: water supplied; no electricity available and no sanitary accommodation.

'Bligh's Lane: water turned on, refuse bins supplied and electricity supplied on payment of a deposit.'

However, these figures were changing by the hour, and when his report was actually delivered to the meeting, a more accurate figure was reported in the local press. They estimated that now upwards of 150 families were in Springtown Camp, making up a total of nearly 1,000 people.

Chapter 3

Early Battles with the Corporation and Rural Council

Meanwhile, the menfolk set about the task of organising the running of all the camps. With Springtown being two miles from Derry, this created more problems than those encountered in the other camps situated in the city. With no transport available, the parents had great difficulties trying to get their children, some as young as five years, to and from their schools in Derry.

However, there was a more immediate problem: the purchase of everyday groceries and other essential provisions. To everyone's amazement, this was soon resolved when an alert squatter, Ronnie Reid, seeing a great opportunity for a business venture, decided to set up a shop in his hut at Springtown. He started selling groceries, milk and other provisions; the response to this initiative was immediate and he reported brisk business. This step by Mr Reid proved to be of immense value to the squatters. It not only solved the problem of acquiring groceries and other provisions on a daily basis, it also brought a sign of normality to life in the camp. The initiative was greatly applauded by the people, and as far as the children were concerned, this was the icing on the cake. Now, not only had they great spacious play areas in the camp, but they had a shop in which to buy sweets.

Word of this highly successful business venture set up by a resident of the camp soon went around Derry. Word on the business front in the city was that Ronnie Reid's shop was a money-printing machine. Local traders and deliverymen wanted a piece of the action and started coming out to the camp. These included Bill Ferry and the Old City Dairy with their milk floats.

Milkman Bill Ferry from Nassau Street was arguably the most popular deliveryman in Springtown Camp. He was paid with milk tokens, as was the

Left: Bill Ferry doing his rounds in the camp in 1959. Right: Bill Ferry's father with the horse and cart which Bill originally used to deliver the milk.

order of the day then, and covered most of the camp, delivering pint bottles of milk and bottles of orange juice. Bill always stopped and chatted to everyone about the affairs of the day, and his delivery sometimes took hours to complete because of this. Another popular man was Jim Moran; he always had plenty of time for a bit of banter. He actually married Nancy Cullen, whom he met while delivering milk to the camp, and for a while was a lodger with his mother-in-law there.

Herbie and Jack Peoples were the first breadmen I can remember, along with Phil McCallion. Their bread vans were always a welcome sight in the camp, carrying fresh bread, buns and cream fingers.

Dessie the 'Blackman', as he was known to all, sold clothes from his car boot – on 'tick', of course. He was a nice man, although I have to say his shoes didn't last very long on the rough roads of Springtown; the clothes he sold also never seemed to fit. Still, he did provide a service to the people of the camp.

Another man who did a roaring trade was Bertie O'Kane the 'Provident' man; he also provided a much-needed service.

Then we had the soft-spoken and humble gentleman, Sam Elder. Sam strolled around the rough, potholed streets of the camp at a slow pace, his horse and cart loaded with buttermilk churns. The people got many an aluminium jug full of buttermilk cheaply from old Sam. He sold other provisions, like his specially homemade fresh country butter, which tasted very salty, probably because it didn't contain any of today's additives. His scallions, lettuce and fresh farm eggs were very popular, especially in the summer months. Gentle Sam always did a brisk trade as he entered the camp with his cart full; and when he left, it was completely empty, simply because his goods were basic and were needed daily by the families. And his prices were always very competitive.

By now, the camp was a Nissen-hut village which not only had a shop, but was visited on a daily basis by quite a few of the local traders. They provided the squatters with all their basic day-to-day needs.

These developments were viewed with great anger by the entire unionist populace of the city, especially so by the unionist-controlled Rural District Council. The reason was that over 90% of the squatters were of a Catholic/nationalist ethos. With Springtown Camp situated 200 yards outside the city boundary, they feared a serious shift in the voting pattern could emerge from the movement of squatters to the camp. This, they argued, had the potential to jeopardise their [gerrymandered] control of the Rural District Council.

Urgent representation from unionists was made to the Stormont Government regarding this issue. Even though it was brought to their attention, any change in the voting in the Rural Council area would not take effect for another two years. This was because the new register would not be subject to revision until 1948/49.

Unionist condemnation of the squatters in Springtown Camp was unanimous except for one dissenting voice, and a very important one at that.

The one exception was Dr Abernethy, the city's superintendent medical officer. He had this to say on the squatting situation. 'While I would not like to say anything that would encourage squatting, I think it was maybe a good thing in the interests of the general health of the whole community, because it was obvious, from a health point of view, overcrowding had reached very dangerous levels in the city.'

This statement by the chief medical officer for the Derry area was viewed as a total vindication of the squatters' actions.

The squatters in the camps in and around Derry decided they would need some spokesmen to represent them at meetings with the authorities. They decided this was the only way for them to achieve the best possible results. They elected a committee to represent them. The committee members would be entrusted with the difficult task of pressurising the Corporation to make the necessary changes that were needed to make the huts habitable. The first Springtown Camp committee was duly elected the week after the first squatter moved into the camp. Their brief was to demand that the huts be converted and basic amenities installed. These would include running water, heating facilities, electricity and toilet facilities.

Sammy Quigley was elected chairman and the rest of the committee was made up of Shaun Fox, Dennis Cassidy, Gerry McCrossan, Liam Moore, George 'Bravo' McIntyre, John Whoriskey, Ronnie Reid, Jimmy Smith and Paddy 'Sauce' Moore.

The other camps also elected their own representatives.

The Springtown Camp committee had a meeting the next day with the powers-that-be in the old Derry Corporation and were made promises. Not trusting the Corporation, they decided to press on with their campaign to have the huts converted. The following day, taking charge of their own destiny, they organised a march to the Painters' Union Hall at East Wall, where a public meeting took place. The meeting was attended by MPs and councillors. It proved to be very successful in highlighting their plight and had the desired effect.

The next day, a deputation from the Corporation, which included Mayor Sir Basil McFarland and Patrick Maxwell MP, visited Springtown Camp and met with the camp's representatives. The mayor suggested to them that the remaining huts that were vacant should be left vacant. He went on to say that no further 'seizures of huts' should take place, otherwise they would greatly hamper any conversions should they take place.

The camp's representatives were of the opinion that this suggestion from the Corporation meant that they were going to go ahead with the conversions. Their idea was that while huts were being converted, the now-vacant huts would be used as temporary accommodation for the families. The committee viewed this as a sensible and workable plan and welcomed it. They readily agreed that it was in the best interest of everyone that no further huts should be occupied. They would, however, like to see any conversion plans for the huts before work began, if indeed the huts were going to be converted.

The Northern Ireland cabinet met at Stormont on Tuesday 27 August to discuss the issue of the squatters; the meeting was lengthy but inconclusive. They arranged to meet again the next day. At that meeting, news was relayed to them that squatters were still moving into the huts as they spoke. It was at this meeting that the decision was made to instruct the Corporation to convert the huts at government expense.

On Friday 30 August 1946, Mayor Sir Basil McFarland made this statement to the press:

'As approved by the Ministry of Health and Local Government, work to convert the huts at Springtown Camp will commence on Monday 2 September 1946. At the moment, approximately 150 huts are in full occupation and work will begin on the remaining 150 huts which are now vacant. When work is completed to these huts, the squatters at present in the camp will be transferred to them, after which the remaining 150 huts will be similarly dealt with. When work on the entire camp is completed, there will be temporary accommodation for around 2,000 people.

'The squatters' representatives have given me an undertaking that no more huts will be occupied until reconstruction is fully completed.

'Part of this scheme will involve the provision of proper sewerage facilities, which are estimated to cost £12,000. In the meantime, the squatters will have to make sure that strict sanitary conditions will prevail, and the Corporation will give them every assistance to attain this. When the entire work is completed, the Corporation will be responsible on behalf of the Ministry for the management of the camp and ultimately for the re-housing of the occupants in permanent dwellings. T McAllister, a representative of the Ministry of Health, who was formerly responsible for the administration of camps occupied by the Gibraltarians, has arrived in Londonderry. He will assist in dealing with problems created in connection with the squatters. JH Wilson, a former ARP officer for the city, has been appointed manager of the Springtown Housing Estate.

'This housing estate will come under the Housing Department of the Corporation. After warnings of certain dangerous, exposed electrical fittings which are connected to the city mains, it was decided to close a number of huts yesterday. Despite this, however, and with the probability of danger to young children receiving a fatal shock, the huts still have been entered by squatters. It is pointed out that occupants of these huts remain in possession at their own risk.'

There was no mention of any conversions being carried out at the various other camps.

The speed at which the Corporation and its masters at Stormont moved to meet the squatters' demands suggested it was to relieve the Corporation of some of the considerable embarrassment that the housing scandal in nationalist areas was causing them. The fact that the beleaguered people viewed huts without running water, electricity or sanitation as a massive improvement to the squalor they previously lived in was confirmation, if confirmation were ever needed, of the appalling housing conditions that prevailed in nationalist areas of Derry, caused by the sectarian housing policy of the Corporation.

The Springtown committee was shown plans detailing the works to be carried out to the huts. Some of them would have to be demolished to facilitate the conversions and the improved layout of the huts. They met with instant approval from all. The works would include a complete change to the huts, both externally and internally. The new front door would be fitted to the side elevation of the huts, with new dormer windows to each bedroom. The huts internally would be partitioned into three bedrooms, a living room, a small kitchen with a jaw box (sink), a toilet and an internal coal shed. The large bedroom would have a dormer window to each side of the hut, with three large windows to the front of the huts. The living room would have a large range, which could burn anything and would be used for heating and cooking. There was also a vestibule door and frame which left a small hallway; electricity was installed in every room.

The cost of the conversions to each hut was put at £1,000.

On hearing the news of the scale of the proposed conversions, the people were delighted. In addition to the above conversions to the huts, safety railings would be fitted throughout the camp. The work was carried out in batches of twenty-five huts at a time. On completion of the first twenty-five huts, the residents who had moved into the newly converted units were very pleased. They were an instant hit with the families. The whole of the camp visited the families to view the new huts. After viewing them, they were over the moon with the new huts. Every family couldn't wait to get into one. What a difference from the rat-infested, overcrowded tenements and run-down houses they previously called home. Now they were living in spacious conditions, albeit huts, and their health, and the health of their children, improved beyond belief.

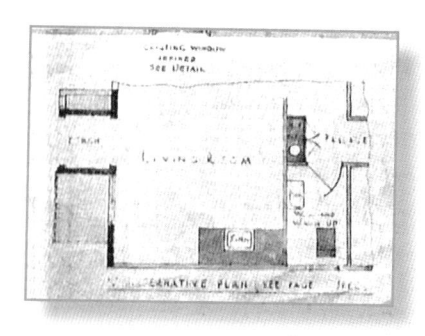

Hut conversion plans.

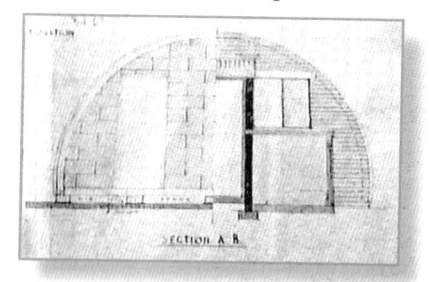

However, there was still disagreement between Derry Corporation and the Rural Council regarding a major sewerage system that was still badly needed in the camp now that the huts were converted. Initially, both authorities refused to foot the cost of such a major undertaking. After some consultation with the Ministry at Stormont, agreement was finally reached. The sewerage system was finally to be installed in the camp. The people were happy, as most of what they had asked for had been granted.

A happy and contented feeling swept over the whole camp and people were smiling again.

Legal Tenancy

On Thursday night of 26 September 1946, a special meeting of all the Derry squatters was held in Springtown Camp. Every camp throughout the city was represented. Samuel Quigley, chairman of the Springtown committee, presided.

The purpose of the meeting was to discuss a letter that camp residents received from James Thompson, the Corporation's town clerk. In the letter, he stated he had been instructed by the Ministry of Health and Local Government to levy a charge of five shillings (25p) per week per hut from Monday 30 September 1946. This was, he said, to cover the cost of water, scavenging and sanitation. However, in order to put this into effect, it would be necessary for each occupier to sign a Form of Licence. On signing this licence, it was to be made clear that squatters were unauthorised persons. Furthermore, they had no right to be in the camp, and their action in taking possession of the huts did not in any way entitle them to priority in the occupation of the huts when they may be converted.

During the meeting, Paddy Fox of the Derry Labour Party had acted as spokesman for the squatters. He told the residents that a deputation had already met with the town clerk and the city solicitor regarding this matter. He went on to say that the five shillings that had been arrived at was a rough estimate agreed by the Corporation at a meeting on Friday. He said he had pointed out the total, which would amount to around £300 per month, was in his opinion excessive in the circumstances. He was promised that when the Corporation found out the actual cost of these amenities, they would then review the levy. The deputation had been assured by the town clerk and the city solicitor that no-one in the camps would forfeit their rights to the converted huts, provided they were prepared to comply with the conditions set by the Corporation. He finished by saying, to his mind, that that was a satisfactory outcome and he could not see the Corporation charging five shillings per family when the proper cost of the amenities had been determined.

Mr Fox advised the people of the camps to sign the Form of Licence and pay the charges for the next four weeks under protest and without prejudice to their rights. They would then raise the matter of the costs with the Corporation at a later date. Sammy Quigley proposed a motion to this effect, and it was seconded by Mr Whoriskey; on a show of hands, the motion was passed.

This was to be the first official agreement between the squatters and the Corporation.

The following week, every family occupying a hut was given a rent book after signing a Form of Licence to Occupy Temporary Dwelling. (The word temporary took on a new meaning in the Corporation's language, as in these cases it meant twenty years.)

MINISTRY OF HEALTH AND LOCAL GOVERNMENT FOR NORTHERN IRELAND

Licence No. 5/65

Form of Licence to Occupy Temporary Dwelling.

This Agreement made the 15th day of September, one thousand nine hundred and forty-seven between the Ministry of Health and Local Government for Northern Ireland (hereinafter called "The Ministry") of the one part and Mary A. McMonagle (hereinafter called "the occupier") of the other part Witnesseth as follows:—

1. In consideration of the payments by the occupier hereinafter mentioned and of the conditions on the part of the occupier to be observed hereinafter contained the Ministry hereby gives its licence and authority for the occupier to occupy Hut No. 219 Springtown Camp from the 15th day of September, one thousand nine hundred and fortyseven until such occupation is determined in manner hereinafter provided.

2. The occupier will pay to the Ministry weekly, at the Offices of the L'Derry County Borough Council the sum of Ten Shillings the first payment to be made on the 15th day of September 1947.

3. (a) The occupier will use the premises for residential purposes only and will not carry on or permit to be carried on therein any trade or business and will not do or permit to be done any act or thing which may cause discomfort or annoyance to other occupiers of the said premises or of any part of the building of which said premises form part or to the occupiers of neighbouring premises and will at all times during his or her occupation keep the said premises in a clean state and condition. No domestic animals, poultry, etc., may be kept on any part of the premises without the prior and specific authority of the Ministry.

(b) The occupier will not permit or cause any damage to be done to the premises and will at or before the end of the occupation hereby authorised make good any damage which he or she has permitted or caused as aforesaid (reasonable wear and tear excepted).

(c) The occupier will not part with or share possession of the premises or any part thereof and will not without the written consent of the Ministry keep any lodger therein.

4. The occupier will permit the Ministry or its agent or agents at all reasonable times of the day to enter into and upon the said premises and examine the state and condition thereof and to effect any repairs which the Ministry may consider necessary.

The first licence agreements between camp tenants and the Corporation. Temporary in this case meant almost twenty years. Hugh McMonagle and his family came to the camp in 1946 and left in 1965.

Group of residents outside the McGuinness hut at Belmont Camp watching the bailiffs removing the furniture. Included is Johnny Saunders on left. Standing at front: Eddie Kelly, Tommy Cooke, Lily and Pearl McGuinness, 12 May 1947.

Evictions

The unionist-controlled Corporation and Rural Council were coming under pressure from anxious unionists from all over Derry and its rural areas. They raised fears of a shift in the balance of power through a major influx of nationalist voters to the camps. This fear was, of course, ill-founded for many reasons. Still, to appease them, the Corporation and Rural Council, after meetings with the unionists concerned, agreed to lobby the War Department, who owned some of the camps. The War Department agreed to institute legal proceedings against the squatters, but, for some unknown reason, none from Springtown Camp.

The first anyone knew of this decision was when a report of the meeting was leaked to the *Belfast Telegraph*. The newspaper carried a report to this effect in their issue of Tuesday 24 September 1946. The Corporation rubbished the report, stating that they had no intention of issuing legal proceedings against the squatters. Town clerk James Thompson said he didn't know where the report emanated from, as the Corporation had never even contemplated summonses against the squatters. Rural District Council chairman Jim Hatrick said he was completely unaware of any proceedings being contemplated by his council. The RUC in a statement said the squatter situation was not a matter for them. Technically, even though they instigated the whole proceedings, they were telling the truth in that they, the Corporation, and the Rural Council themselves would not be taking legal action against the squatters.

Mary B Kelly and Maggie McGowan with their children at Belmont Camp, 1946.

Despite their denials, the people of the various camps simply did not trust either authority. Their mistrust was well founded as just two weeks later, seventy-four people from different camps received summonses. The summonses ordered them to either vacate the huts they were occupying or face immediate legal action. With nowhere else to live, the squatters had no alternative but to stay put and wait and see what would transpire.

The powers-that-be, without delay, carried out their threat of legal action.

The Derry courthouse was filled to capacity on Wednesday 9 October 1946 with people from the Belmont, Clooney and Eglinton camps summonsed to appear in court. The prosecutions, at the behest of the unionists, were brought by the British Secretary of State for War. Further proceedings against the people from the Bligh's Lane, Bishop Street, Mabuoy and Corrody camps were adjourned pending the outcome of the cases against people from the other camps.

The squatters were charged with 'wilfully entering upon the premises of the said complainant, with intent, wrongfully, to take possession of, or use, the said premises'.

The cases got off to a controversial start when the presiding resident magistrate (RM), Mr Bell, was asked from the outset of the court proceedings by HC O'Doherty, solicitor for some of the squatters, 'Did the British Government talk to you regarding these cases?'

Halloween party group at Belmont Camp on 31 October 1946. Included are: Tommy Cooke, Eddie Kelly, Kevin Scanlon, Hugo Lewis, Minnie Lewis, Charlie McMonagle, Florrie Divin, Mona McMonagle (with son Lornie), Jock Brennan, Wilfred Brennan, Charlie Carlin and Sonny McGlinchey.

Mr Bell replied angrily, 'That is an improper suggestion. Judges and magistrates are solely responsible for the administration of the law. Therefore, the public can have the fullest confidence in the fearless and impartial administration of the law.' He did admit, however, that he had had the benefit of talks with Colonel Davison of the War Office. 'I think it is right to say that the Secretary of State for War was most anxious to help people in their housing difficulties. However, they themselves were confronted with difficulties too technical to explain. Therefore, I wish to assure the people commonly known as squatters that their interests are not being overlooked by those responsible for the administration of the War Office.'

Their interests were not being overlooked, either, by those who, like himself, were charged with the great responsibility of administering the law.

'I hope that at the end of the six months, some solution will be arrived at for your comfort and wellbeing.'

Later, the RM interrupted a heated debate between HC O'Doherty for the Belmont Camp people and EH Babington for the Crown. He asked Babington why now, after eighteen months lying vacant, the War Department suddenly wanted the huts. 'I gathered that this camp lay unoccupied for the best part of two years while people were dying from diphtheria, TB and other diseases, the complement of overcrowding conditions. I must say, it had often occurred to me why those huts were allowed to lie empty when people were living twelve to a room, but this is a matter for the government and not for the courts.' Mr Bell went on to state that he would hear each case separately.

Frederick Thompson, a squatter from Belmont Camp, giving evidence, said he was an ex-serviceman and that he was living in a small room with his wife and five children at 25 Governor Road. 'I had to leave that address and was then on the street before entering the hut. I had nowhere to go. We were sleeping in the bus depot. My intention was to move into the hut to get temporary shelter for my wife and children.' He finished his evidence by asking the court: 'What father wouldn't have done the same thing?'

Another man charged said the huts would not have been seized if the local authorities had done their job properly. He asked who in their right mind would prefer a hut to a proper house. 'We would have had to go to the workhouse if we didn't move into this hut.'

The RM, fining all defendants one shilling, said, 'I am sorry, but there is nothing I can do. You can only have six months to stay.'

Dealing with Belmont Camp, prosecuting solicitor EH Babington said the camp had been offered to the Corporation by the War Department but they had refused the offer.

'Then why don't they give the camp to the squatters?' asked the RM. 'Nobody else seems to want it.'

Seventy-four squatters were each fined one shilling.

With regard to Clooney Camp, evidence was given that the British Army wanted the huts by the end of the year. The RM gave a decree for possession with a stay of execution until 31 December. A similar decree was given against the people of Eglinton Camp, but the stay of execution was reduced to two months. The same was the case for the Belmont Camp residents, but they had a stay of execution of six months.

Babington asked the RM to evict the Belmont Camp people with immediate effect.

'No,' replied Mr Bell. 'They will have six months to leave the huts.'

'That means the War Office will have to be landlords for six months,' replied Babington.

'I cannot help that. Where are these poor people to go?' was the RM's response.

The people left the court disappointed but not surprised by the outcome. They returned to their huts to deliberate on their next move.

A meeting was held the next night in Belmont Camp to discuss the implications of the court's ruling. After long discussions and deep thought, they came to the conclusion that there was nothing really they could do at this particular time. They decided to deploy a 'wait and see' policy, as the next move was really up to the authorities.

The squatters returned to their everyday chores in the camps and waited for further developments. With the threat of eviction hanging over their heads, they felt trapped; despair set in. Some people started leaving the other camps, most emigrating to England. Nevertheless, a large number of families remained.

The months passed without any major development, and the time allotted to the people by the court to vacate their huts was now nearly upon them.

The appointed bailiff let it be known that he had planned to target Belmont Camp first.

On the weekend beginning Friday 9 May 1947, Derry was a city of tension. The people waited to see what the outcome of the terrible state of affairs at Belmont Camp was going to be. The situation had the potential to explode, because who could envisage a more dramatic or emotional scene than that of poor families, with children as young as three months, being evicted from tin huts? The fact they were being evicted from tin huts that had lain empty for months made the decision to evict them all the more puzzling.

The people of Belmont Camp were sick with worry when the bailiffs came to evict them on the Monday, as they would be rendered powerless and homeless. With nowhere to go, what were they supposed to do? Where would their children sleep that night? Where could they take their young children to have some food? These questions ran through their troubled minds; they had no answer to any of them.

Yes, their plight was the main talking point all week: on the factory floors, in every shop, street and indeed in every work place in or around Derry.

Yes, the local newspapers carried headline articles reporting their situation in the camps, and yes, all were sympathetic.

Yes, Paddy Fox of the Derry Labour Party, along with some nationalist politicians, worked round the clock that week to try and find a solution.

Still, at the end of the day, apart from the few mentioned notables, it didn't change the frightening fact that they were on their own.

Unionist politicians didn't care and stayed silent. The authorities were not only unhelpful, they were determined to evict the residents of Belmont Camp.

A meeting was hastily convened that Saturday 10 May by the people of Belmont. In attendance were Paddy Fox, a few other politicians, and James

Thompson, the town clerk. Thompson relayed the news to the people that seventeen huts would be made available to them at Springtown Camp on Monday. This was because seventeen families in huts there were being transferred to the newly converted huts. He went on to say to the camps' representatives and spokesmen that assuming two families agreed to share a hut, that would mean thirty-four families could be accommodated at Springtown. He further stated that if they agreed to this proposal, then each family would get a converted hut when they were ready.

The people rejected this compromise, solely on the grounds that it still meant that sixteen families would be evicted with nowhere to go.

They decided to stick together.

However, spokesmen for the Belmont people agreed to allow the first four families evicted on Monday to take up the offer of huts in Springtown. They would then review their position later on Monday night when they expected an answer to telegrams sent by Paddy Fox to the British prime minister and the Stormont prime minister regarding their plight. They also passed a resolution at their earlier meeting on Friday night protesting against the evictions; this was sent to both prime ministers and also to unionist Westminster MP, Ronald Ross.

The resolution sent read: 'We, the homeless families of Belmont Camp, protest in the strongest manner against the War Department decision to evict us from our temporary accommodation. The Corporation has promised us homes in the converted huts at Springtown Camp. Why can't we be allowed to stay in Belmont Camp until these are ready? Two hundred and fifty people must not be left homeless. Intervention is needed now, as eviction begins on Monday.'

Over that weekend, Alderman Patrick Fox, Alderman Frank McCarroll and Eddie McAteer MP worked all hours to try to find a solution to the terrible situation facing the 265 people living in Belmont Camp.

Their last throw of the dice was the meeting with James Smyth from the Stormont Ministry, but they found him uninterested, unsympathetic and unwilling to interfere with the court's decision to evict the people.

The Belmont Camp residents returned to their huts to make last-minute arrangements. They would have to sit their children down and try their best to explain what was about to happen on Monday.

'How do you explain to a child that men will come to your home on Monday, throw your furniture onto the streets and force you out of your home?' asked one angry father.

Sleep didn't come easily that Sunday night to the beleaguered people of Belmont Camp. That weekend, they were surely the most harassed people in Ireland as they awaited the arrival of bailiffs on Monday morning.

Mr and Mrs Sweeney and family on their way to Springtown Camp after being evicted from Belmont Camp on 12 May 1947. Johnny Saunders is on the extreme right.

The sun was shining brightly that May Monday morning as the bailiff arrived right on time at the camp. He was accompanied by four RUC men, who were there for his protection. The British Army had soldiers from the Royal Enniskillen Fusiliers there in force to dismantle the huts immediately the families were evicted. As the bailiff approached the huts, one father called out to him, 'I hope you sleep better tonight than I did last night.'

Photographers from the local papers were taking photographs of the bailiff at work. He objected strongly to this, telling the photographers that on no account would they be allowed to print them. The photographers took no notice of him and continued taking pictures of him going about his work. This annoyed him to such an extent that he angrily approached the RUC men and asked them to remove the photographers from the camp.

They refused, and this brought loud cheers from the squatters.

With fifty families still in Belmont Camp, the bailiff's intentions were to evict four families per day. He encountered an immediate problem on the first day: as he was on his own, he was unable to lift some of the heavy furniture from one of the huts himself.

The British soldiers and the four RUC men present watched him struggling with the heavy furniture but refused to assist him. With no-one from Belmont Camp about to help him, he left that day, succeeding only in evicting three instead of his intended four families. However, he returned the next day with an assistant and evicted five families so he could keep to his schedule of four families per day.

Bailiff at work in Belmont Camp as the children look on in bewilderment, 12 May 1947.

Above: First to be evicted from Belmont Camp were Abbie and Eva McGuinness and family. Photograph shows the McGuinness children – Lily, Pearl, Abbie and Billy – beside the belongings where the bailiffs placed them outside their hut. Below: Baby Billy McGuinness rests in his cot as bailiffs remove his family's furniture from their hut, Monday 12 May 1947.

The first family was evicted from Belmont Camp at approximately 10.00 am on Monday 12 May 1947. They were the family of Mr and Mrs Abraham McGuinness and their six children. They became the first camp squatters to be evicted in Northern Ireland. Mr McGuinness and his family had previously lived in the attic room of a terraced house in Bishop Street, which had only one small skylight window, before moving to a hut at Belmont Camp.

Also evicted that day was the family of Mr and Mrs John Sweeney and their three children; they came to Belmont Camp after living in one small room at Orchard Lane. Eddie and Mary B Kelly and their three children became the last family to be evicted on that first day. (Mr Kelly had served with the Royal Ulster Rifles for six years and had been discharged owing to disablement.)

The three families moved to Springtown Camp within hours of eviction.

Bailiff carrying furniture from Abbie McGuinness's hut in Belmont Camp, 12 May 1947.

Delivery man saying goodbye to Mrs McGuinness at Belmont Camp on the day she was evicted, Monday 12 May 1947.

British soldiers demolishing huts at Belmont Camp after the bailiffs evicted residents on Monday 12 May 1947. Ninety-nine per cent of families evicted from Belmont went to Springtown, where they shared huts with existing families.

John Moore, his wife and nine-year-old daughter were due to be evicted that day also, but as the bailiff was on his own, he ran out of time. He and his family were evicted the next day when the bailiff returned with an assistant.

The scene was a harrowing sight as furniture lay outside their huts, the children looking on in bewilderment. British soldiers climbed onto the roofs of the huts, started to strip the corrugated tin from them and proceeded to demolish the gables of the huts, thus rendering them useless.

The evictions continued unabated. Patrick and Sadie Campbell and their children were among four other families who were evicted from Belmont Camp on Tuesday 13 May 1947. Again, mothers, fathers and their children could only look on helplessly while bailiffs removed their furniture from the huts and left it on the street. At the same time, British soldiers were on the roof dismantling the huts. They again proceeded to knock down the gable ends of each hut first; although not regarded as normal work for a soldier, they carried out this distasteful task with enthusiasm.

It was ironic that the British soldiers who were assisting the powers-that-be that day were from the Royal Enniskillen Fusiliers, the very regiment that one of the evicted fathers, Patrick Campbell, had joined the previous day.

Also evicted that day were James McCarron, his wife and ten children. Mr McCarron said they were up until 3.00 am preparing for the bailiff. The other two families evicted that day were the families of James Cassidy and Sam McGowan. Again, the families were told there was accommodation for fourteen families at Springtown in huts which had not yet been converted. They would have to share a hut between two families. It was suggested that the authorities would build a partition separating the huts. The good news was that a further fifty huts were being converted at the time and would be ready for occupation within a month.

All the evicted residents again moved to Springtown. The families cast out had been opposed to sharing a hut in Springtown because they said the huts there were smaller than those at Belmont. However, all the families were united in the opinion that their children's health had improved immeasurably since leaving the squalid small rooms of tenements and squatting in the huts.

The families were now organising the removal of their furniture, which was lying at the side of now partially dismantled huts. Some families moved by van, some by horse and cart, and some simply walked the short distance to their new home. Thankfully, the weather was kind to them as they entered their new camp surroundings at Springtown.

Alderman Paddy Fox, who was present throughout the week at Belmont Camp, said that the suggested partitioning of the huts at Springtown Camp, which enabled two families to occupy one hut, should be a temporary measure. Soon, each family would have a converted hut of their own to look forward to in the new camp.

The squatters' champion, Alderman Paddy Fox, with an evicted family at Belmont Camp, May 1947. Paddy Fox, above all others, fought day and night for the families' rights.

Group photographed on 12 May 1947 at Belmont Camp. All were on their way to Springtown Camp. Picture includes: Eva McGuinness, Abbie McGuinness, Hugo Lewis, Minnie Lewis, Eddie Kelly, Charlie McMonagle, Sadie Campbell, Maggie McGowan, Eddie Kelly and Mary B Kelly.

Tommy Cooke was nine years old and oblivious to the serious situation that had developed at the camp. 'Sure, as a nine-year-old boy, all I was interested in was playing in the plantation there,' he recalls. 'The surroundings to the camp were lovely. We even had a tree-lined avenue from the Culmore Road entrance to the huts in Belmont Camp. The huts at Springtown were better because they were lined with mesinite, as opposed to the huts in Belmont which had only the bare tin inside. We had to pull the beds out to the centre of the huts at night in Belmont because of the condensation coming from the tin. It was the only way to keep the beds dry.

'A big potbelly stove was in the middle of the hut and, when lit, it gave out good heat. Actually, the stove would be red hot at the sides when fully lit, and we would toast bread on the sides of the stoves. Toilet facilities were the same as would be used in building sites – just a shed built over a sewer. Sometimes there was a queue and you just had to wait beside the shed until it was your turn to use the toilet. Water came from a stand-up water tap in the centre of the camp, and it was the job of the men and boys to fetch the buckets of water to the huts. It was while playing around the camp that the children came across old shower facilities used by the soldiers. After every football match, the boys would take a shower while someone kept watch for any adult approaching. If we fell from a tree or got a cut knee while playing football, it was straight over to Danny Hasson, the first-aid man.'

Danny was a kindly man and was always sympathetic when treating you. Tommy had fond memories of his short time in Belmont Camp and said the community spirit was second to none. 'For instance, I remember the committee organised a lorry load of coke to be delivered and it was stored in an empty hut. It was just one of the signs of community awareness that prevailed in the camp, and it saved the long journey to and from the Gasyard with a handcart for the normal half-bushel of coke.'

When it was their turn to be evicted, Tommy remembers it was Hill's removal van that ferried their belongings to Springtown. 'I enjoyed the short trip to the new camp, sitting at the back of the removal van with my legs dangling from the tailgate,' said Tommy. 'Anyway, sure all the people from the Belmont Camp, like Kevin Scanlon, Eddie Kelly, the Morrin, Lewis, McMonagle, Sweeney and McCarron families, were going to Springtown. So all we were doing, really, was moving to a better hut and taking all our old pals and neighbours with us.

'However, I still thought the camp at Belmont was better for us as children to play in,' he recalls, looking at me with an almost apologetic smile before quickly adding, 'but I still had a great time in Springtown. I loved following the workmen Freddie and Joe Begley around as they were felting the dormers and roofs during the conversions of the huts,' he concludes.

A little girl watches as British soldiers demolish her hut at Belmont Camp after her family were evicted by bailiffs, 12 May 1947.

    Squatters in the various other camps watched on in horror as they witnessed the callousness of the authorities, under the protection of the RUC, evicting the Belmont Camp residents. The speed at which the British Army dismantled the huts after the residents' furniture was removed by bailiffs shocked them. After witnessing these evictions, these residents knew their fate would be no different. This proved to be the case as the bailiffs moved into Mabuoy camp on Monday 2 June 1947. The bailiffs, once again under the protection of the RUC, moved swiftly, as did the British soldiers of the Royal Enniskillen Fusiliers, who instantly dismantled the huts once the bailiffs had removed the residents' belongings.

On entering the camp, the bailiffs and their entourage glanced at a large board with the inscription:

WELCOME TO BELSEN

One of the first to be evicted was Ralph Adcock, his wife and family. Mr Adcock, an ex-petty officer in the Royal Navy for eight years, when asked where he intended to stay the night, replied, 'I don't know, I have no place to go to.'

Also evicted that day: Mr and Mrs Freddie Wheeler and their children, Charles Lynch, his sister Sarah and brother Patrick, Tom Burns, aged seventy-eight, his elder sister, who was on crutches, and her daughter and niece. It was not a very nice sight to see an evicted seventy-eight-year-old man assisting his elderly sister from their modest hut.

Mr Wheeler, chairman of the Mabuoy Camp committee, said he had been told by Mayor McFarland that the Corporation had no accommodation to offer them. However, if any of the occupants at Springtown could offer them facilities, the Corporation would assist in any way they could.

Children looking confused as the bailiffs evict Freddie Wheeler and family from Mabuoy Camp in June 1947. Most of the families went to live in Springtown.

Given that Springtown already had housed in excess of 300 people from Belmont two weeks previously, it was thought the camp was already overcrowded. Nonetheless, with nowhere else to turn, a deputation from the Mabuoy Camp visited Springtown in the hope of finding somewhere to stay. They met with committee members and talked to some residents who were already aware of their plight. The Mabuoy deputation, to their utter delight and sheer relief, found people who had been in the same predicament as them prepared to offer them help.

The Springtown residents said a partition could be erected to divide huts, thus making way for a family from Mabuoy to live in the other half. The Corporation readily agreed and, in truth, were let off the hook, courtesy of the generosity of the Springtown people.

The Mabuoy families returned to their camp with the news that they had found people in Springtown willing to help them. Just as had happened in Belmont, all were re-housed in Springtown that week.

Bailiffs at their work, evicting families from Mabuoy Camp in June 1947.

On leaving Mabuoy, the people praised the efforts of Eddie McAteer MP, Alderman Patrick Fox and Councillor William Barr. They also thanked Henry Wilson, camp manager at Springtown, for his sympathetic attitude towards them. But they had harsh words for the Rural Council, who they said had given them no assistance or help of any kind.

The remaining squatters in other camps, seeing there was little or nothing they could do to influence the inevitable outcome, knew they were in an impossible situation. After some consultation between the squatters and the authorities, there was an agreement that the evictions would stop immediately and that the remaining squatters from the different camps would be moved to Springtown, where they agreed to share a hut until such times as the last huts at Springtown were converted.

Each family was promised they would get tenancy of a converted hut.

A few short weeks later, Springtown became home to the last fourteen families from Clooney Camp, five families from Bligh's Lane Camp and twenty-five families from the Beech Hill Camp. Their camps were dismantled by the British Army within minutes of the squatters leaving.

Chapter 4

Getting Acquainted

One year after the first squatter moved into Springtown, it was filled to capacity, with all 302 huts occupied and housing 319 families.

With scores of new families once again moving into the camp, getting to know their new neighbours was again a priority. There were people from different communities and different backgrounds, city people and country people. Nevertheless, they had one thing in common: they had all been previously living in squalor.

The coming weeks would be a learning process for many of this new and emerging community. People were meeting new neighbours for the

Pearl, Lily, Billy and Tony McGuinness posing for the camera, July 1952.

first time and forming friendships – some that would last a life time. It was story time once again in Springtown, each family relating to the other their particular tale and family history. They told of their own individual circumstances which forced them to squat into the different camps and the trauma of their evictions. The new inhabitants were busy finding their way around this new Nissen-hut village, locating where the wee shops were, who the deliverymen were and what they sold. They also had the important task of relocating their children to different schools in the city. It all added to new and exciting times for all concerned, especially the children with their new-found freedom and great play areas.

Aerial view of Springtown in 2010. Shaded section indicates site of original camp.

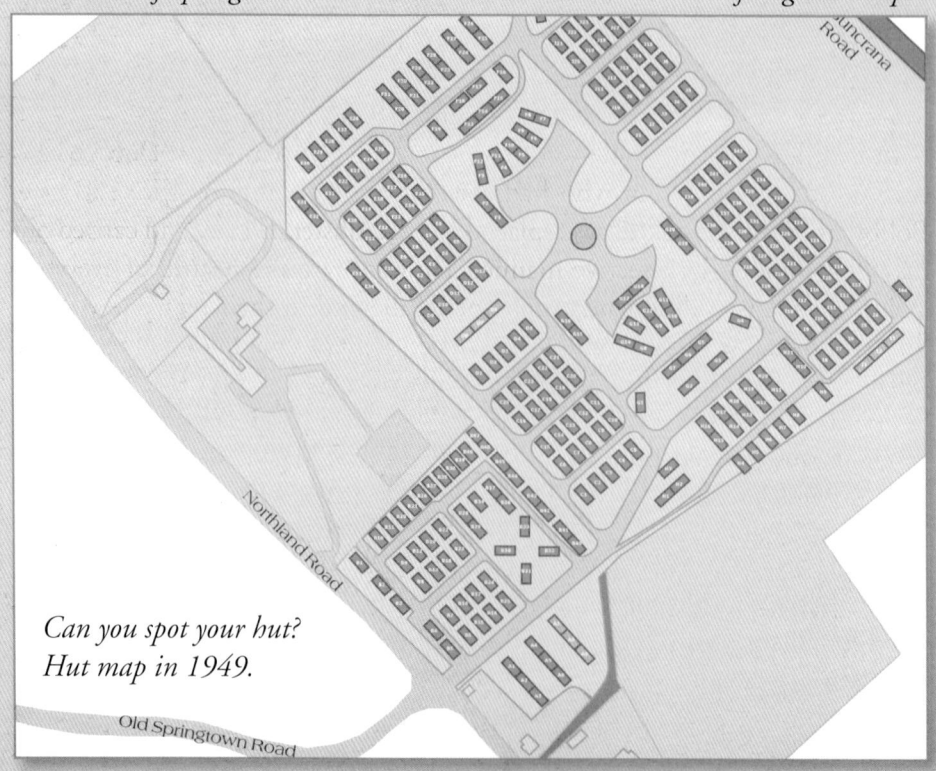

*Can you spot your hut?
Hut map in 1949.*

With the camps at Belmont, Clooney, Bligh's Lane, Mabuoy, Creevagh, Beech Hill and Bishop Street demolished and now but a memory, nearly all the original squatters from the nine different camps throughout Derry and the county were now living in Springtown, many sharing a hut with another family. This left one fully occupied camp in Derry, which now had the population of an average Irish town.

Springtown Camp, which had been converted for 'temporary accommodation', was to remain intact for a further twenty years.

Bob Hutchman relaxing at home with his wife after work in his small office at the top of the camp, 1956.

At the beginning of 1948, when the conversions of the huts for 'temporary use' were completed, there were a total of 302 huts in Springtown, housing 319 families. The Corporation, in their wisdom, employed two men to look after the maintenance of the huts. An impossible task by any standards, but in hindsight, it should have forewarned of the Corporation's future intentions regarding the upkeep of the huts. The men entrusted with the task of the maintenance of the 302 huts were Paddy 'Sauce' Moore and Mick Powers; both men became legends in the camp. Every man, woman and child was very fond of both men, who were always very helpful when called upon. Of course, the task they were set by the Corporation of keeping the huts in good repair was impossible, but both men remained in their positions for many years, with Mick Powers staying until the last residents left the camp.

In addition to them, there was 'rent man-cum-camp manager' Bob Hutchman, a decent, civil man who had a wee office near the top-gate entrance. Bobby, as he was known to all, replaced Mr McAllister in 1949 and carried out his duties in a quiet, effective manner. He was always respectful of everyone and very understanding when someone fell behind in their rent. He was the first port of call if you wanted any repairs done. His reply to everyone was the same: 'I will look into it.' To be honest, the people sympathised with him, as he had only two workmen to look after 302 huts – a daunting task.

The future seemed bright for the people of Springtown as they now had moved into the newly converted huts. Their standard of living had improved immensely and they were experiencing a new lease of life. The memory of overcrowded wee rooms with one Primus stove and their subsequent evictions was now relegated to the dustbin. The families were now in spacious living quarters, had separate bedrooms and a range and other amenities that made life much more comfortable in their tin huts.

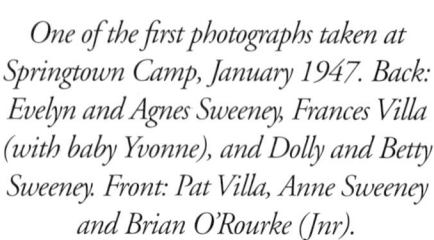

One of the first photographs taken at Springtown Camp, January 1947. Back: Evelyn and Agnes Sweeney, Frances Villa (with baby Yvonne), and Dolly and Betty Sweeney. Front: Pat Villa, Anne Sweeney and Brian O'Rourke (Jnr).

Sammy Quigley with daughter Isobel and son Liam in one of the first huts to be converted, 1947. Sammy was elected camp committee chairman in August 1946, days after the people squatted into the huts.

Big Jimmy Jennings arrived in the camp in January 1947, and he recalls the winter that year was one of the worst in living memory, with heavy snowfalls lying for weeks. Jimmy recalls they had to search for the water taps (which were attached to a 3ft stand-up pipe), the snow was so deep. Along with his friend John Moore, he started a newspaper round in the camp; it was a very popular and much-needed service for the people.

'It was a luxury having the daily paper handed to you at your doorstep each morning,' remembers Mary McMonagle, who also fondly reminisces about the beautiful maple dancefloor in the recreation hall. 'It was so clean and shiny we could slide up the floor at our ease.' Mary with a glint in her eye recalls her old neighbours the Clingans, McLoones, Browns, Killens and Duddys.

In the early years at the camp, people were coming and going at regular intervals, some leaving for England and further afield. Their reason for leaving was twofold: to find employment and to find a proper house in which to rear their children. The sad part of this was that some never, ever returned to the city of their birth.

With new houses now being constructed in Creggan, some families were lucky enough to be allocated one of them. This movement out of the camp left vacant huts, but they didn't stay vacant long, as the housing shortage in Derry was still endemic. There were still many families living in tiny rooms in slum areas of the city; these people were only too glad to avail of the opportunity to move into the huts.

Many of the parents took advantage of some light entertainment when they attended dances in the recreation hall. Dances were organised by the camp committee and Johnny McBride's pipe band from Fahan Street often entertained the people. The idea was that such functions not only gave them an opportunity to get to know their new neighbours, they also provided temporary respite from the recent upheaval to their lives.

Things went along smoothly for the next couple of years with families coming and going. Throughout the camp's existence, tenants regularly flitted from hut to hut for one reason or another. I suppose the main reason was they thought the other hut was in better condition, or simply because they wanted to move to be beside a relation or friend. One family was to move no fewer than eight times!

The wooden huts, of which they were seventeen in total, rarely became vacant; the odd time that one did was because the family were re-housed. They were much sought after because, being made of wood, they were warmer in the winter and the rooms and ceilings were square which made them easier to decorate, as opposed to the curved walls and ceilings of the tin huts. When decorated, the wooden huts looked really nice and were very comfortable.

William and Maureen Duddy with their twin girls Bernie and Kay outside Hut 216, 1948.

Kay and Bernie Duddy outside their hut in 1952. Soon, they would be on their way to a new house in Creggan.

The corrugated-tin huts, which had curved walls, had no demarcation lines to separate walls from ceilings. They were just one big curve from the floor level at one side to floor level at the other side, making it very difficult to paper walls. I don't remember ever seeing paper on any ceilings in a tin hut!

***

With Springtown being over two miles from Derry, it meant a round trip of between four and five miles to the schools and work each day. The next on the committee's agenda was a meeting with the transport department of the Corporation with a view to getting a bus service to and from Derry. This proved to be very difficult, and the buses continued to come only as far as Eden Terrace. However, in 1948, a new transport authority was set up incorporating all the small independent transport companies throughout the North. This new company, called the Ulster Transport Authority (UTA), was to serve the whole of Northern Ireland. It was a timely venture for the residents of the camp. After several meetings with UTA over a period of several weeks, they agreed to start a limited service to the camp; the first bus route to and from the camp began in July 1948. The bus stop was situated 150 yards inside the camp near McConnell's shop.

BUS SERVICES Nos. 151A

BUS SERVICE No. 151A.—LONDONDERRY—SPRINGTOWN.

WEEK-DAYS

LONDONDERRY (Strand Road) dep.:—

a.m.	a.m.	a.m.	a.m.	p.m.	p.m.	p.m.	p.m.	p.m.	p.m.	p.m.	p.m.	p.m.
7 30	7 55	9 45	11 45	12 10	12 50	1 10	2 45	4 15	5 40	6 45	7 10	9 5 10 40 ...

SPRINGTOWN dep.:—
SX

a.m.	a.m.	a.m.	a.m.	noon	p.m.	p.m.	p.m.	p.m.	p.m.	p.m.	p.m.	p.m.	p.m
7 40	8 5	9 0	10 0	12 0	12 20	1 0	1 50	3 0	4 50	5 50	6 55	7 20	9 15 10 50

SUNDAYS

LONDONDERRY (Strand Rd.) dep.—p.m.—12 45   2 45   5 15   7 15   8 45   ...   ...

SPRINGTOWN   dep.—p.m.—1 0   3 0   5 30   7 30   9 0   ...   ...

SX—Saturdays excepted.

The Ulster Transport Authority bus schedule for Springtown Camp.

66

The UTA bus depot on the Strand Road from where the 151a bus service to Springtown Camp departed. The last run to the camp – the famous 10.40 pm bus – left from the rear of the depot.

A direct route to Derry now established, life became a lot easier for the people and their children. With the service being a big success, as most buses were packed, UTA increased the number of buses to the camp. Soon, they were running approximately every hour, the first one leaving the camp at 7.40 am and the last bus leaving Derry at 10.40 pm. There was a total of fifteen buses timetabled to and from the camp on weekdays and five buses on a Sunday. This made visiting relatives, going to dances or the pictures, and shopping in the city much more accessible for the residents. The daily bus service to and from Derry provided a further normalisation to people's lives in the camp.

Chapter 5
Jane Russell Adoption

Film star and screen goddess Jane Russell made sensational news around the camp in November 1951 when the news filtered through she had adopted fifteen-month-old Thomas Kavanagh. Thomas, born on 29 July 1950, was the son of Hannah Florence McDermott from Hut 69b Springtown Camp and Dubliner Michael Kavanagh. Hannah, sometimes called Florrie, had been working in London when she met Michael, a carpenter from Dublin working on the London building sites, at a dancehall in Cricklewood, a frequent haunt of the Irish in London. They married a short time later and went to live in a

Jane Russell, the film star.

small two-room flat at 8 St Stephen's Terrace, South Lambeth, London. They had three children in quick succession: daughter Theresa and sons Michael and Thomas, who was the youngest at fifteen months.

Things were very difficult for the young married couple with three young children living in a very small second-floor flat in London. They found life a struggle bringing up a young family in this enormous and unforgiving city. Hannah had earlier moved to London in search of a better life, but things had not been easy. With her husband unemployed, they were struggling to make ends meet; the family were suffering real poverty and they were now on the brink. Hannah wanted to give her children the best possible chance in life. She wanted them to have everything in life, all the things she'd wanted but never had, the best education money could buy and a standard of living she knew in her heart neither she nor her husband could give them.

The British general election that year returned Winston Churchill to power. Newspapers carried news of his victory on their front pages alongside his photograph, and on the same front page, they carried a picture of bejewelled American film star and sex symbol Jane Russell. Russell was in London to take part in the Royal Command Performance before the King and Queen of England. The caption above Russell's photograph read: 'Jane Russell in London to Adopt Baby Boy'. She didn't mind these headlines, as she had made no secret of the fact that she wanted to adopt a baby boy between the age of one and two years.

Jane Russell, the mother, with her adopted children Thomas Kavanagh and Tracy, shortly after adopting Thomas in 1952.

The front-page story caught the attention of Hannah Kavanagh. This was her chance to give her son everything she'd ever wanted for him in the land of opportunity.

Jane Russell was one of the world's biggest film stars, and she had the resources to give her son all of these things. 'It would be like heaven for him,' Hannah confided to a friend.

Hannah dashed out to a phone box and phoned London's Savoy Hotel, where Jane Russell was staying with her mother, Geraldine Jacobi, and asked to speak to her. The hotel receptionist put her call through to the actress's room. Russell wasn't there, as she was at rehearsals for the Royal Command Performance, but her mother was, and she took the call.

Hannah told the star's mother she'd read the article in the papers and that she had a healthy, fifteen-month-old boy whom she would like Jane Russell to adopt. The actress's mother promised to pass on her message, suggesting she should phone back in a few hours.

Russell returned to her hotel room after rehearsals and her mother told her an Irish woman had phoned her hotel. She relayed to her daughter what Hannah had said and Russell waited in anticipation for the call.

Hannah, as promised, phoned the hotel again, and this time got to speak to Jane Russell in person. After talking for several minutes, they decided to meet in two hours, Russell asking Hannah to bring the baby with her. Russell knew that only a British subject could adopt a British child, but this was different, as this couple were from Ireland.

Standing in the lobby of the Savoy Hotel with baby Thomas in her arms, this small, slim Derry woman must have attracted some odd looks. Glancing around the posh, luxurious foyer, Hannah would have thought this was heaven compared to her two wee poky rooms on the second floor of a drab tenement block.

Russell was later to admit she felt a lot of trepidation when the mother arrived with her baby boy. The film star said, 'She was a very sweet little woman, and she placed the baby boy on the bed. He had lovely blue eyes and a mass of golden curls. He looked straight through me, and he looked just like my brother Billie, who'd died at sixteen months.'

Hannah explained to her that she had other children and would never be able to give her young son the life or education he deserved, and she wanted him to go to America with a Christian family. Russell went on to say, 'I was standing there, scared and numb. I let my mother do all the talking. I finally told the baby's mother I would let her know. When they left my hotel room, I went to my bedroom and prayed hard. All that I heard myself saying was "take him, take him". The day before the Royal Command Performance, I phoned the parents and told them I would take the baby boy.'

That night, Jane Russell was standing talking to the Queen of England, but her mind only gave space to a little fifteen-month-old Irish baby boy. She recalls the show was a success but her head was spinning and she had a sore throat. Russell thought it would take weeks to get the baby cleared and that he would have to follow her later.

Tuesday 6 November 1951 was to prove to be not only an extraordinary day, but a life-changing day to the lives of Thomas Kavanagh, his mother Hannah, and film star Jane Russell. That morning, the phone rang in Russell's hotel room; British publicist Gordon White was on the other end. He told Jane that miraculously they had got all the papers cleared and an Irish passport for Thomas had been issued by the Irish embassy in London that morning. They told her if she came down now and signed the papers, the baby could, after all, go home with her that very night. Jane said she left her mother to do the packing and continued, 'I staggered to the waiting car, where Mr White and a Mr Bayeux were waiting. I couldn't believe what was happening. I was too sick to worry. As I signed the paper, I saw his birthday was almost the same date as my husband Robert's.'

When they got to the airport with the baby, they were on the tarmac and about to board the plane. They looked around and there was the baby's mother, Florrie Kavanagh, standing crying, a photographer following her. She wanted to say a last goodbye to her baby.

Russell said it was very emotional indeed. 'I was crying, the mother was crying and the baby was crying. As we boarded the plane, she was walking away. Then she turned around and said, "His name is Thomas. Take good care of him." I will, I called back to her.'

As the plane roared away from London airport, Hannah watched through tear-filled eyes as her son Thomas was on his way to San Fernando Valley in Southern California and a new life.

***

When the plane touched down in New York, the news of Thomas Kavanagh's adoption had reached America.

Personnel from RKO (a major US film company) were there to meet Russell as were hordes of photographers, reporters and television camera crews. They fought, screamed and climbed on boxes to get pictures and a story.

To try to calm things down a bit, Jane sent the baby with her mother to Albuquerque before facing husband Robert. Things happened so fast in London that she didn't have time to tell her husband of the adoption, although by now he would have heard the news.

Word got to Russell that her home was besieged by reporters and photographers, all looking for an exclusive. One alert photographer followed her mother all the way to Albuquerque where he managed to get a photograph of Thomas. Russell later commented that you would have thought nothing else was happening in the world other than her adopting a baby.

She told her friends that when she brought him home and sat him on the floor, everyone just stood there and looked at him. He was a nice baby and not at all shy, and he settled down and adapted quickly to his new surroundings.

News soon broke about the adoption, and the Kavanaghs were visited two days later by Superintendent Reginald Spooner, a top-notch officer from the Metropolitan Police. He was there on the orders of the British Home Secretary. The news was carried by every newspaper, television and radio station all over America, Britain and Ireland. The home of Jane Russell and the studios of RKO were snowed under by dozens of press and television crews.

Over the next few weeks, the Kavanaghs had a torrid time in their tiny flat in South Lambeth. Hannah received scores of hate mail from women all over the country who criticised her for giving her son up for adoption. Her close neighbours also vented their anger at her decision to let her young son go to America with Jane Russell. The story was to dominate the front pages of the national dailies for weeks. Most of the letters arriving at the offices of the newspapers were about Tommy Kavanagh's adoption.

That week, Hannah, responding to people who asked if she thought she had made a mistake letting her son leave with Jane Russell, said, 'No, I don't. I'm certain I did the right thing for my son, and I would do the same thing again. Do you not think Thomas is going to a better place than this? I actually told his sister and brother that Thomas has gone to Fairyland. It was the only way I could explain it to them.'

Her husband Michael, twelve years her senior, said they had received some nasty letters from people, mostly women, criticising them. Hannah said she gave up her son Thomas because she loved him dearly, because she knew he would have a much happier life with Jane Russell. She told reporters, who were constant visitors to her small second-floor flat, 'I had always wanted to make something of my own life but I didn't have a chance. I want my children to have a better chance than I had. That is why I gave up my son.'

The storm clouds were also gathering around the corridors of power in the British houses of parliament. On Thursday 15 November 1951, Colonel Marcus Lipton, Labour MP for Brixton, stood up in Westminster and demanded that American film stars stop snatching British children. This comment made the Russell family angry and Jane replied: 'I would like to inform Colonel Lipton that Thomas is not British, he is Irish and he travelled on an Irish passport.'

Still, the American papers had a field day with this. What an international storm this wee son of a Springtown Camp mother was making!

The US press were relentless in their pursuit of news and photographs of Russell with her adopted baby. It seemed the whole world wanted to know the ins and outs of young Thomas Kavanagh.

As the media attention reached saturation proportions, Jane Russell was summoned to the studio office of RKO, where billionaire owner Howard Hughes and his attorneys and managers were waiting for her. There was only one item up for discussion: young Thomas Kavanagh. They suggested to Russell that she should return Thomas to London; otherwise, this had the potential to cause an international incident. At this stage, Jane's husband Robert, panicking about the media attention it was attracting, agreed it might be for the best in the circumstances. Jane reacted angrily and steadfastly refused; instead, she called the Immigration Department and explained all the legal details to them. She was relieved when told that if England didn't push the issue, they certainly wouldn't, as they had no problem with the legality of the adoption.

Hannah Kavanagh (née McDermott) bathing her children Theresa and Michael at her two-bedroom flat in a tenement building in South London the day after her son Thomas, adopted by film star Jane Russell, flew to America.

Hannah's other children, Theresa and Michael Kavanagh.

Nevertheless, back in London there was another twist in the tale. Shortly after an MP brought the question of the adoption to the floor of the British legislature, the Kavanaghs were charged with breaking British adoption laws. Hannah and her husband were summoned to appear at Bow Street Magistrate's Court on Thursday 24 April 1952.

Russell was furious at this development. She hired a top London barrister to defend the Kavanaghs. Throughout the trial, the Kavanaghs rigidly stood by their story and never wavered, although some people criticised them. The judge finally decided Thomas should stay in America with his adopted parents, as it was best for the child. The Kavanaghs were discharged conditionally, and the British were later to change their outdated adoption laws. It had proved a difficult six months for all concerned. Only after the court case could Russell complete the legal adoption of Thomas and claim American citizenship for him.

This saga with the British authorities led Jane Russell, with the support of her husband, famous professional American footballer Bob Waterfield, to campaign to make adoption laws simpler and quicker for suitable parents. Russell, unfortunately, was unable to have children, after a near-fatal personal tragedy at the age of nineteen. From that moment on, she took a staunch pro-life stance against abortion, as she cared for children deeply. This was borne out when she championed the passage of the Federal Orphan Adoption Amendment of 1953 in America. This allowed children born to American servicemen overseas to be placed for adoption in America. She also founded the World Adoption International Fund, an organisation which placed children with adoptive families. She later pioneered the adoption of children from foreign countries to American families. Her organisation has placed over 51,000 children with adoptive families.

Hannah Kavanagh's son Thomas Waterfield, aged seventeen, playing a roll on his drums.

    Thomas Kavanagh, by all accounts, apart from the normal teenage rows he had with his father, was to have a very happy childhood living with his new family in California. Later, as a teenager, he grew interested in music and became a keen and talented drummer. He formed his own rock band, Toucan Eddy, and they were moderately successful playing the Arizona pub scene. His adoptive mother Jane was, of course, a cabaret singer as well as a film star. There were times when Thomas appeared on stage with her, playing drums as she sang.

    It was while Jane was doing cabaret work in London and Wales in October 1968 that Thomas, eighteen at the time, decided to accompany her on tour. In London, he took the opportunity to meet up with his biological mother, Hannah, and his sister Theresa. This was the first time he had set eyes on his mother and sister since being adopted in November 1951. Both Hannah and Theresa were delighted to see Thomas, and he was over the moon at meeting his biological family. Jane Russell said the meeting made everyone very happy; the Kavanaghs were very proud of him and so was she.

Thomas himself was not at all interested in talking about his adoption or indeed his roots, and I suppose that is understandable: he, like everyone else, is entitled to his privacy. I phoned his brother Buck, who lives beside their mother in the Santa Maria Valley, California. While very pleasant during our conversation, when I told him of this book, he seemed guarded when talking about his brother.

Thomas's adoptive parents Jane Russell and Bob Waterfield divorced in February 1968. Both he and his sister Tracy elected to live with Jane, while Buck went to live with his father. They all remained close friends right up until Waterfield's death. Russell was to marry actor Roger Barrett in August 1968; Barrett died three months later. She married for the third time in 1974 to millionaire John Calvin Peoples; the marriage lasted until his death in 1999.

I remembered young Thomas Kavanagh's uncle, William 'Sandy' McDermott, as a restless, questioning and unknowingly witty person in the camp. He still is, to this day, a well-known character about town. His matter-of-fact attitude regarding the hype that surrounded the adoption of his nephew typifies Sandy. He maintains the craic about his dear mother Frances is a much more interesting story. She provided a very important service to the people in the camp. Reminiscing about bygone days, he told me: 'My mother sold bread and buns from the wee front room in our hut. Anyone could knock on our door at all hours of the night and still get served. People, you included,' he smiles, pointing a finger at me, 'would come knocking on our door at ten or eleven at night looking for a loaf of bread for the breakfast in the morning. If my mother said it may be a bit stale now, the response was usually, "Sure, we can make toast with it."'

Sandy chuckles loudly as he recollects his mother Frances buying pawn tickets from people in the camp. 'I'm not kidding you, my mother had more pawn tickets than Barr's pawn shop. When she bought the pawn tickets, she would go into the pawn and pay the money that was due on the goods. She then would re-sell the items to her neighbours. To tell you the truth, I think most times she was lucky to get her money back. Sometimes, she had to sell them at a loss, because if she had kept all the clothes she bought with the pawn tickets, we would have had more stock than Willie Scanlon! But she didn't care; she just liked the wheeling and dealing. Sure, she loved the people in the camp.'

To this day, Sandy says he could never understand what all the fuss was about his nephew being adopted. 'Sure, look at some of the poor wee wains from the camp who were taken into care . . . and some of them were treated badly. My wee nephew was going to live in America with a millionaire film star, to be treated like a lord, with all the best that money could buy. Swimming pool out their back, sunshine daily. Tell me, was there not a difference?' he asked, arms outstretched.

Jane Russell today, at the age of eighty-nine, lives in retirement in the Santa Maria Valley on the central coast of California, near her son Buck.

Hannah Kavanagh, who visited her mother, sisters and brothers in Springtown several times a year, continued to live in London. She was to meet her son Tommy in London in 1968. After the meeting, she was asked if she'd do the same thing again given the chance; her answer was an emphatic no. Hannah was to have a hard life; she separated from husband Michael and controversy followed her to her grave. She died on Friday 4 January 1980 in a fire at her flat on Forster Road, Clapham, South London, where she lived alone.

However, a post mortem was to reveal she had been strangled before the fire had started at her flat. Police launched a murder hunt for her killer, who they thought had started the fire to cover up the murder. Commenting on his biological mother's murder, Thomas said, 'I was all churned up inside. I just felt sick that a woman, who has had more than her share of suffering, should be snuffed out like this. Although we were virtual strangers, you can't throw off a bond with the person who gave birth to you.'

Her estranged husband Michael was buried next to her in 1998.

Thomas Waterfield (Kavanagh) is living happily with his own family in Tucson, Arizona, working as a florist and playing with his band Toucan Eddy at night. There is little doubt that Thomas in his youth had received all the material things in life that money could buy. Did he find in the USA the Promised Land that Hannah Kavanagh thought it would be for him?

Only he can answer that.

***

Just a short few months after her nephew Thomas Kavanagh was adopted by Jane Russell, Maureen Elizabeth McDermott was being fostered to a childless couple living in Leicester, England. The couple applied to adopt Maureen, but the authorities were of the opinion they were too old at forty-six and fifty-six, so they continued to foster Maureen.

Maureen was born at 69b Springtown Camp in 1949. She lived with mother Frances and father David McDermott until 1952 when, at the tender age of three, she was taken to Leicester to be fostered. She went to school there and later qualified as a hairdresser.

Maureen takes up her story: 'My natural mother wrote to me and sent me gifts, but my foster parents withheld all correspondence from my mother to me. Despite this, I did on several occasions manage to intercept the mail, but I had no way of returning the mail; my foster parents forbade me. After a considerable length of time had passed, the correspondence stopped.'

After completing her training as a hairdresser, Maureen went on holiday to South Africa. On returning to Leicester, she told her foster parents that South Africa was a wonderful place with sunshine all year round. Her parents were so impressed by her glowing reports of life in this sun-drenched country that they decided to emigrate to Port Elizabeth, South Africa.

However, by this time, Maureen had changed her name by deed poll to that of her foster parents, Mary Poshydaew. Her foster father was a Russian refugee from World War II, and her foster mother was a Russian translator.

Mary set up residence in Port Elizabeth and in 1975 she met and married local architect Frank DeMeuse. They had a son, Jonathan, and a daughter, Claire. Both have come through university and are now qualified in physiology and chemistry.

Sandy McDermott with his sister Maureen, who flew from her home in South Africa to meet with Sandy, whom she hadn't seen since leaving Springtown in 1952. Maureen had been fostered by a couple living in Leicester in 1952.

Mary, despite her and her family's success in their chosen careers, still carried the 'want' to contact and meet her brothers and sisters. The urge never left her heart and mind, so she set about the task of locating her family from Springtown.

With the support and help of her understanding husband Frank, she wrote to everyone and everybody she thought could shed light on her search. The determination of this close wife and husband team brought fruit, as they soon discovered that Mary's long-lost brother, William 'Sandy' McDermott, was still living in Derry.

After fifty-three long years, Mary decided it was time she made the long trip back home to Derry. Her daughter accompanied her on her emotional journey to see her brother. Sandy was over the moon to see Maureen, as he still fondly calls her, as he showed her around Derry and took her to see the school she would have attended. Both keep regular contact with each other now and will continue to do so.

I must say, despite Mary's happy contented and successful life in sun-drenched South Africa, it is very refreshing to see and hear of her commitment in seeking out her Springtown family.

It is also very satisfying to know she has never forgotten her roots.

Chapter 6

Early Childhood Days

The location of the camp was ideal, and indeed to us children it seemed like a gigantic adventure park. It had trees, cornfields and orchards full of apples situated just outside the wire fence that surrounded the camp. There were lots of green areas for us to play – with a large open hard stand down at the square that made a perfect play area in wet weather – and all in a safe environment. With no shortage of open spaces, we could play any game of our choosing; we were in our element. Clean, fresh country air filled our lungs.

The Ward children: Liam, James, Mary and, front, Anne, 1952.

The sight of the Buncrana train passing daily was always greeted with pure excitement.

Our parents would open their front doors all day long and let us roam our part of the camp to play in complete freedom and safety. The surrounding scenery was breathtaking, with the sight of dozens of green fields, all nestling at the foot of the Donegal hills.

The adults were also pleased that the border was just under a mile away from the camp; it made smuggling that little bit easier.

With so many things to do and explore, the overcrowded, gas-fume-filled rooms in run-down tenements was now a fading bad memory. The chain-link wire fence erected by the US Navy stood eight feet high around the entire perimeter. There was a concrete bridge over the Lough Swilly railway line at the bottom entrance leading on to the Buncrana Road. In the very early days, parents would take their children onto the bridge to watch the Buncrana train pass under it. It was a great thrill as the smoke bellowed up around you from the steam engine.

The camp was made up of 95% green corrugated-tin huts and the rest were the more 'lavish' wooden huts. Rough, uneven roads and footpaths ran through the camp. The streets were lit up at night by a total of nineteen telegraph-type poles carrying large tungsten filament bulbs of 150 watts inserted inside a rectangular metal shade (the bulbs were later reduced to 100 watts by the Corporation).

At night, the camp was a grim-looking place, but in summertime, it became a very pretty sight as colourful buttercups, bluebells, and daisies surrounded the green tin huts.

Lily Jennings with children Ted and Esther.

With the camp situated about two miles from Derry, it was obviously too far to walk into and out from the town daily. Some residents saw the prospect for a business venture and set up wee shops in their huts. Ronnie Reid was the first to do this.

With a population now approaching 2,000, one shop was simply not enough. Soon, others followed Ronnie's example and opened shops of their own. Down the years, we had many wee shops, including Reid's, McCrossan's, Hasson's, Smith's, McConnell's, Moore's, Canning's and, last but not least, Mary Ann Meehan's shop. I was to get my first pair of blue jeans (on tick, of course) in Mary Ann's; although they were about six inches too long for me, I was still on cloud nine with excitement.

I think probably everyone in the camp had a 'book', which was another name for tick, or as it is known today, credit. It was a little red book and the shop owners used to keep a record of the groceries a family got in his shop during the week. Families would pay the total amount each Friday (well, that was the theory, anyway). I'm pretty certain some cute customers may have had a book in a couple of shops, or indeed all of them!

I can say without fear of contradiction that my 'little red book' was a big favourite in the camp long before the Drifters even thought about recording it!

The shop owners were generous to a man, and all very understanding. They were on many occasions a lifesaver, as were the many deliverymen who supplied their services. Back then, deliverymen brought their services by van, car,

Hugo Lewis and Charlie Crumlish outside Hugo's wooden hut, 1952.

Frances Clarke with her sons Bobby and John. In background: John Friel and pals, 1953.

horse and cart, or simply just a push cart, and on a few occasions with their wares simply carried on their shoulders. As the people of Springtown ushered in the 1950s, the deliverymen increased in number.

Hugo Lewis recalls, as a young boy, leaving Belmont Camp and coming to live in Springtown. He reminisces about going up to the camp gate with his pals Willie 'Inkin' Canning, Kevin Scanlon and Brian McMenamin every Saturday morning where they would count the number of horse-drawn carts that passed the gate on their way to Derry to sell their turf and buttermilk. Other carts were stacked high with potatoes, vegetables and fresh eggs. They got so friendly with the deliverymen who passed the camp that when returning home, if the traders had any spare apples or other items left, they would give them to the young lads. Hugo remembers when one of the cartwheels got stuck and wouldn't turn. They helped the cart owner to remove the large wheel as they put their youth and strength to good use by holding up the cart while the owner greased and refitted the wheel.

'We got six fresh eggs each for helping out,' he said with a smile. Hugo went on to say: 'During the school holidays, every Monday morning it was normal for us to stand at the gate and count how many people went by. This time, however, it wasn't the deliverymen with their horses and carts we were counting, but the men and women of the camp with their wee brown parcels under their arms on their way to the pawn shops in Derry.'

Happy campers on a summer's day, 1951. Included: Carmel, Michael and John Kerrigan with Maureen, Ann, Kay and Bernie Duddy.

Behind our hut was a big chestnut tree on the property of Henry Jackson, who lived in Springtown House. Standing in its own grounds, it was a hugely impressive, large house. Beautiful gardens full of flowers of every colour of the rainbow, they looked stunning in the sunlight. However, more importantly and to our delight, he just happened to have an orchard full of delicious apples. The only things separating us from those delicious-looking apples were an 8ft-high wire fence, two large Alsatian dogs, and the serious problem of Mr Jackson's two big sons. His orchard was visited by both boys and girls from the camp on a regular basis.

The many battles of wits that took place between Mr Jackson, his two sons and the children of the camp were a source of delight to us. They certainly kept us occupied on many a night as we sought some childish excitement. On the odd day we actually got spotted by Mr Jackson himself, it was not uncommon to hear the odd shot being fired from his shotgun, albeit in the air. This put the fright into us, and on such occasions, our jumpers full of apples, we quickly dropped them and ran for our lives as we scarpered over the fence as fast as an Olympic pole vaulter. We vowed we would never prog (rob) his orchard again.

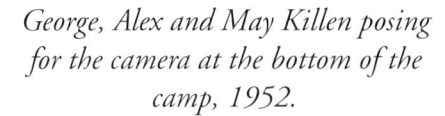

George, Alex and May Killen posing for the camera at the bottom of the camp, 1952.

John Magill, George Deeney, Liam Ward, James Ward and Pat Mitchell playing during the summer holidays, 1952.

More often than not, it was his two sons and his two Alsatian dogs that were normally let loose on us. With the dogs (encouraged by their masters) at your heels, the fear you felt was something else. Constipation certainly wouldn't have been a problem, that's for sure!

After finally escaping over the fence to the safety of the camp, the relief felt was enormous. In truth, the feeling of a lucky escape didn't last long. The temptation to taste once again those juicy apples was too much for us, and soon we were back to robbing his orchard. This scenario went on for years, and was part of growing up in the camp for a lot of boys and girls. In hindsight, I think Mr Jackson and his sons enjoyed the battle of wits as much as we enjoyed his apples.

The big chestnut tree was a different matter. Although on Mr Jackson's property, it was so big it spread way over the fence and into the camp area. Half of the children in the camp came there for the chestnuts. Most of us were content to throw a stone or a stick at our chosen chestnut in the hope of bringing it tumbling to the ground. Other, more determined boys chose to risk injury by climbing the large tree to pick the biggest and best chestnuts.

Throwing a stone or stick at a particular chestnut was a fine art that would entail a lot of practice to perfect. Somehow, we always managed to get a good supply of chestnuts. The following procedure would then take place. We would peel off the surrounding layer to get to the actual chestnut itself. It then was a matter of placing it in a jam jar full of water and letting it steep overnight. This, we thought, would strengthen the chestnut. Whether it actually did or not was another matter.

The next day we would pierce a hole in the centre of the chestnut, thread a piece of string through the hole and tie a knot on the end of the string. Now

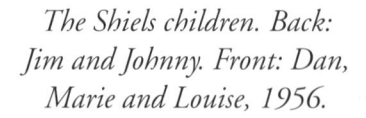

The Shiels children. Back: Jim and Johnny. Front: Dan, Marie and Louise, 1956.

The Gilmore family outside their hut, 16 Springtown Camp, in 1952. Floyd, Tony, Bernard and May with little Sarah at front.

the chestnut was ready to do battle, so out went a challenge to every other boy or girl to a game of chestnuts. Once the challenge was accepted, one combatant would hold his chestnut on a string while the other hit it with his chestnut. The winner would be the one who smashed the other's chestnut. These contests would take place in the middle of a circle of boys and girls looking on. If your chestnut was very strong and came through a few contests unscathed, it soon went around the camp and resulted in every boy or girl challenging you.

It was like a duel in the sun – or a High Noon, if you like – and a lot of childlike prestige rested on the result. I remember one boy who went to the extreme when his chestnut, which he had had for a long time, finally succumbed after many contests. He put the crumbled chestnut into a box and buried it beside his hut. The person who beat him had the name of having the strongest chestnut in the camp, a much sought-after title among us.

The big chestnut tree was utilised as support for one of the largest swings in Derry. It was absolutely colossal, and no-one, no matter how daring they were, would ever attempt to swing it to its full capacity. The long, strong ropes were tied around the top of the tree, and even with the softest of pushes, it would easily clear the 8ft fence. Many an arm and leg was broken on that gigantic tree. Hours of pleasure on a hot summer's night was enjoyed by all on that swing.

Just beside the chestnut tree was a field which had golden corn one year and potatoes the next. The famous song with the lyrics 'the corn is as high as an elephant's eye' wasn't exaggerating as far as this cornfield was concerned.

With the corn's height in mind, we devised a fun game that was enjoyed by all. Two children would stand at the edge of the cornfield with eyes closed.

Another child would shout out instructions: take ten steps forward, four steps to the right, five more straight ahead, three to the left, two to the right and so on. Then you were told to stop and open your eyes. The first to find their way back was the winner. At times it would go wrong, as when one or both children couldn't find their way back. When that happened, it was time to call in our pet dogs. The person 'lost' would call the dog and the dog would soon find them. Someone at the edge of the field would then call the dog again, and the 'lost' child just followed the dog back to the edge of the field and safety. It was a very popular game among the camp children.

The railway line, on which the Buncrana-bound train passed daily, was situated at the bottom of the camp. After the Lough Swilly Railway company disbanded the service, old bogies (that is what we called them) were left on the railway line. These were just wooden boxes with small steel wheels, and were used to transport workmen and repair parts along the railway line. They were a great attraction for the children and we played on them regularly. They moved along the railway line at a speed determined by how fast you operated the levers on them. The lever was pushed groundward, and the bogies would travel along the railway at an exciting speed. The thrill could be compared favourably to the excitement of a ride on a Big Dipper at a fairground.

After playing on them on a hot summer's day, we would strip off and jump into the nearby burn, which ran parallel to the railway line, for a dip. The fish had to give way as we splashed and dived under water. As for the cleanliness of the burn, it would be fair to say the environmental health officer of today would not have been impressed!

Below: The Lough Swilly Railway line which carried the Derry to Buncrana train. Right: Buncrana train passing Pennyburn Church.

Back then, we were bathed once a week in a big tin bath and washed with a bar of Sunlight soap. Our hair was 'fine combed' with a steel comb to evict unwanted squatters from our heads. After a football match, with sweat running from us, we drank one wee bottle of lemonade between four or five pals; we all drank from the same bottle. We rode makeshift trolleys, without helmets, ate bread and butter laced with sugar. We walked to school and back, in hail, rain and snow, some of us with shoes with holes in them, and without coats. We fell from trees, broke bones and teeth, and we didn't run to solicitors to claim.

When we fought as kids, we didn't bite, pull hair, scratch, or hit on the ground, and only girls had pierced ears. None of us ever died from any of these activities, as a Mrs Cullen's powder was the cure for all ills. Then, grass was for walking on, coke was drunk from a bottle, crack was laughter among your mates, and LSD was pounds, shillings and pence! I think all four words may have different meanings today.

Two innocent little Springtown Camp boys, Brendan Wilkinson and little brother Stevie. Both went on to become talented sportsmen, August 1955.

In the mid-1950s, things were good and in the main, most people were happy with their lot in the camp. Clean, fresh air filled our lungs, and looking over the mountains of Scalp and Eskaheen was a sight to behold. We took turns in the maintenance of our swimming pool, as the sods that were used to build the dam to retain the water levels needed to be changed every now and then. When changing the dam, we would let the dirty water flow away and replenish with clean, clear water. This maintenance work included clearing away any old, rusty bicycle wheels, discarded prams and the like. After we cleared the designated area, we could swim till our hearts were content.

The only drawback to a great afternoon's dipping, apart from someone's dog deciding to jump in and join in the fun, was the chance of being caught by Bob Chambers; he was the farmer who owned the land the burn ran through. Bob would chase us from the burn because we had stopped the flow of clean water getting to his cattle further down the field. This stoppage affected fields further down the railway line also, and his cattle needed drinking water.

If truth be told, we thought all farmers were millionaires, and we had little sympathy for poor old Bob. It gave us little concern as we swam and played in glorious sunshine. At times, Farmer Chambers crept up quietly and caught us unawares; he would grab our clothes, leaving us to run naked to our huts. He would later return our clothes, on condition we would not swim there again. As with Mr Jackson, who owned the orchard, we always agreed, but never kept our promise. The battle of wits between the camp children and Farmer Chambers was also part and parcel of everyday life during the summer holidays. To be honest, it added to the excitement.

Bob was a nice, inoffensive man, really, and anyway, the whole camp bought their potatoes and turnips from his mother. His mother, wee Mrs Chambers as we called her, was a lovely woman, and all the children were very fond of her. Every Saturday, there was a steady flow of children, bags in hand, walking down the Buncrana Road to her small farm cottage.

Our shopping lists would be mostly the same: a stone of spuds, a big turnip and a big York cabbage for Sunday's dinner. She had a set of weighing scales in her wee shed next to her cottage, which was 200 yards from the Buncrana Road entrance to the camp. The potatoes were stored in a large heap in the corner, just the way Willie Scanlon stacked the old clothes he bought and sold in the corner of his hut. Unlike old Willie, she would go on her knees and hand-pick the best and biggest potatoes for the people of the camp. She gave great value and would always say: 'I will add a few extra to compensate for the mud.' After serving me, she would always warn me: 'No swimming in the burn, you hear?'

Mates and muckers: Carmel, Michael and John Kerrigan with Maureen, Ann, Kay and Bernie Duddy, 1951.

The years the field next to the camp was growing spuds, some of us 'craftier' children saw the opportunity to make a few bob. We would open a few potato drills in the field at the bottom of the camp. Well out of sight of prying eyes, we would proceed to fill our bags with spuds and pocket the spud money. The money would be used for a card school, toss pits, or to treat ourselves in Mc-Connell's, Moore's or Mary Ann Meehan's shop.

We were doing great for a few weeks and everything was going to plan until the day Brendie Wilkinson told me his brother Eamonn was sent to Farmer Chambers for the spuds and he decided to do likewise. Filling his bag full of spuds from the field, he then made a fatal mistake when he decided to wash the spuds in the burn. Bringing home spotlessly clean spuds from the Chambers farm was unheard of, and naturally he was caught. That finished the wee earner for us all: as word was now out, no-one would take the chance again.

In later years, I met Bob Chambers down the Buncrana Road. He didn't look any different, with his old torn coat on and a bit of rope doubling as a belt. He complained to me that his lands were being vested by the authorities. I told him that he could probably get millions of pounds for them. He said, 'They can keep their millions. I just want my fields for my cattle.'

I brought up the subject of our swimming pool in the camp, and his sad face lit up as he laughed. Looking me straight in the face, he said, 'You lot broke my heart when you were in the camp. But I have to say, when it closed, it took part of me with it.'

I have no doubt he meant that sincerely.

The Mooney sisters Kathleen (with baby Lily in her arms), Maureen and Bernadette, 1949.

Martin Fleming pictured with his little sister on the day he made his First Communion. Martin was a keen footballer and played for local team Oxford United.

Fanoly, Lynn, Pat and Jimmy McCarron playing behind their hut on a summer's night in 1958.

During our school holidays, most of the children at one time or another would walk to Grianan Fort to make a wish at the wishing chair. The fort was about four miles from the camp; we would set out in a group of maybe ten, each with a piece of bread and jam, and an empty bottle. Among the regular trippers were Molly and Christine Dunne, Angela McCloskey, Rosaleen Doherty, Kathleen and Sally Bradley, Danny Feeney, Jim English, Paddy McLaughlin, Frankie Doherty and Yours Truly, all from our part of the camp. More likely than not, we would meet other children walking the same course. The usual suspects from top of the camp were Peter and Johnny Divin, Jim Campbell, Patsy Moore and Stanley Colby accompanied by the Campbell girls, the Deane sisters, and Martha and Kathleen Lynch.

I am sure almost all of the children at one time or another made that trip.

It was a must to stop at the well at the Branch Road to fill our bottles with fresh spring water. In the unlikely event that we had a few pennies, we would spend it on sweets at Mrs Callan's shop, which was facing the well. More often than not, we never made it to the fort. When we ate our bread and jam and drank our water, we would be about halfway there; that normally was the place to turn and head back to the camp. Still, it was a healthy walk and good fun on a bright summer's day.

I can recall the Wade Brothers, Christie and Herbie, who lived at the Branch Road; both were frequent passengers on the Springtown bus, the only bus that came close to their home. They, like us, always had this notion that the gateway at Jackson's big house was haunted. When they got off the bus, especially in the dark nights, they would sprint as fast as they could until well past it. Rumour had it that someone had died at that spot and their ghost, which was supposed to be a 'bad' ghost, would attack you at the gate. All childhood fantasy, of course. Still, we would never delay too long in passing that gate.

Chapter 7
Setting Up Shop

As early as September 1951, the huts were showing signs of dampness and severe condensation. At a Corporation housing sub-committee meeting, the Corporation's architect submitted a report on the dampness. He suggested treating the damp with seculate paint, and that alterations were needed to improve the huts if occupation of these huts were to continue. The Corporation's response to his report was to instruct the architect to purchase seculate paint to the value not exceeding £5 for experimental treatment of the damp. The first huts were demolished the following month.

On further inspection of the huts by the Ministry of Health and Local Government in January 1952, a report was sent to the Corporation intimating that the closure of Springtown Camp should now be considered. The Corporation's reaction to this report was to carry out minor repairs to some of the huts and to re-house the odd family every six or seven months. However, as soon as a family was re-housed, and on removing their last piece of furniture from their hut, some other family would carry in their first piece of furniture to the same hut and squat in it.

It would appear that the Corporation's housing committee tolerated, if not condoned, squatting into the huts at this particular time. This view was confirmed when, in April 1953, six families squatted into vacant huts before the Corporation could demolish them.

The Corporation without delay authorised the housing manager, Dennis Arthur Murphy, to negotiate completion of licence agreements with the six families concerned. They further instructed Murphy not to demolish any further huts that may become vacant until such times as there were no families prepared to reside in them. They also announced that twelve huts at Springtown were to be rewired at a cost of £158 14s 0d (£158.70). When a further announcement was made that other minor repairs were to be carried out to selected huts, this led to a feeling in the camp that the Corporation were about to carry out some renovations to the huts. Residents viewed this as an attempt to placate them while delaying further any policy of re-housing them. They rightly assumed that the camp would be there for a considerable length of time.

With this in mind, in late 1953, Mrs Margaret Hasson of 139 Springtown Camp, through her solicitor Claude Wilton, applied to the Corporation for permission to open a temporary shop in her hut. The application was refused. However, the Corporation said they would consider letting a separate site for the erection of a temporary shop at the camp. They actually suggested a block of five shops could be erected in the camp on a special site. This option was never taken up.

With minor repairs being carried out to the huts, a five-man deputation sought, through Councillor Doherty, a meeting with the Corporation's housing committee. The deputation was seeking assurances that if renovations to the huts did go ahead, it would not delay the transfer to permanent houses for the families of the camp. The Corporation refused to meet with the deputation, saying that it would give the residents of Springtown up to 10% of houses that became available for re-letting.

One resident who did get a positive response from the Corporation in January 1954 was businesswoman Margaret Hasson. She, through her solicitor, agreed to erect a temporary shop in accordance with the Corporation's architect-prepared plans. The housing committee then agreed to let shop space to Mrs Hasson at a rate of three shillings (15p) per foot frontage. This became the first 'official' shop in Springtown Camp. However, at the same meeting, the committee refused an application from her husband Alex, who asked the Corporation to let him a vacant hut to garage his car. Alex Hasson was later to open a betting office in the camp without seeking their permission; he accepted bets from all comers. The daily newspapers with the horse racing programmes were pinned to the wall of his hut, just like a normal betting office in the centre of Derry. It certainly

Maggie Lynch holding Celine, with Maureen, Willie and Kathleen, pictured in 1951 when a photographer visited the camp and charged half a crown to take your photo.

may not have been regarded as a legal betting office from the law's point of view, but if you placed a bet, and it won, you got paid, and that was all that mattered to the punters.

There were other budding entrepreneurs emerging in the camp. The father-and-son team of Francie and Jimmy Brandon were both larger-than-life characters. They sold their wares around the camp, and twice weekly you would hear them shouting at the top of their voices: 'Fresh herring, fresh herring,' and 'Shell dulse, shell dulse. American apples, American apples.' We were always called in from playing, handed a plate and told to go and get fresh herring and dulse. No prizes for guessing what was for dinner on those nights.

Son of Francie: Jimmy Brandon with wife Maisie.

In the hot summer days, we would sit on the footpath, pennies in hand, waiting patiently for the appearance of Gormley's ice-cream bicycle. This was a three-wheeler bicycle with a square box to the front full of ice cream. When he finally appeared, there would be a mad rush to his bicycle and we would wait our turn to buy a poke or a wafer.

A carnival atmosphere would go round the camp when the colourful 'rags for balloons' men visited. Gangs of children would follow them like a Pied Piper around the camp. They carried with them balloons of every shape and colour, and they did a roaring trade as children brought old rags to them by the bagful.

Another group of men to visit us would be the 'oilcloth men'. They would have rolls of oilcloth (floor covering like vinyl) and big rugs to sell. When money was unlikely to appear, which was quite often, they would agree to exchange the oilcloth or rugs for a good supply of rags. As far as we children were concerned, we now had everything we ever needed within our camp confinement.

The Hasson business partnership of husband and wife, who were convinced the camp was there to stay for many years, were proved correct as the Corporation gave warning of this in October 1954. That winter of '54 was a wet one and the wooden huts started to leak water, the row belonging to the Gormley, Deery, O'Kane and O'Hagan families at 63a, 63b, 63c and 63d being hit the worst. After inspection by Bob Hutchman, the huts were re-felted very quickly. The Corporation also agreed to replace broken or fused bulbs to the street lighting but ordered the workmen to reduce the seventeen existing bulbs from 150W to 100W.

The one-and-only Francie Brandon astride his donkey, waiting for the fish to land.

Reproduced from an article in the Irish News, *1927. Supplied by the Brandon family. The judge ordered Francie to re-pay the four pounds!*

On This Day/January 14 1927

Absent-minded romantic

FRANCIS Brandon of Hogg's Folly, Derry, who was arrested 10 days ago in Enniskillen, appeared before the Derry magistrates yesterday on a charge of stealing four pounds from his employer, Robert Woods, a fish dealer of 1, Windmill Terrace.

The evidence of Woods was that Brandon, who had been about a fortnight in his employment, was sent to Buncrana on Boxing day to buy fish. He received four pounds from witness. Brandon did not turn up and he had not seen him since that date except in court.

The defendant said he was willing to pay back the four pounds. It was through drink he did it. Explaining the circumstances, defendant said he found on arrival at Buncrana that no fish had been landed, and accepted an invitation from two buyers to accompany them to the Lough Swilly Hotel for a drink. When he came out he had lost his senses and forgot all about his employer's pony and cart.

District Inspector Cahill said instead of returning to Derry and giving back the money to Woods, Brandon had gone to Enniskillen, and had it not been that he was arrested there he might never have returned to Derry at all. He got married for the second time in Enniskillen on the day he was arrested with the money he took from Woods.

Mr Arthur, JP - Did he use the money for that purpose?
Defendant - No, I did not.

Chapter 8
New School and Making Do

Meetings with Bishop Neil Farren regarding the schoolchildren didn't run as smoothly as expected; people found him very stubborn and unsympathetic to their situation. With the families now residing at Springtown, Bishop Farren wanted the children to attend the Lenamore School, which was over two miles away. With no bus service to that school, it meant children, some as young as five years, would have to walk four miles a day. That, of course, meant they would have to leave the camp in the darkness of morning and arrive home in the darkness of night in wintertime – and in all types of weather.

The parents rightly thought this was most unreasonable and made the bishop aware of their feelings. For weeks, the bishop refused to budge, insisting the children of the camp should leave their respective schools in Derry and attend Lenamore School. It was only after elected representatives and other people of influence made representation to him that he finally agreed to let the children stay at their own schools in Derry. The children found it difficult enough walking to Eden Terrace in all weathers to catch a bus to school without walking miles to and from Lenamore School. The reason the bishop chose to put the parents in the camp through weeks of anguish was baffling, and without any sense of reason. The older ex-residents of the camp still, to this very day, remember the bad feelings that prevailed in the camp regarding this issue of the schoolchildren.

***

Life went on as normal in the camp, with parents turning their attention to preparing for the transfer of their children from schools in Derry to a newly built school at nearby Pennyburn. This meant that for the first time, every child of school-going age (under fifteen) from the camp would be attending the same school.

When the people squatted into the camp in August 1946, their children went to different schools throughout the city. The Bridge Street and Rosemount schools were probably the two most attended. Daily bus fares for the children to and from the city were a drain on the weekly income of families, so the new school was very much welcomed.

Soon, the normally quiet Buncrana Road and Messines Park would come alive in the mornings and mid-afternoons. Both would be transformed into busy thoroughfares, with hundreds of children from Springtown walking to and from their new school. Barney Norby's shop at the Collon and the wee shop beside the school would soon do a roaring trade in sweets.

That Sunday night, we were all called into our huts early as the tin baths and bars of Sunlight and Lifebuoy soap were out in force, parents pouring jugs of cold water in first, then adding boiling water from a kettle that was simmering on the hot range. All the young children were scrubbed down by the fathers before moving to the mothers with the dreaded steel fine comb in her hand.

Tin bath time wasn't so bad, as the heat from the range was always so warm, even in the coldest of nights, but once you stepped outside the living room, you were hit with the fierce cold. The huts had two extremes: either they were too hot or they were freezing cold. Come Monday morning, Buncrana Road would be packed with hundreds of children, ages ranging from five to fourteen, all walking to their new school at Pennyburn.

Brothers Jim and Winston Thompson outside their hut, 224 Springtown Camp, 1951.

Danny Doherty, son of popular and much-loved Mary 'the Hen' Doherty, 1957.

Left: Getting ready for a gun battle, 1956. Back: Noel McDonald, Alex Killen and Danny McMonagle. Front: George Killen and Gerry McDonald. Right: Mary McMonagle babysitting in 1956.

On Monday 7 June 1954, St Patrick's School in the parish of Pennyburn opened its doors for the very first time and all the children from the camp transferred to the new school. At 9.15 am, the children were marched down to the assembly hall, where we said a prayer. Then, one by one, our names were called out and we were marched to our class in a line of pairs holding hands. Our teacher was a lovely, humble nun; hands clasped together, she walked in front of us. We marvelled at the bright colours of the walls and ceilings of the school – pinks, reds and yellows were on the ceilings, with creams, greens and blues on the walls. With so much natural light shining in through the massive metal-framed glass windows, the brightness and multicolours took our breath away.

The new teachers of St Patrick's boys, girls, and infants schools seemed more nervous on that, the first day of school, than the children. Children from ten different schools throughout the city had enrolled at the new school and teachers were naturally concerned about how children from so many different schools – and from such a variety of homes – would get along together.

This new, modern school had three different sections. Both boys and girls attended the infants school from their first day until they reached the age of eight. Then they were transferred to either the boys school or the girls school. They stayed there until they were eleven, at which time they either transferred to St Columb's College or the Christian Brothers' School for the boys or, in the girls' cases, to Thornhill College. However, if you didn't transfer to one of

Teachers at the Big Boys School in Pennyburn. Back: Jim Ramsey, Sean Mellon, Jim Flanagan and Michael Quigley. Front: Neil McMahon, Freddie Campbell, Dermot MacDermott (headmaster), Jim Quinn and Kieran McFeely.

those colleges, you just stayed on until you reached the age of fifteen, at which time you left school to start work. The children attending St Patrick's Primary School simply called it 'Pennyburn School'.

Of the 354 new arrivals to the boys school, 154 were from Springtown Camp.

Mr Dermot MacDermott was the principal of the boys school and Sister Mary Augustine (family name, Mullan) was principal of the girls school; her vice-principal was Sister Mary Philomena Donaghy. Sister M Stanislaus (family name, McGurk) was head of the infants school; her vice-principal was Sister M Aloysius (family name, McVeigh).

There were, in total, twenty-five teachers at the combined infants, boys and girls schools.

The boys school (to my fading memory) had one female teacher, Mrs Farren, who started several months after the school opened, and eight male teachers. They were Neil McMahon, Michael Quigley, Kieran McFeely, Jim Quinn, Paddy Flanagan, Jim Ramsey, Sean Mellon, and Freddie Campbell.

Brian Friel, world-famous playwright, also taught at the boys school for a couple of years.

The girls school had eight teachers in total. After the principal and vice-principal, there were Sister Mary Immaculata Mulholland, Margaret Gillen, Patsy Casey (née Devlin), Kathleen McGettigan, Aine Friel and Marie McCrossan.

Class of 1958, St Patrick's Boys School, Pennyburn. Pictured left is headmaster Dermot MacDermott and right, class master Brian Friel, the world-famous playwright. Springtown boys in the photograph include in back row, sixth from left, Mickey Bridge and Malachy Cullen. Third row: James Moore, Liam McConnell, Francie Brandon and Davy Magill. Second row: Peter Divin, Guido Delpinto and Bernie McGinley. Front row: Charlie Sweeney and, fifth from left, Liam Ward.

The dreaded school photograph every family had to pose for. The Wilkinson family: Mary, Annie, Eamonn, Hughie, Stevie and Brendie at St Patrick's, Pennyburn, 1956.

The infants school had a total of seven teachers on that first day. After the principal and vice-principal, there were Sister Theresa (McLaughlin), Martha McGuinness, Mary Catherine Devine, Mary Christina Spellman and Margaret Lagan.

It was the practice in the infants school to award or praise a pupil if they did well in class in a particular week. The top pupil of that week would get a thin red cloth sash to put around him or her; the second-best pupil was awarded a yellow one. Each kept possession of the sash for one week, unless they were exceptional and were allowed to keep the red sash for a couple of weeks. However, it was normal for the yellow sash to change hands weekly.

At the other end of the scale was a dunce's hat, a big pointed hat made out of light cardboard and painted black. This was worn by the pupil who may have answered a series of questions wrong, or, in the nun's opinion, was not paying attention in class, or simply not giving their best effort. I never got to wear the red sash, but I did once get to wear the yellow one. I washed it every night before going to bed and placed it beside the hot range to dry. I was so proud; I wore it to and from school for the entire week, even while playing football. I did, however, on several occasions get the dubious distinction of standing in the corner of the classroom wearing the dunce's hat. I must say, I never did like the infants school for some reason.

The children quickly settled into their new school. It was a sight to see the camp children walking in their droves down Buncrana Road, up Messines Park, onto the Racecourse Road and into Pennyburn School. Some of the older boys soon devised a shortcut down by the railway line. They would jump over the burn that flowed at the bottom of the camp and come out near Heaney's big house, which led them directly into Messines Park. This route was to become the main one for most of the boys of the camp. However, most of the fairer sex stuck to the Buncrana Road route, as it was cleaner and more ladylike.

It is fair to say that some pupils from the camp, mainly boys, were of the opinion that they were treated differently by some of the teachers because they came from the camp. I personally don't subscribe to that train of thought. I believe that while we may have been looked on as being from a deprived area, namely Springtown Camp, I can honestly say I found the teachers to be even-handed in their dealings with all the pupils.

Michael Quigley was regarded as probably the 'toughest' teacher in the boys school. Yet I can say with a fair degree of certainty that he treated all the boys the same, whether they were from Culmore Road, Strand Road or Springtown Camp. Step out of line and you were dealt with accordingly. Actually, I am of the belief that my education progressed more, to a larger degree, in Mr Quigley's than in any other class.

The pupils' favourite place in St Patrick's School – the canteen.

**Gregorian Chant Winners
Derry Feis 1963
Mr. Quigley**

Michael Quigley, teacher at St Patrick's Boys School, Pennyburn, with his Derry Feis winners of 1963. Springtown Camp boys include in back row: Patsy Callaghan and Gerry McDonald. Third row: Paddy McLaughlin, Danny Craig and John McBrearty. Second row: Tommy Mooney. Front row: William Craig.

One teacher was above reproach in any context and viewed by everyone, be they pupil or parent, as being an absolute gentleman. He was Mr Dermot (Dickie) MacDermott, principal of the boys school. I can remember he would buy presents and pay for them out of his own pocket at Christmas time. He would go to every class in the boys school and ask the teacher: 'Who has worked hard all year? Who is the most improved boy?' Those boys chosen by their teacher would receive a present, courtesy of Mr MacDermott.

Dickie, as he was fondly known by his pupils, was a very decent and fair-minded man who treated all his pupils as equals. Wherever or whatever background they came from, rich or poor, they received equal treatment from him. I have yet to hear anyone say an unkind word about him. He indeed was a man of his word and a true gentleman.

Several years after he retired, he was invited to attend a school prizegiving night. He had this to say: 'Of all the thousands of boys that have passed through Saint Patrick's School, one boy has kept coming to my mind since I

Class of 1960, St Patrick's Girls School, Pennyburn.

started to look back over my time here. He came to us on the fourth of October, nineteen fifty-four and left on the ninth of May nineteen fifty-six and made, in all, one hundred and twenty-four attendances. On the day he came to us, he was twelve years and six months old and had never been to school before in his young life. He could neither read nor write, and two plus five meant nothing to him. But he had done many things in his young life, and we discovered that if we asked him what two shillings plus five shillings was, the correct answer came easily. Money, he understood. He was the only child I have ever taught whose education was based on his monetary knowledge. I have not seen him since he left school, nor have I heard of or about him. I wonder where Michael Jackson from Springtown Camp is now. I hope he is well and prospering.'

Unknown to Mr MacDermott, Michael Jackson was at that time indeed well and working in Scotland, where he had decided to stay after being one of the original 'taddy hoakers' (spud pickers) from Springtown.

He concluded by saying: 'Springtown Camp is now gone, with its children spread to many corners. No harm. They were good children, but Springtown was not a good place to grow up in.'

Of course, that point of view was shared by many. But for the children of the camp, as we knew no better, we enjoyed growing up there. We look back

Back: Noel McDonald and Hughie McMonagle. Middle: John Friel, Thomas Brown and George Killen. Front: Martin McDonald (now Fr Martin), Robin Brown and Willie Brown, 1955.

with nothing but fond memories of our childhood days there; innocent, carefree days. We may have lacked many material things; to deny that would be silly. However, we were taught the basics from our beleaguered parents: work hard, retain your humility, be honest with yourself and everyone around you. Simple advice, yet so effective if carried out. And it is true to say there are some people who were reared in the camp and would prefer to forget about their time there, and indeed may not have pleasant memories of Springtown. That is their choice and one which they are entitled to make and which has to be respected, although it is also true to say that they are in a very small minority.

Did it harm us? No, I don't believe it did. Did it give us resolve to do better in life? Yes, most certainly and without doubt. Did our lives improve when we left the camp? Well, that depends on your point of view. It's undeniable that the conditions we lived in improved considerably in that we had damp-free homes, hot water, baths and open fires and a decent kitchen, not to mention upstairs bedrooms. We were soon walking on carpet, as opposed to cold, damp oilcloth; the streets we walked on were level, smooth and free from water. Nonetheless, one major thing in the negative was that while all the front doors in the camp were open, all were now closed in the new housing estates. This, naturally, reduced the daily contact somewhat from that which had existed in Springtown.

Rosaleen Jennings, Danny McCloskey and chums, 1956.

Twins enjoying the sunshine on the green.

One well-known woman from the camp told me about the time she began to suffer from depression soon after leaving Springtown. Her doctor visited her in her new home and asked her to stand up and look out her window. The woman stood up, looked out her window, then looked back at her doctor. 'What do you see out there? How many front doors are open?' he asked her.

She looked back at him and didn't answer.

'Now, how many front doors in Springtown Camp would be open at this time?'

Bobby Doherty with daughter Marie in his arms and son Frankie, 1955.

She sat down without saying a word.

'There is no need to ask how many neighbours' homes you have visited today or how many you would have visited had you been still in Springtown. That is your problem, and one, I'm afraid, that will take some getting used to.'

In general, as far as physical health and living conditions were concerned, life improved dramatically for all the former campers. The major downside, however, for all the families was the loss of a close-knit community. This, above all things, is, to this day, the biggest regret from former Springtown people spread all over the globe. I suppose this may have been because the families in the camp had the same social standing. Now we were out in the big, wide world, with wall-to-wall carpet, fitted kitchens, Venetian blinds and coloured bathroom suites the norm.

The face of Derry was changing dramatically, with people being re-housed, not only from the camp, but from terraced homes due for clearance under redevelopment schemes. It placed a different kind of pressure on families to make sure their houses didn't get left behind in the 'style stakes'.

***

In my day, there wasn't a football team at the boys school, but they had one when I was in the infants school. It was a successful one too, as they finished runners-up in the Derry schools' league. That team had three players from the camp: Alex Killen (goalkeeper), Willie Curran and Eugene McLaughlin.

Class of 5th standard in 1954, St Patrick's Boys School, Pennyburn, with teacher Jim Quinn and nine Springtowners. Back row: Seamus Fleming, James Ward, Paddy Lynch and Alfred Cullen. Middle row: fourth from left, Maurice Dunne, Phillip Killen; seventh from left, Liam Fleming, Seamus Morrison. Front row: third from left, John Brown.

The school itself had green fields to the rear, with just a sprinkling of houses to the front, and the old Shantallow on the left and the Collon to the right. As you stood in Classroom 8 of the boys school (the last class you attended before leaving school), you had a clear view of the whole of Derry, while on the other side of the classroom, you had the hills of Donegal as a backdrop. To the rear of the playground lay a sloping embankment, and at the foot of the embankment was a slow-moving brown burn.

At 10.30 am we were brought out of class to the long corridor, where we would get a small bottle of milk. After the milk was drunk, we got the chance to go to the toilet.

Dinner was served at 12.50 pm, the cost of which was 9d (4p), and I think it's true to say that most of us from the camp were receiving free dinners, as our fathers were on the 'broo' (dole). Without doubt, dinnertime was our favourite part of any school day, especially Friday, as we always got chips for dinner with apple cake and custard for dessert. I can't remember too many plates that were not cleaned at our tables in the dining hall. Strange, you may think, but as we were paraded to the dining hall, we could always tell what was on the menu by the smell emanating from the hall. Christmas dinner was extra special, as the canteen staff excelled with extra fare for all. It was always a full house for Christmas dinner; everyone went, including the pupils who had to fork out 1s (5p) for it. Why they increased the price for Christmas dinner, I'll never know!

Class of 1961, St Patrick's Girls School, Pennyburn.

Susie McWilliams from Hut 201 Springtown Camp on her First Communion day, 1953.

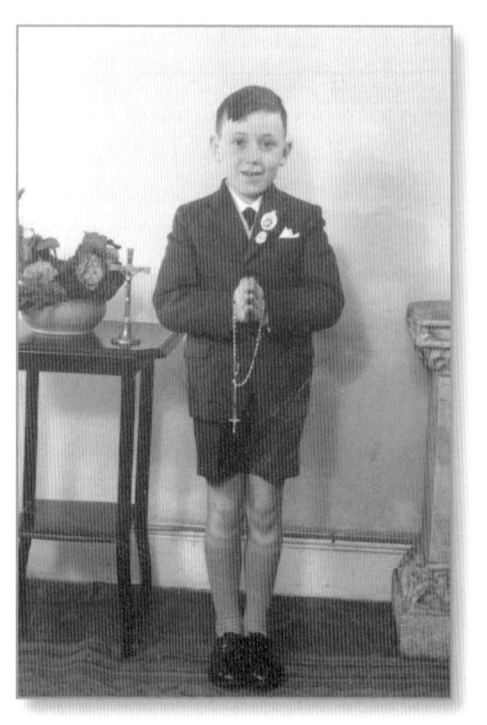

Frankie Fisher of 63a Springtown Camp on his First Communion day, 1957.

I recall the great excitement we all felt on the days preceding our First Holy Communion. That was the day I got to wear my first new pair of shoes and a brand new suit (short trousers, of course) and shirt. We looked smart with our Sacred Heart badges pinned to our lapels.

The girls wore a lovely white dress with a head veil, just like a wedding dress. In Springtown, no matter how poor a family was, it was of paramount importance that the children were put out in new suits or dresses for their First Holy Communion. This took precedence over everything, and no matter what or who went behind, our parents made sure we would be looking a million dollars. After receiving our First Communion, we went back to the school canteen for tea, buns and pastry. The highlight, of course, was visiting your friends and relatives and getting a few bob in every house or hut as the case may be.

It was another two years before I got my next pair of new shoes and that was on the occasion of my Confirmation.

In the intervening years before and immediately after my Confirmation, I, like some of the camp's other children, but not all I must stress, had to make do with the clothes and shoes our mothers bought at jumble sales. Those were like mini-fairs: items of clothing would be placed on a stall and people would offer a few pence or shillings for each item; the offer was either accepted or a price was agreed after further negotiations. It was the cheapest way of clothing a large family, and for a few of the large families, mine included, the only way.

Although the clothes were second-hand (the jumble sales were held by charity organisations or youth clubs to raise funds), we children didn't pay too much attention to that, or indeed didn't care, maybe because we simply knew no better. What mattered to us was that the shoes kept out the water and you didn't leave a puddle behind you with every step you took. The same can be said for the big coats, which doubled for blankets on a cold winter's night when the huts were freezing. We didn't ask or care who had owned them previously. Again, all that mattered was they kept us warm. To be quite frank, in my early years I truthfully thought the saying 'two up, two down' meant two at the top of the bed and two at the bottom. But like all the other children there, I was happy and contented in the knowledge our parents always did their best for us in the circumstances they found themselves in, and we just got on with enjoying life in the camp.

> Some parents were very religious, and the family rosary was a nightly must. At designated times, they would call their children in for the rosary. If by chance you were playing with someone from another family, then you had to go to their hut for the rosary.
>
> The perfect example of that was the Porter family; they would say the rosary without fail every night. Mrs Porter, a lovely woman who hailed from Donegal, made sure all the wains around her hut joined them in saying the evening prayer.

Actually, our biggest worry was getting a thru'penny bit (about 1p), which was the admission fee, to see the pictures in James O'Hagan's hut. We had some brilliant nights in that hut watching the Royal Canadian Mounted Police do battle with the criminals, or the Cowboys outgunning the Indians. Who cared if it was a silent movie? Sure, we had James O'Hagan narrating the whole story to us. He did so in great detail and we were spellbound watching the movies in the wee room in his hut. The windows were covered with a blanket to keep out the daylight; it was a truly remarkable experience. Most of us had never even been in the city in our young lives. This was just a fantastic treat for us, and the memory of such occasions we would cherish all our lives. It is still one of my fondest memories of growing up in the camp. He catered for all age groups, as there was also a midnight show for the adults and, of course, Housey (Bingo).

Eddie and Jim Fox, Stevie and Annie Wilkinson, Bridie Bridge, Kathleen Fox and Mary McDonald outside the Wilkinson hut.

Sammy and Sarah Holden with children Raymond, Vera, Ann, Patricia and Dolores snapped by renowned photographer Bert Hardy in December 1955 for Picture Post *magazine. The interviewer was world-famous journalist Woodrow Wyatt.*

    In the winter months, Housey was a big attraction for a lot of women – and a few men! It was played in several huts; arguably, the most successful and longest-running was held in Paddy and Mary Ann Meehan's hut. It was a joint-venture by Paddy and Jack Jennings, and the full house was normally worth £2. This was the best prize money in the camp at that particular time. It was also a great pastime for the people, who viewed it as their weekly entertainment, and it got them out of their huts for a couple of hours. This gave them the chance to chat with the neighbours from other parts of the camp. The fact that you could win a few bob was an added bonus. It was only a few shillings a night and people brought their own wooden Housey card. The organisers collected a few pennies before each game and there was great excitement when they announced the amount for the winner of the last house. I am reliably informed that on one occasion when it was announced the last house would be worth £2 10s (£2.50), a gasp went up, followed by a nervous silence. In any case, the lucky winner's name would go round the camp like wildfire.

    Not too many men went to the Housey sessions; they left that to their womenfolk. There were also a lot of very modest and quiet men in the camp, men whom you wouldn't hear raise their voice or speak an angry word. Men like Johnny Parkes, Ted Bridge, Elkie Clark, Barney McGinley, Willie O'Hagan and Johnny English, to name but a few.

The incomparable John Moore with wife Cissie and friends Peter O'Hagan, Eddie O'Hagan, Jimmy Jennings and Andy Doherty outside John and Cissie's hut, 1951.

One who also fell into that category was big Jimmy Jennings, a gentle giant. Jimmy was one of the first residents of Springtown and was a close friend of John Moore's, the O'Hagan brothers, Willie Morrin and Tommy Mooney. They formed a weight-lifting team and were keen trainers, pumping iron. Eddie O'Hagan actually broke the Irish record. Unfortunately, it was done at an unregulated sports event and thus wasn't recognised. It was a pity, because his achievement deserved to go into the record books.

One of the funniest men in the camp, and a great one-liner man, was the unforgettable Harry Feeney. Wherever he went, he had everyone in stitches and it was a laugh a minute. Many of the people who went to watch the Sunday afternoon matches at the Rushie Field went with the intention of getting close to Harry just to enjoy his banter and craic.

Harry brightened up many people's day with his quick-fire humour. He and John Moore would hold centre stage in the huts on long winter nights. When both were present, a great night of fun and laughter was assured. On those particular nights, John would select a topic for discussion, which would be written on a board and form the basis of the night's banter. It was a novel way to spend a winter's night in Springtown.

When the camp was in decline, depleted and badly run down, and with no prospects of a house for anyone, John Moore and family joined the emigration trail to Bradford, like dozens of Springtown families before him. It's a testament to both of these men that their names never fail to crop up when ex-Springtowners get together and reminisce about the camp.

Occasionally, Springtown men could get seasonal employment as dockers working at the quay when the coal, spud or grain boats docked there.

There was widespread unemployment in the camp with approximately 80% of the men out of work, which, of course, was the main cause of the poverty. Some families, especially ones with fewer children, were slightly better off than the larger families. A few men did have steady jobs, but most would have had to make do with some casual/seasonal work.

Seasonal employment included dockers working in the quay when coal boats, spud and grain boats docked there. Some went to England in search of work, even if only for a few months of each year. The men, naturally, missed their families while away, and their wives wanted them home as soon as possible, as rearing a big family on their own was tough.

The men then had to prioritise their needs. First off, they needed employment so they could send money home to their families. They also needed at least thirteen weeks' work to get the required number of stamps on their cards, which entitled them to 'standard benefit' when returning home. Back then, thirteen stamps was the golden number needed to receive extra money on the dole, which would made a big difference to the weekly income to each home. If you didn't have the required thirteen stamps on your cards, all a man would receive was National Assistance, which only entitled them to the bare minimum amount of money each week. Still, the short time the men were working did bring welcome and instant relief, albeit briefly, to their households.

Being sent to McConnell's, Moore's or Mary Ann Meehan's shop for a quarter-pound of butter, half-dozen eggs and one cigarette was a regular thing in our hut. When things were really tight, asking your neighbour for a 'wee taste of sugar' or a 'wee bit of butter' or a 'fag' was not uncommon.

It was widely felt, rightly or wrongly, and it was certainly my opinion, that the mothers of the camp had to contend with much more than the fathers had to. That was the case in our hut, anyway, simply because some fathers got out one day a week for a few drinks. Or if they didn't drink, a game of snooker or a hand of cards, and could at least escape the everyday pressures for those few hours each week. Most of the mothers maybe got to the pictures two or three times a year – if they were lucky. It is not to say that there was anything wrong with a man getting out for a few hours a week – every man is entitled to that – but some of the women, in my opinion, didn't have that luxury.

Molly Smith and her daughter Tina. Molly was a shopkeeper for many years in the camp.

I think that was a sign of the times everywhere in the 1950s, as it was a man's world in those days. Those were the days when women were expected to be at home, to look after the children, cook, clean and do the washing, be the first up in the morning and last to bed at night. If truth be told, it was an era when women maybe got a raw deal everywhere.

Granny Fisher with grandson Bobby on her knee in the camp in 1955.

Of course, there were exceptions in the camp, as there always are, as some men didn't drink, smoke, or gamble, and seldom left the camp. Our parents in Springtown, although living through poverty and terrible conditions, remained very close. This was maybe the main reason they got through the very harsh times that existed in the camp. When I transport my mind back to when I was a boy growing up in the camp, most of the men were in long-term unemployment. Then, family numbers tended to be on the large side, with six, seven, eight children, or in many cases even more. And hardship was never far away from the doors of the huts. Some of the privation was so severe that it led to a small number of families having their electricity disconnected because they just could not afford to pay the bill. I can vividly remember such a time in our hut when our electricity was disconnected because we didn't pay our bill. With no electricity in our hut, life was very difficult indeed, for parents and children alike.

The overriding concern of the parents was to provide food and clothes for their children. For some, poverty was a part of everyday life; I have had some very sad stories about abject poverty in the camp relayed to me from a host of different people.

Frances and John English with their children Margaret, Jim and Ann on Ann's First Communion day, 1950.

Some of the instances of the poverty were very detailed, and a lot worse than I had experienced. However, I have decided to focus on my own personal experiences. In that way, it will not give rise to any embarrassment or offence to anyone, as that would be the last thing I would want to do.

***

One of my very first recollections of the lack of money and poverty was at meal time one day. I can remember my father giving each of us a half of a boiled egg and toast for tea.

He tore up the egg carton in which the eggs were boxed and made them into egg cups.

There were nine children in our family, so half a dozen eggs just about covered us on that particular occasion. Other times, I remember him cutting a loaf of bread into as many slices as was needed to give each of us an equal portion of the bread. As the oldest boy, I got to get the heel part of the loaf; it was a little bit bigger.

I can't honestly recall ever going without food in the camp, but I do remember occasions when I could have eaten a lot more if it had been there. There were times when, if you broke a cup, you had to drink your tea out of a jam jar; then again, you were glad to drink it out of anything in those days. The free school dinner and milk we received on school days, to some extent, took the pressure off our parents. Each pupil got two small bottles of milk, mid-morning and mid-afternoon, and it was regarded as a godsend in those days.

Christmas time was, of course, a very special time for the young children. On Christmas Day, we would get up out of bed feeling excited, in anticipation of what present we would get. More times than not, it was a toy gun for the boys, a wee doll for the girls and the usual orange for everyone. I remember one Christmas, Danny Spratt and his brother Junior each got an Indian outfit and half the wee boys in the camp were after them with their cowboy guns. They never, ever got another Indian outfit again.

As for clothes, the jumble sales were our main providers and we made do with second-hand clothes obtained from them. I suppose a lot of families in Derry were the same, as unemployment was a scourge then. It was the norm when you got a hole in one or both of your shoes

Junior and Danny Spratt at their front door wearing the Indian outfits they got for Christmas 1950.

that you just did some instant repairs by tearing off a piece of cardboard from a box and sticking it in your shoes. It was really no big deal and you just got on with it.

At night, we had the situation where we were drinking our tea out of a jam jar by candlelight in our wee tin hut, all contented and happy as Larry! The lack of lighting had its advantages at times as when I broke a cup and had a readymade excuse: I couldn't see in the dark. I remember my mother saying that we only had four cups left now. It was jam jars to the rescue after that!

It crossed my mind it must be only film stars or very rich people who drank tea from a cup and saucer. We had candles lit all over the place, and the smell of burning candle wax filled our hut on those winter nights. We had three candles in our living room, one in each bedroom, one in the toilet and one in the kitchen. Each candle would last for about two hours and then they were replaced with new ones. When we got into bed, my father would blow them out and remove them in case of fire.

Fire was a major risk in the camp and some huts burned to the ground; they would burn in minutes, just like a bale of straw. I think, on looking back, we must have spent more on candles than we would have on electricity. It was a fun time for us children and we were oblivious to the embarrassment obviously being felt by our parents. It must have been a bad time for them, always hoping something would turn up and that things would improve, but on that occasion they didn't and our electricity was disconnected. Still, we children were always happy with our lot.

One thing that was never missed, however, was the stipends money paid to the Catholic Church. Nobody, but nobody, would be 'disgraced' by not paying that. That duty was sacrosanct, as the names and the amount each family gave was read out from the pulpit by the priest at Mass every Sunday. It was money they couldn't afford to give! But, fearing embarrassment, they somehow managed to find it.

Patrick Gormley of Hut 31a Springtown Camp, seated left, voting at an unemployed meeting in the Union Hall in December 1955.

Down Memory Lane...

Hugo Cullen, Seamus Fleming and George Lynch on their way to the closing of the Men's Retreat in St Patrick's Church, Pennyburn.

Springtown Camp's Fr Martin McDonald, happy and contented.

Sheila Brennan with her mother Margaret.

Frances Doherty and Davy Harkin. Note Sally Fleming's wooden hut in the background.

Dolly Sweeney, with her cousin Effie, and daughters Mary Saunders, Ann, and Evelyn McCarron, 1954.

Mary McClean and Dan Hegarty relaxing on 'The People's Stool' in the early 1970s.

Brian Parsons took his hut with him when he left the camp in 1967.

Charlie O'Hagan with his wife and two small children. Charlie was on the camp committee in 1964.

Two unknown young ladies.

The Kelly family.

Ordination of Fr Andrew McCloskey, born and reared in the camp. Also pictured are his parents, Annie and Jim, and his aunt and uncle, Louise and Johnny Shiels, 9 June 1974.

Martha and Steve Dunn on the green in front of their hut with their children in 1960.

Charlie and Sarah Lynch holding Frances Lynch's twins George and Margaret.

Jenny Deery (née McCarron), Fanny McCarron, Ann McColgan (née Sweeney) and Evelyn McCarron (née Sweeney) just home from the bus run to Rathmullan on August Monday 1958.

Jim 'Sixty-Niner' Campbell of 33f Springtown Camp.

Maureen Duddy with daughters Kay and Bernie outside her hut, July 1952. Maureen's young son Jackie was murdered on Bloody Sunday by British paratroopers.

The Entertainers at a Springtown Camp reunion dance in the Stardust, 1983. Back: John Gillespie, Stanley Colby, Tony Nash, Jackie McConnell and Seamus McConnell. Front: Jimmy Deery, Hughie Harkin and Andy Wilkinson.

Chapter 9
Changing Seasons

One of my very first recollections of the camp was when I must have been about four or five years old. It was a winter's night; my mother got a potbelly stove from Rose Ann Bridge. I can vaguely remember a young man, I believe his name was Eddie Doherty, pushing this stove on a wee truck to our hut. He later went back with the truck and I went with him to fetch the flue pipe. What excitement in our hut the next day as my father went on to the roof to cut a hole in the tin for the flue pipe. It was installed that day in our big bedroom. My father lit the stove using twigs from the tree at the back of our hut. He added some coke, which we got from the Gasyard, and soon it was glowing red hot and gave out a tremendous heat. The big plus was now the family had two places in the hut warm enough for us to sit or read or do school homework. It was a big difference to six or seven of us huddled around the range in what we called the living room.

Lots of boys would go into the Gasyard in the Lecky Road for a half-bushel of coke every Saturday morning and we'd have old prams in which to ferry it out to our huts in the camp. The coke was needed for the potbelly stoves that most families had in their big room; it was the only way you could heat the huts. At one end was the main range, which was used for cooking and heating, and at the other end was the potbelly stove. The reward for us was the entrance money for the Derry City match at the Brandywell.

Prior to us getting the stove, the living room was used for cooking, eating, doing homework and even getting bathed. The stove certainly gave us more options and more freedom of movement within our hut; it improved our quality of life, for sure. At times, we would take the wireless down to the big room and listen to the *Clithero Kid* or *Dan Dare, Pilot of the Future*. That was a few years before we were introduced to the world's first superstar, *The Lone Ranger*. It also meant my mother had loads of room to bath us on Saturday nights.

Those were the days our parents were fighting against seemingly impossible odds: still dreaming impossible dreams, but always settling for much less; scraping every penny, yet somehow still finding enough for a wee bet on a Saturday afternoon in the hope that it might come up. On the very rare occasion it did, our family was rich for that weekend: it was fish and chips on that Saturday night from John McGowan's fish and chip shop down at the Collon. A fry was made for Sunday breakfast and after Mass we had all the trimmings for Sunday dinner. We children were never told how much was won, but we knew it was a big win if our mother went to the pictures on the Monday night.

I can remember my father's bet was nearly always a 'bob' (5p) each-way treble which, in today's money, would have been 10p in total. Not very high stakes, but they always bet in the hope of 'landing a rise' (winning a few pounds). The most memorable occasion when my father did win was during the time our electricity was disconnected. I was playing Cowboys and Indians with my friends out on the street. I caught a glimpse of my father hurrying, almost running, down the camp towards our hut and carrying a big brown parcel and smiling like a Cheshire cat. He beckoned me with a nod to follow him. I ran with my makeshift bow and arrow into our hut to see what he wanted me for. I watched, mouth open, as he excitedly told my mother his horses had won, at the same time handing each of us children a bar of chocolate. It was obvious from his excitement that he had won a tidy sum. He soon blurted out that he had already paid the electricity bill and the lights would be switched on the next day.

That night, our old brown table was to resemble a table at a Roman banquet feast; it was barely able to hold all the food.

The electricity was duly switched on again the very next day and that night our hut was lit up as bright as Piccadilly Circus in London. I only realised that night, while lying on top of my bed reading the *Beano*, what we were missing. My mother even got to go to the pictures that night, a very rare occurrence for her, and for the first time in over a year. That was a happy week in our hut and we felt 'rich', if only for a short time. Our parents vowed never again would our electricity be disconnected, and it never was.

I often smile to myself when thinking back to when Mrs McCloskey had a 'book' with Herbie and Jack, the breadmen. As we didn't have a book of our own, she used to get our family bread and buns on tick. Our parents would pay her at the end of every week, and she in turn would pay the breadmen. Mrs McCloskey, a kindly woman, later arranged with the two breadmen to call at our house, so we then became customers in our own right. Saturday mornings were always my favourite, as I got a cream finger; it was a great treat then, I can tell you.

A young Uncle McLaughlin leads his donkey under the watchful eye of his father and nieces, 1949.

Summer nights were always good in the camp with everyone outdoors and it was a regular sight to see some women having a quiet game of cards on the doorstep of one of the huts. The men played rings (throwing horseshoes at a bar sticking up from the ground; if you got the horseshoe around the bar it was called a ringer) up at the gate. Ernie Collett was a regular player, with Phil Burns and Oliver Brown.

The young boys played football and, like everywhere else at that time, the late 1950s, it was normally fifteen goals each half. We would play the football on the green just at the front of our hut. On the odd time one of our windows was broken, my father would nail a piece of wood over the broken pane. It stayed like that until he would measure it with a piece of string and go into town to buy a pane of glass and some putty. He would put the pane of glass in and smooth the putty with a knife. At a later date, at times a much later date, he would paint the putty to match the rest of the windows, which would normally be emerald green or white.

While the boys played football, the young girls – among them Grace and Ruby Porter, Lena and Kathleen Kelly, Kathleen and Sally Bradley, and Annie Wilkinson – were playing 'cheevies' (someone tipped you on the shoulder and then it was your turn to run after someone else and tip them on the shoulder and so on), hopscotch, hula hoops or just plain skipping, or at times they would simply watch the boys playing football, especially if they fancied one of them.

Another feature in those long summer nights in the camp was the races we used to have around a wee ring road; we raced, two at a time, and would run in opposite directions. At the halfway point, you could see the other runner between the huts and you then knew if you were in front or behind. The races with old bicycle wheels and wire cleats were always great fun. We would strip the wheels of their tyres and tube and bend a piece of wire into a 'U' shape, put the wire cleat against the wheel and run with it; it could be tricky on the rough, uneven roads.

There was always great rivalry between the top and bottom of the camp with no-holds-barred football matches; these matches were not for the faint hearted. Tackles that were the norm then would now get you jailed!

The many toss pits we had were popular with all ages – even some of the fairer sex enjoyed them. The beauty about a toss pit was you could join in even if you only had a penny, and if your luck was in, a few shillings could be had. There were always ways and means to get a few pence to try your luck: collecting lemonade bottles was the quickest way, as you got a penny on each return at one of the wee shops. We later progressed to collecting 'porter bottles' and a few rags and taking them to Morgan's rag store over the Lecky Road. How much you got sometimes depended on the rag-store man's mood. When he found out we were from the camp, he would check the pockets of the coats in the rags to see if we put

Patrick and Kathleen Friel holding baby Eileen with Mary Ann, Dan and Pauline in front, 1949.

The McGee family at their front window at 65 Springtown Camp: Tom and May with children Tom, Evelyn and John, 1952.

Seamus and Molly Smith, who provided a great service to the people from their shop in the camp.

Sadie, Rebecca and Ruby Clingan, Agnes Rabitt and young Ben Clingan in front of the fence that surrounded the camp, 1951.

stones in them, or check the rags to see if they were wet. Of course, the wetter they were the heavier they would weigh. I have to admit he had good reason to, as we tried every trick in the book to make them heavier. In general, though, he treated us fairly enough.

One summer's night, Tommy Donnelly was tossing the two pennies in the toss pit and it just seemed he couldn't lose; he was winning everything in front of him. The next day was the same – not one single boy won. That night, we left the toss pit, bemused at how he could never lose. Again, the following day started off the same way, Tommy winning galore, never losing. However, things were to take a bad turn for him when one of the lads grabbed the pennies out of his hand. We all soon found out why he never lost: one of the pennies had a head on both sides!

Poor Tommy returned to his hut with a beautiful black eye, and all the money he had in his pocket was confiscated and shared out. Suffice to say, he took a few punches over the next few days, as boys who were not present when he was caught sought retribution of some sort.

In the wintertime, with all the rain, the grass areas were damp and not suitable for playing on. We then turned to the large hard-stand pitch of tarmac in the square in the middle of the camp which was our all-weather pitch. Poor Johnny Parkes must have had his heart broken in the wet weather, as about fifty children congregated outside his hut to play on the hard stand. He was a quiet man and had the patience of a saint; he never bothered us at anytime.

We had many advantages over children of the same age in other parts of Derry. There were so many large, open spaces in which to play, both grassed and tarmac areas. In fact, the play options in our Nissen-hut village were almost endless. We were fenced in, and with only about two cars in the camp, were free to roam the wide-open spaces in total safety. Of course, we had other options to occupy us, not all of them strictly legal, mind you, like Jackson's orchard, the swimming pool, the cornfield, the plantation with the many trees there. Not to mention the many railings around the camp we could swing on, our Old Faithful bridge, and close to the bridge we had the tunnel beneath the Buncrana Road where the train used to pass under. It was a favoured place to explore, where we could catch 'sprickly backs' or tadpoles.

***

The Rankin family, a large family of both boys and girls, lived just a few huts from us. They were a popular family and had many friends in the camp. Sad times and tragedy struck their home when the children were all still of school-going age. Their mother, Mary, a decent, hard-working woman, fell ill and died after a short illness. Both Joni McKeever and Kathleen McLaughlin helped the family at this sad time as much as they possibly could. But eventually, the family was taken into care by the authorities. Tommy, who was thirteen, with his sisters Joan, Martha, Annie, Patricia, Bridget and young brother Daniel, who was seven years old, were taken to Termonbacca Home in Derry. They were later transferred to the Dhu Varren home in Portrush. It was from that point on that the family lost contact with Daniel, the youngest member of their family.

As the years rolled on, and despite being fostered out to different families, they managed to keep in touch with each other, with the exception of young Daniel. The Rankins tried to locate him on many occasions, but without success. With the years passing by at an ever-increasing pace, the family intensified their search. Unfortunately and despite their best efforts, Daniel's whereabouts remained a mystery. Every piece of information, no matter how small, every lead, no matter how distant, they followed up, but sadly, it all ended in tears. With every avenue explored and with each passing Christmas, the Rankin family started to despair of ever finding their wee brother.

Even after forty years had passed without a sighting of Daniel, still the family refused to give up and their search continued. Springtown Camp website owner Hugo McConnell posted a message on the web seeking information on Daniel's whereabouts. He visited every ex-children's home in Derry in an effort to get a lead but drew a blank. Then out of the blue in July 2008, the Rankin family got a break. Tommy Rankin, now married and living in London, received a phone call from charity organisation Adopt NI. They said that by pure chance, they had come across a person who was searching for his family, and the words 'Springtown Camp, Derry' made them take notice; they put two and two together and finally, after forty-five long years, the Rankin family's search was over when it became clear it indeed was their long-lost wee brother Daniel, the brother they hadn't set eyes on since he was seven years old on that fateful day all those years ago when they were parted as a family. It was with some excitement that Tommy and his wife relayed the message to other members of the family and soon they were planning a big family reunion. The gathering took place on Sunday 27 July 2008 in Manchester. That day, they met up with their long-lost wee brother.

Unfortunately, they still don't have contact with their whole family, as way back in 1952, eldest brother Billy left Springtown Camp to seek employment. The Rankin family have never heard of, or seen, Billy since that day.

Daniel Rankin meets his older brother Tommy in Manchester after forty-five years of separation. They had lost all contact when they were fostered out to different families in 1963.

Charlie Sweeney, however, was perhaps even more unfortunate, as his search for his younger brother Billy, whom he hadn't seen since leaving the camp, had an unhappy ending. Charlie tried the Salvation Army's missing persons department and all the other agencies who specialise in finding missing persons – all to no avail. Again, the years passed by without any word as to Billy's whereabouts. But Charlie wouldn't admit defeat in his search, so he kept trying. Eventually, with the help of the various agencies, he traced Billy to London. Sadly, though, Charlie was just a few weeks too late, as Billy had passed away a mere six weeks before Charlie found out where he lived.

Several families have lost contact with each other over the years and Ray Donnelly's family is one of them. They were a popular family in Springtown and sold toffee apples, icing squares and blackjacks from their hut in the camp. Ray told me he hasn't seen or heard from his older brother Tommy for a long time. Tommy was a keen toss-pit lad, card sharp and, like most of us, enjoyed a wee flutter on the horses. He took up the job of selling *Tillies* (short for *Belfast Telegraph*) after legendary *Tillie* boy 'Snooker' Cullen retired and moved on to the building sites. Tommy, however, wasn't as clever as Snooker (who was?) at outfoxing the sailors by getting top dollar for a *Tillie*.

Samuel McGowan, Willie Scanlon and George McGowan on a brisk December morning in the camp, 1948.

One man who never strayed far from the camp, and who was a saviour on many occasions for the people of Springtown during the hard old times, was Willie Scanlon.

Willie was already an elderly man when I was a young schoolboy, but his contribution to the life of those around him was immense.

He was a wheeler dealer, buying any item you had to sell, like old clothes and shoes. He was, as one woman put it to me, the difference between going hungry or having something to eat. When a family was short of money, they would take some item of clothing or footwear over to him and he would buy them – often knowing they were not much good to him, as the chance of re-selling them was remote. Nevertheless, he very

May McMonagle with Pauline Friel.

rarely, if ever, refused to buy an item. In hindsight, I now know it was his way of helping people.

I was a regular customer of his. I'd take an old pair of shoes or a coat that maybe my mother had bought at a jumble sale, but because they didn't fit any of us, I took them over to old Willie. Honestly, it really didn't matter what I would take over to him, I never got more than two bob (10p) for it. Knocking on his door, he would roar, 'Come on, on in!' He would be, as usual, sitting in his chair, chewing tobacco. The conversation would normally go like this.

'What is it you have this time?' he would ask.

'I have a great pair of new shoes,' would be my normal reply.

Susie McDonald with children Noel, Gerry, Martin and Ann. 1957.

'New shoes?' he would say with a chuckle. 'You mean new to you, son.'

I would hand him the shoes for his inspection.

'Son, these shoes are older than you,' would be his remark while asking in the same breath how much I wanted for them.

'I need five bob for them,' I would answer in a flash, knowing I hadn't a snowball's chance in hell of getting five bob off Willie for a new suit, never mind a pair of second-hand shoes.

Back he would come at me. 'Son, you will make a good comedian when you grow up. Look, the sun is shining and I'm in a good mood today. Throw them in the corner, here's two bob for you, and what's the money for? Horses, card school or a toss pit?' he would inquire.

'Just three doubles and a treble, an ice pop and a dainty,' I would answer truthfully, a smile on my face.

Old Willie had lots of clothes and shoes piled in the corner of his living room; there was so much stuff there they reached the ceiling. He re-sold some of them to different people in the camp, or at times did a deal with the oilcloth men, who sold their wares in the camp at regular intervals. I thank God for him, as he was my personal banker when I was a boy.

Some people went to him if they needed, say, a pair of shoes in a hurry, and he would normally charge them four bob (20p). A buyer would go to him for an item of clothing or a pair of shoes and would have to search through all

Samuel Holden pictured in thoughtful mood, with wife Sarah holding baby Sharon, Christmas 1955.

the stuff he had piled up in the corner. That, at times, would take about ten minutes alone, as the buyer would find one shoe but have difficulty finding the match for it.

Old Willie had an answer for everything. He would always say, 'If there's a right, there's a left, just keep looking,' while continuing to smoke his pipe. He had every type of clothing, every colour, every shape and size; matching them up could be a problem, though. It definitely wasn't Austins Stores, but most times, you got what you wanted after a bit of searching – and at a discount price to boot!

The smell of old Willie's tobacco was the hardest to stick as he sat there, smoke bellowing out of his pipe, reading the paper while you searched his lot in the corner. He occupied one end of his hut while his daughter Ginny, her husband Willie McBride and their children occupied the other half. Ginny, like her sister Mary Edgar, liked to play cards, mainly stud poker. Actually, it was there that I was introduced to a flush or a straight run as I played cards at the ripe old age of thirteen. Making a few shillings there was very difficult; more often than not, I got 'rooked', which was another word in those days for getting 'busted', or in today's terminology, 'skint'. Sometimes it was a difficult choice to make: take my chances at the card school or stuff my face with sweets. Being an optimistic young lad, the cards normally won.

It's fair to say Willie Scanlon was a safety net for some of the people – in more ways than one. For instance, he was always available to buy most anything at any time, day or night, when money was needed in an emergency. On the other hand, if your shoes suddenly gave way to the camp's rough roads and the rain, it was straight to Willie Scanlon's hut for an emergency fitting.

> *I sighed and looked around me, and gazed in disbelief,*
> *For I saw poor people living through poverty and grief.*
> *And standing gaunt and broken, the old tin huts of green,*
> *And looking o'er the mountains of Scalp and Eskaheen.*

***

Holidays from school in the summer were always a great time and eagerly awaited. The long, carefree summer days that were always (rose-tinted memories) sunny and warm and full of happiness. This was probably because we children had so much to occupy us in the camp. Those were the days of endless matches, swimming in the burn, watching the men playing football down at the Rushie Field – all happy memories.

The big event of the year for most of the children under twelve was the annual August Monday bus run. This was our summer holiday: one or two buses would be packed to capacity going to Buncrana, Moville or Rathmullan. Normally, our parents would pay a small weekly amount of a few shillings until our fares were paid in full. We children were always eager to run messages for people several weeks before the bus runs in order to get a few bob. The money earned would become a prisoner until August Monday.

The week before August Monday was always a very exciting time for us and sleep was hard to come by, as the feeling of excitement was overwhelming. Most of the boys were dressed in short khaki trousers and sandals on our feet. On the morning of the bus run, it was customary for the young boys to gather at the gate of the camp and wait for a sighting of the buses coming from the Northland Road.

Maggie Mooney, Molly Slater and Joanie McKeever on a bus run, August Monday 1956.

August Monday 1953 and half the camp are on their annual holidays in Buncrana. Rose Ann Bridge is surrounded by friends and neighbours including Togo Moore, Eileen Colby, Molly Smith (holding Charlie Smith), Nan Kiernan, Molly and Philip Killen, Florrie Divin (with Johnny Divin), Tina Smith, Betty Smith, Marley Bridge, Kay Bridge, Margaret Killen, Pat Killen, Brian Kiernan, Patsy Moore, Mickey Bridge, Stanley Colby and Peter Divin.

Group at a bus run on August Monday 1955: Hugh McMonagle, Jimmy Jennings, Celine Deeney, Charlie Curley, Patsy Long, Sally Fleming, Mary McMonagle, Bella Carlin, Jimmy Brown, Hughie McMonagle, Moira Carlin, Margaret Brennan, young Mooney and Fleming girls, and Sean Fleming.

With the first sighting, we would roar down to our parents and the rest of the children waiting in a big queue. As the buses entered the camp, we would run alongside them until they came to a halt. The parents would usher all of us on first and it was always a dive to get to a window. Next, our parents would board, their baskets and bags filled with flasks of tea and sandwiches. A head count would take place and when all were accounted for, it would be around 10.00 am and time to move off. Although the journey probably only took about thirty-five minutes, it seemed like half a day to us children. As the buses moved through the camp, the singing would start. We would slide the wee window at the top open, stick our hands out, waving to everyone and anyone who saw us. It was a huge adventure to us and one which we thoroughly enjoyed to the full.

When the buses arrived at their designated destination, they always stopped at the road fronting the beach. We all piled out, and after selecting our own wee family spot on the beach, a rug or blanket was spread on the sand and baskets and bags placed on them. All the families stayed close to each other, just like one big, happy community. Within five minutes of reaching the beach, everyone stripped off and ran to the ocean for a swim. The sight of upwards of 100 Springtowner men, women and children in the sea together would stay with me forever. The men and children were swimming and splashing each other while most of the women were content just to paddle in the water, shoes in hand.

Philip Killen was a super swimmer, and I have clear visions of him diving from high rocks at Rathmullan into the sea.

After about two hours of frolicking in the water, and with the sea air making us hungry, it was time to dry off and get changed back into our clothes. We were now ready to eat our tea and sandwiches. After we were fed and watered, it was the children's job to clean up any mess we made on the beach and put any rubbish into bags and bin it.

Sadie Clingan, Kathleen Diamond, Ruby Clingan and Ben Clingan, 1952. The Clingans emigrated to Iowa, USA, in the early 1960s and remain there to this day.

A visit to the shops up the town was next on the itinerary; most families went up together. Our mothers would normally stay with the younger children while some of the fathers might disappear for an hour to have a drink. This was the time the children would enjoy most of all, as we were let loose to spend our few shillings. I experienced a feeling of great freedom, as I was able to spend my own money as I saw fit.

Any Sunday was a big day for the local shops, but August Monday was an extra-special day, as daytrippers flocked to the County Donegal resorts. The shops with their big net bags hanging from their doors and displaying the different colours of football and beach balls were a big attraction to all of us. They were like a magnet to us, and after first buying a poke of ice cream and a bar of rock, it was straight to them we would go. Being able to buy a ball or a gun with a roll of caps was a big thrill for us. The gun and caps were a very popular choice for the boys, as they looked and sounded like real cowboy gear, and it added to our enjoyment playing Cowboys and Indians when we got back to the camp.

A few hours later, those fathers who went for a couple of pints (not all fathers went) would appear and meet up with the main squad of mothers and children. Fish and chips were then the order of the day, and boy, did we enjoy them! August Monday in the mid-1950s was a roller coaster of a day and as far as we were concerned, that day, Buncrana, or wherever we went, belonged to us.

With all the excitement, the day would fly in lightning fast. Before we knew it, 8.00 pm had arrived and it was time to start walking back to our bus. Before boarding, we would all show off to each other the different toys, footballs or dolls we'd bought.

I can remember we always had to wait on somebody; when they finally appeared, a loud cheer would go up in the bus, as it meant we could begin our journey back home. As the bus pulled out from the resort, the singing would start up; this time our fathers would join in, a few pints in them by now and their shyness long gone.

Some man with cap in hand would make his way through the bus, collecting a few bob for the bus driver; everyone gave a few coppers as a thank you to him. For nearly all of us, it was the only time of the year that we as family units got out together. It was a fun time for all the family and a great bonding exercise for all the camp. It was something we looked forward to for weeks – plus the antics of the day were talked about for ages afterwards.

The camp would be awash with dolls, guns and footballs for the next few days after the bus run. We would be up at cock crow to play with our new toys. To my mind, these days were always long, warm and sunny; whether they were or not is another matter. In hindsight, I suppose the bus runs were a slight escape from the pressure of everyday life in the camp for our parents, but to the children, they were just magical in every way. If my memory serves me correctly, I believe the buses only ever went to about four or five places, changing each year.

Back then, Buncrana, Moville, Rathmullan and the Downings sounded like far-off exotic places to us. The bus runs and all the great craic will live long in our memories.

***

Getting repairs carried out in the camp proved a difficult task, the Corporation consistently refusing all requests. They were very reluctant to spend any money on the camp and would do so only in extreme circumstances. One of many instances of this took place in August 1955. The roads were in such a bad state that camp manager Bob Hutchman complained that he considered them to be dangerous to walk on, especially at night. The Corporation instructed the city surveyor to carry out an inspection of the roads. Early the following month, he informed his superiors in the Guildhall that they were indeed in a serious state. He further went on to report that in his opinion the only solution was to re-surface them, and that extra road gullies would need to be installed in order to remove surface water, which was causing bad flooding.

The city surveyor advised the estimated cost of such works would involve an outlay of approximately £2,300. The housing committee flatly refused to even consider spending such an amount of money on roads in the camp and they rejected his proposal and authorised the surveyor's office to execute works to the roads to a value not exceeding £300. They further instructed him to advise the district traffic manager of the UTA (Ulster Transport Authority) that buses must cease forthwith from using any roads inside the camp.

The 'repairs' to the roads were carried out but were totally inadequate, as all they did was fill in a few potholes. After the winter months, the roads throughout the camp were again in a terrible condition. The potholes returned worse than ever, loose stones and chunks of tarmac strewn all over the roads. Never a day went by without some child falling on them and getting bruised and cut.

The following year, the UTA made an application to the Corporation seeking permission to use a small portion of road inside the camp for a bus terminal; the submission was made on the grounds of passenger safety. The application was refused on the grounds that the buses would 'damage the roads'. The decision beggared belief and was greeted with bemusement by the residents.

Here is the response from the Corporation:

'That the permission sought by the UTA be not granted, as the Corporation is of the opinion that the proposal would result in undue wear and tear to the carriageway of the roads within the camp.'

This reply was so laughable that people didn't believe it at first. However, it was consistent with the Corporation's attitude towards the people of the camp over the years.

Jackie Fisher holding his nephew Bobbie Fisher, with Mick Powers and 'Sauce' Moore, on their rounds in the camp.

Chapter 10

Exodus

Around the late 1950s, the huts had fallen into a serious state of disrepair, and the chances of getting them renovated were about the same as winning the pools. The Corporation maintained their policy of refusing to employ any additional workers in the camp. It was obvious to all concerned that some of the huts were now beyond repair and could only get even worse with the passing of each winter.

With this in mind, some young families were now seeking a home and employment in England and were leaving the camp for good. Most of these families went mainly to Bradford in West Yorkshire while a few others left for Scotland. They seemed to get on well there, securing houses and employment, and it was no big surprise when some of their immediate family decided to follow suit. Soon, complete families were on their way to Bradford and a new life.

The Corporation, fearing the vacated huts would be squatted into, would waste no time in having them demolished or sold. The few who did manage to squat into the huts were swiftly removed by the bailiffs and the huts auctioned off to farmers who wanted them as shelters for their animals.

The farmers, with their workmen, lorries and massive trailers, would come from as far away as Sligo to the camp on auction day. Auctions were held beside each of the vacant huts, with farmers bidding against each other as dozens of campers looked on. Bidding normally started at £10, with most huts being sold for around £20–£25. As soon as the auctioneer put down his hammer, the winning farmer would instruct his men to start dismantling the hut.

During the dismantling, it was a source of some considerable amusement to us to watch the evicted mice scrambling everywhere, seeking safety.

By nightfall, as the lorries and trailers loaded with corrugated tin and steel-angle iron made their way out of the camp, all that would remain would be broken concrete slabs where the huts used to stand. We had the sad situation

May Sweeney and Bridget Costello training John McBrearty's donkey for the Pennyburn sports day donkey derby, 1956.

where a hut that was home to eight or nine of a family on a Tuesday was to be the home of the farmer's animals by that weekend. Of course, the significance of this was lost on the children, simply because we knew no better.

This pattern continued as more huts were vacated, auctioned and dismantled by farmers from all over the country as families were slowly re-housed or emigrated to England or Scotland. After the dismantling, the camp became an eyesore with broken concrete bases and debris strewn all over the place. The hut floors had about one inch of asphalt covering on them; I soon found out this material made for a good bonfire, the only problem being such fires emitted clouds of black smoke, much to the annoyance of the residents.

Among some of the people who emigrated were the Saunders family, who left for Scotland after their eldest daughter Ellen, who was already married and working there, sent for them. The Stewart family, with the popular Alex and Benny, being Scottish, soon followed suit and returned to their homeland after years in the camp. After meeting and marrying Scottish girls, Johnny Divin and Patsy Moore also moved there and to this day still remain in their Dundee homes.

This mini-exodus was gaining momentum as people began searching for a better way of life and saw their future being brighter in a foreign land, with Bradford eventually becoming home to many Springtown families. They took this course mainly to escape the living conditions and chronic unemployment that existed in their home town.

Alex Hasson and his family were among the first to venture to Bradford, taking up employment in the building industry. Soon, Phil Green, Jimmy 'Di' Doherty, his brother John 'Chada', Ken Nash, along with Jimmy 'Stinker' Canning and Willie 'Inkin' Canning followed suit. Their womenfolk, Sarah and Bernie Bridge and Annie Scanlon, either went with them or followed soon after. The Doherty brothers, Chada and Di, were married to two sisters from the camp, Bernie and Sarah Bridge. The list grew bigger by the month as Eddie Kelly and family, Willie and Jenny McBride and family and Maggie Kelly and her family all crossed the Irish Sea to sample life in the West Yorkshire city.

Willie McBride and wife Ginny (née Scanlon), who emigrated to Bradford in the early 1960s, back in Derry on holiday with friends.

Most of the men worked on the building sites in Bradford. Some worked their way up the ladder, eventually becoming very successful in their chosen fields. The Springtown clan were to grow stronger and stronger over the coming months and years. In truth, they once wielded a lot of power and indeed became a major influence on many of the large building sites there.

With the advance party of ex-campers paving the way, a steady stream of families, impressed by their success in securing steady employment and on being allocated a house, quickly continued to take the 'Bradford Trail', with the Moores and the Burkes leaving the camp for a new life there.

Sarah Doherty (née Bridge) holding baby sister Mary.

Sadly, it says a lot about their home town when all of them to this day remain there. Chada Doherty and Bernie Bridge met and married while growing up in the camp. Their son John joined a boxing club in their adopted city of Bradford and showed great promise as a teenager. After years in the amateur ranks, he fulfilled his early promise, going all the way to become British Champion. He proudly holds a famed Lonsdale belt which he won outright. He fought under the name Paddy Doherty to avoid confusion, because there was another boxer at the time called John Doherty. His grandmother and granddad were none other than Ted and Rose Ann Bridge, a well-known and much-loved couple in Springtown. John brought over a team of young boxers to compete against a Derry select a short time ago and paraded his Lonsdale belt in the Stardust.

Andy Doherty was another ex-camper who boxed professionally in England. Andy, a talented sportsman, played football for the Springtown team and was a speedy winger. I remember 'Neekie' Henry training Andy in the camp; Neekie would ride his bicycle while accompanying Andy running the roads.

Bradford now boasts a large Derry contingent, with most originating from Springtown. The first families that arrived in Bradford from the camp way back in the 1950s now have daughters and sons, and in some cases many grandchildren, born there.

Lena and Kathleen Kelly, who lived facing us in the camp, relayed to me their memories of the day they left Derry for Bradford. Lena takes up the story:

'This day Kathleen and I were coming home from Pennyburn School. As we approached our house, our mother met us halfway down the street, shouting for us to hurry up. When I asked my mother what the hurry was, she just said, "Pack all your clothes and be quick about it. We're going to Bradford. Eddie has a house for us there."'

Eddie was their older brother who was already settled in Bradford with his wife Aggie and their children.

'Well, being young girls, this seemed quite exciting stuff, really, so we did as we were told and soon we were on the train on our way to Belfast. There, we caught the boat to England. We finally arrived in

Well-known Springtown resident Jenny Scanlon with a friend on a night out in Bradford, 1960.

Bradford the following day and Eddie and Aggie were there to meet us. It was all so sudden, we didn't even have time to say goodbye to our friends. Now we found ourselves living in a different country, miles away from home. At first, we were definitely not at all impressed with Bradford, and to be perfectly honest, the first question we asked ourselves was, what the hell are we doing in this place?'

They began attending a new school, the transition made easier by the fact they were some way ahead of their British classmates of the same age. Although Kathleen and the rest of her sisters came back to Derry often, Lena didn't return to her home town until all of forty-five years later.

Their brother Eddie came to my rescue one day when he saved me from a certain thumping from a few bigger lads. I had been involved in a kids' fight in the Glen area with a boy of my own age a few days earlier. While walking out the Northland Road, I was spotted by this boy's older brother and his friends. I wouldn't have been fit for one of them, never mind the three of them. They approached me menacingly and their intentions were clear – they were about to attack me – when I heard this voice from behind me: 'What's wrong, young Deery?' I turned around and, to my relief, there was big Eddie Kelly. I told him the boys were about to hit me, and with a quick, open-handed slap to the bigger boy's head, the threat was over as they took flight. Boy, I sure was glad to see Eddie Kelly that day.

Around Springtown, we had many a good friend
In this friendly camp of huts, that had no end
But the days pass by and the months rush on
And before we know it, the years have gone
To keep in touch, we did faithfully promise
But we never did, like Eddie or Thomas
Tomorrow comes and tomorrow goes
The distance between us grows and grows
A few short hours, yet many miles away
A telegram arrived, your friend Eddie died today
Flashbacks to the camp, yet no goodbye at the end
A few short hours, yet many miles away, died our vanished friend

Andy Doherty (partly hidden), John 'Chada' Doherty, John McLaughlin, Jimmy 'Di' Doherty and Willie Deery in a working men's club in Bradford, 1988.

Uncle McLaughlin, Willie Deery, John Doherty (British Flyweight Champion and winner of a Lonsdale belt), John McLaughlin and Willie Edgar in Bradford, 1988.

Chapter 11

Tip, TV and Teens

Eddie 'Tip' Canavan was a well-known character not only in the camp but in Derry everywhere. Tip was an alcoholic but a harmless human being. He regularly staggered off the 10.40 bus to the camp with a bottle in hand and one sticking out of each pocket. Despite his tragic circumstances, he was always in good form, smiling and happy.

He was given the nickname Tip because his father came from Tipperary. Most days, he could be seen wandering along or standing at a corner in William Street. His trademark was if he saw a person who looked sad or down in the dumps, he would put his arm around them and say, 'If you worry, you die; if you don't worry, you still die, so why worry?' The person would invariably brighten up and soon have a smile on their face again. Derry people were always generous to him and several would bring him sandwiches and at times a cup of hot soup.

A very witty person, his one liners were legendary.

One day in William Street during the No Go era (the time when the British Army didn't go into the Bogside or Creggan areas of Derry), he was receiving some abuse from a British Army foot patrol. As the banter flowed between them, a small crowd stopped to listen. Tip told the soldiers, between sips from his bottle, 'Shut up or I will join the Provos (Provisional IRA) and shoot the lot of you.'

The soldier replied, 'We are much too intelligent for the Provos.'

Tip roared with laughter at this, and with bottle in one hand, he put his other arm around the soldier, and, smiling into his face, said, 'Listen, son, the Russians put a man in space, the Yanks put a man on the moon, and you British can't even put a man in Creggan.'

The crowd burst into loud laughter and the soldiers left with their tails between their legs. I don't believe they ever engaged Tip in a one-to-one again!

Tip not only drank daily, he drank hourly for years, and sadly was unable to overcome his illness; as the months and years passed by, it finally got the better of him and he died a relatively young man. It is fair to say the only harm he ever did was to himself. Tip lived in the camp for many years with his mother, father and brother Steven. They were actually one of the last dozen families to leave the camp before being housed in Creggan. To this day, Tip's name stills crops up in conversations, especially by those from the camp and those who still carry out their business in William Street.

This is a lovely tribute to Eddie written by the very talented Seamus McConnell, himself a well-known camper, for the reunion dance way back in 1986. It really sums up Tip very well.

Well, listen and I'll speak of a character unique
Who used to walk the troubled streets of Derry
He always wore a smile, his manner could beguile
And everyone called him Tipperary
From Springtown Camp he came and each night was the same
At all hours you could hear him loudly singing
No sooner off the bus until there was a fuss
For all the children to his coat were clinging
Down William Street he'd sit, a man of charm and wit
The stories he could tell were quite amazing
With bottle in his hand, he didn't give a damn
If all around him half the town was blazing
The life he led was tough, always sleeping rough
And too hard on the nicotine and bevy
In rain and snow he'd lie and as the years rolled by
The burden on his health, well it grew heavy
Well, poor old Tip did sink beneath a sea of drink
And some days you could see him softly crying
Till his body weak and sore could not take anymore
They found him lying in the street dying
Though time it marches on and old Tipperary's gone
No more will he walk the streets of Derry
But on my life I'll bet that no-one will forget
That gentle soul they all called Tipperary.

Right: The legendary Eddie 'Tipperary'
Canavan relaxing with a drink.

Arrival Of Television

The arrival of the first television in the camp was such a joyous occasion that the people who came to install it felt like royalty. There were about fifty children surrounding their small van as they delivered the TV set. On entering the hut, carrying the television, there were gasps from the children, who marvelled at the size of it. When the engineer came out of the hut to get some tools from his van, they were bombarded with questions.

'Hi, mister, is it working now?'

'Not yet, but soon,' came the reply from the workman. Eventually, he came out and said it was switched on and working well with a great, clear picture. The poor family were tortured that first night, as everyone was glued to their window in the hope of catching a glimpse of this new phenomenon.

I do believe Snooker Cullen's family were one of the first to get a television; soon a few other families followed suit.

When the affable John Moore got a television, we children knew we would get a chance to see it, as John was a very kind man. This happened the night after he got it installed. I remember it well, a Sunday night and we were playing football right outside John's window. I suppose John took the view we

Eddie Kelly, Pat Nicholl, and Snooker Cullen in London, 1972.

would be quieter if he brought us in. Calling us over, he asked if we wanted to see a cowboy show that was starting in five minutes. 'Yes!' came the roar from a bunch of excited young boys.

That Sunday night, I sat with my pals on the floor of John Moore's hut and watched the wonderment of television for the first time. The programme was a fantastic cowboy show called *Rawhide* (right). One of its stars was Clint Eastwood, who played the part of Rowdy Yates. Good as James O'Hagan's silent films were, this was something else. I mean, they were actually talking and you could hear everything; it was a new horizon and another new experience for us growing up in the camp.

The battle cry from then on while playing Cowboys and Indians was *get 'em up, move 'em out*, which were the last words spoken in *Rawhide* after every show. It may have made James O'Hagan's silent-movie matinees obsolete, but they still played a major part in the lives of both the children and adults. We were always grateful to James and his lovely wife, Rosie, for giving us the opportunity to see them.

The scene was repeated every Sunday night as we crowded around John Moore's hut to watch *Rawhide*. John would let us in to watch the cowboy show if we agreed to stay away from his hut on the other nights. We readily accepted and rigidly stuck to the bargain, and Sunday nights in his hut soon became one of the highlights of the week.

Ann McColgan (née Sweeney) with daughter Bettine outside their wooden hut in 1964.

Sundays in the camp were now transformed from being just a match day to a day of non-stop excitement. Our normal Sunday was to go to Mass in the morning, the afternoon taken up by watching the big match down at the Rushie Field. Then we had two or three hours of playing football before we headed to John's hut to see *Rawhide*. Sundays were certainly roller-coaster days for us. Later on, Saturday afternoon was to be an exciting time as well as we looked forward to listening to Ronald Rosser giving out the football results on the wireless. Then it was time to watch the world's first superstar, *The Lone Ranger*, on television. If we were playing football, the minute we heard *a fiery horse with a speed of light, a cloud of dust, and a hearty Hi-Ho, Silver, the Lone Ranger rides again*, it was the signal to grab the ball and make a dash to a hut to watch this wonderful superstar with his pal, Tonto, his horse, Silver and, of course, his silver bullets.

During the week, we were put to bed early when a programme called *Quatermass* was scheduled to be shown on television, as our parents deemed it unsuitable for our tender eyes.

Our Early Teen Years

When we all reached the age of thirteen, we ran messages (errands) for some of the women in the camp. Danny Feeney, Paddy Parsons, Stevie Wilkinson, Paddy McLaughlin and Yours Truly all had our own favourite people we ran messages for; it was a way of earning a few bob. I was Bella O'Hagan's message boy and Bella was a legend in the camp. She would give me a dollar (25p) plus the bus money every Saturday morning to go into town to get her messages.

Sometimes, I would meet the other boys on the bus, all on our way to Derry. I would plan my route: William Street was the first port of call – to the butcher's to get her meat; I always had instructions to tell the butcher

The one-and-only Bella O'Hagan with granddaughter and husband Johnny outside her wooden hut, 63d.

to give me a good shinbone for soup. Beside the butcher's was the bookie's shop, where I would ask some man to place Bella's bet for her and, of course, not forgetting to place my own 'bob double'. After safely tucking the betting slips into my pocket, I'd walk over to Bigger's pork store in Foyle Street.

Bigger's pork store in Foyle Street.

This is where I had to be extra careful as I ordered the pigs' feet and parin's (thick bacon). I had to make sure the pigs' feet were not too small; Bella hated small pigs' feet. At times I would have to say to the pork man, 'Mister, gone give us bigger feet than that, otherwise I will get the bake ate off me.' Smiling, he would always give me great value.

Last stop was the vegetable shop for Bella's soup vegetables, then it was straight to the bus station and out to the camp. Bella was easily the best payer in the camp and it was a job much sought after by all the young lads who wanted to earn a few bob.

In addition to my instructions for the butcher, I was firmly told to take a good look at the man I entrusted to place the bet in the bookie's. Bella left nothing to chance. 'Look for Willie Edgar or Jack McLaughlin or anybody from the camp,' she would advise me. It was also imperative I bet the horses in John Joe McGeady's bookie's and nowhere else. She reckoned she had better luck there than any other betting shop. Anyway, they were in William Street, so it was handy enough, and Jack or Benny McLaughlin or Willie Edgar would normally be about on a Saturday morning, so that didn't present a problem. When I eventually got back to Bella's hut, especially in the wintertime, she would have a big bowl of soup ready for me. I watched the sport on her television as I ate the bread and soup. Willie, Eddie and Jamesie, her big sons, would be training with weights in the room with the likes of big Jimmy Jennings and Tommy Mooney.

Bella always backed the favourites; she never named a horse, just the favourite in a particular race. One Saturday as I was eating my soup, I could see from the television that the favourites were doing well and seemed to be winning right, left and centre. I drew Bella's attention to this.

Squinting her eyes, she moved closer to the television screen to have a look, at the same time putting her finger to her lips, the sign for me to keep quiet. She didn't want anyone to hear me saying some of her horses had won. When all the results came in, all her horses had won and I asked her if she wanted me to go into the bookie's to collect her winnings. 'Naw, I will go in with you,' she replied. I might have been only thirteen, but I was no mug and I was aware she must have won a good few pounds. When she thought it would be too chancy for me to send a stranger into the bookie's shop for her winnings, we set off for Derry again that Saturday afternoon, and on the bus, Bella quizzed me on who placed the bet for me. It was big Jack McLaughlin, I told her.

I waited outside while Bella went into the bookie's; she came out with a grin as wide as the Foyle. She gave me another dollar (25p); that made it a full ten bob (50p) I got from Bella that day.

On returning to her hut, I had tea and biscuits and watched *Dixon of Dock Green* on the TV. After it was over, it was straight to McConnell's shop where I bought some sweets. I was a happy camper as I ran to our hut with money in my pocket and a bag full of blackjacks, dainties, and lucky dips.

Bella was a generous woman, but I couldn't say that about everyone who wanted you to run errands for them. There was one lady in particular and when she called someone to run a message, we let on we didn't hear her and would clear off. She didn't pay you most of the time; she had always plenty of excuses, like: 'I will give you a dollar next week', or 'he only sent half of the money this week', or 'the wire boy (post office boy who delivered money sent from England) hadn't come yet with the money'. Next week never came, as far as she was concerned, so all the boys tried to avoid her.

***

Of course, boys being boys, many a fight broke out in the camp, and when this happened, which was often, a crowd would form a big ring and each would roar on their pal. The rules were simple: no biting, no pulling hair, no kicking, and no hitting when the other boy was on the ground. Oh, how times have changed! These fights would normally take place coming from school or after a football match, but the next day, all was forgotten.

Confirmation Group

Confirmation day, May 1959. Front row: Paddy Parsons, Johnny O'Donnell and Jimmy McCarron. Second row: Tommy Duffy, Martin Deane, Tommy Mooney and Christopher McClelland. Fourth row: Paddy Kelly, Willie Lynch, Frankie Doherty, Hubert Porter and Daniel Bradley.

There were times when you had to be cute when buying sweets from either Fanny Canning's or Mary Ann Meehan's shops. Both shops faced each other; if you went into Mary Ann's shop first and she hadn't got what you wanted, you would naturally go over to Fanny's place. This was where problem started – neither of them would serve you if they'd seen you going into the other shop first! We soon got wise to this and had to sneak into the shops separately.

It was the done thing on every St Patrick's Day to have our shamrocks and a small green, white and gold cloth badge pinned to our jumpers. For some reason, we gathered stones from the crumbling roads of the camp and a crowd of boys and girls would go into the estate with the aluminium bungalows just over 200 yards away where predominantly Protestant families lived. We would throw stones at the young boys who were playing there and they in turn would throw them back at us. It was a sort of 'annual battle' between the children which lasted all of fifteen minutes. Years later, both sides had a good laugh about the episodes.

I often recall the day I was asked to run into the pub now known as the Argyle Arms for a half-bottle of Mundies wine for a gentleman. I was about thirteen years old but still in short trousers and would be known to run errands for people. I was getting half a crown (about 12p), big money then for running a message, so I didn't think twice. I was told to knock at the small side hatch on the wall of the pub on the Argyle Street end. I duly knocked and was answered straightaway by the barman, who inquired what I wanted.

'Half a bottle of Mundies wine,' I told him.

'Who is it for?' he asked.

When I told him the name of the man, he obviously knew him, as he said, 'Okay, wait a minute,' as he took the money off me.

He came back about two minutes later and gave me the bottle wrapped in brown paper. I was told to put the bottle up my jumper by the barman. On walking out towards the camp, I had the bottle up my jumper and keeping a tight grip on it being careful not to drop the bottle. As I was walking past Templemore School, I nearly fainted when I saw a policeman cycling towards me on the Northland Road. I didn't know what way to turn, so I just stopped and picked up a paper and pretended to read it. I was so nervous I didn't realise I was reading brown paper! I dropped it and looked at the football pitch at the school, hoping the policeman would just ride on by on his bicycle. He didn't. He stopped and asked me what I had up my jumper.

'A bottle of lemonade,' I replied.

'Let me see it,' said the policeman. I showed him the bottle and he unwrapped the brown paper around it and asked who it was for. I told him and he ordered me to come with him to the police station on the Strand Road. When we arrived in the barracks, I was asked the number of the hut where the man who sent me lived. I said I didn't know the number, but when they suggested I knew where he lived, I told them I did. As they put me in a police car and drove out to the camp, on the way out I thought to myself, *the first car you were ever in and it had to be a police car!*

Looking back on the incident, you would have thought I had committed a hanging offence instead of a slight misdemeanour by today's standards. Both the man and I were summonsed to appear at court in Bishop Street. I laugh at the thought of it now, but back then it was serious enough for my mother to borrow a pair of long trousers from my cousin, as she was of the opinion I would look older in long trousers while attending the court.

At court, the gentleman in question was fined five shillings (25p), and I was let off and told to stay away from public houses. When the judge, who didn't take the case too seriously, asked the gentleman who owned the bottle if he had anything to say, he responded, 'Can I have my bottle back?'

Smiling, the judge said, 'Of course you can. It's your property.'

The man, my father and I left the court together and went straight out to the camp.

After about nine months running Bella's messages, I progressed to gathering brock (leftover food from meals). I was given a donkey and cart loaded with three large bins by the Barbers, who had a wee farm on the Collon Lane beside our school. I recruited Colm Wilkinson to take over my message-boy job for Bella; I wanted someone reliable for Bella, because Bella had treated me well, and it was the least I could do. Colm was mister reliable and as honest as the day was long, and he was perfect for Bella. Colm was to run Bella's messages for a couple of years after that.

The job with the donkey and cart was a six-days-a-week job. After school, I went straight to Barbers' wee farm, where I would harness Nelly the donkey and within fifteen minutes, I was on my way to do my run.

I started off my run at the terraced houses in the Collon, then around Messines Park and back to the Collon Lane farm. My target was ambitious as I tried to get three bins of brock per day; with me getting paid two shillings per bin that made six shillings a day and a total of £1 16s 0d (£1.80p) for the week. It was great money for a fourteen-year-old boy but very hard work. I didn't always achieve my quota, but more weeks than not, I did. I gave my mother £1 per week, and it was needed in our hut.

Football At The Rushie Field

Between the railway line and the huts lay a big field full of rushes where the children would pull rushes from the ground and make batons by binding them together. The men of the camp decided they needed more recreation facilities; as they were thinking of getting a football team together, they would also need a football pitch. The Rushie Field was the only site that was big enough to facilitate a football pitch.

Scores of men and children set about the enormous task of clearing the rushes from the field. This was a difficult task indeed, but after many days and nights resulting in many a blistered hand, they finally succeeded. Heavy rollers were pushed up, down and across the pitch until it was flat; a nice, level pitch was now ready. Goalposts were now needed; the men soon secured round steel posts and got them welded in to goalposts. Bags of lime were purchased and the men set about lining the pitch to the necessary measurements.

Young footballers down at the Rushie Field in the summer of 1955.

Standing at the top of the banking, you had a grandstand view of the complete pitch and it looked an impressive sight. Now it was ready for some exciting football matches. The responsibility of selecting the team and inviting teams out to the camp to play fell on Jim Reilly, Willie Edgar and Neekie Henry.

Sunday afternoons (evenings in the summertime) were the designated times for such matches. The men needed a football strip and they decided to give a bob (5p) each week, which would be used for the purchase of a football rig and two tube and covers (footballs). Sometimes if the ball went soft or was punctured, the leather cover would need to be unlaced and the tube taken out and patched. The tear was repaired with a solution used as an adhesive to stick the patch to the tube; when dried, it would be placed back into the leather cover and re-inflated. However, when the leather cover itself got torn, then a specialist (like a shoemaker) was needed to stitch it together again. That specialist was Bertie Downey, who had his shoemaker's shop in Waterloo Street; he never charged a penny for his service, something the Springtown team were grateful for. Bertie hailed from the nearby Collon and was a regular at the Springtown matches, and he enjoyed the craic like everyone else on many a Sunday afternoon.

Neekie Henry's hut was used as the changing rooms for the team, and as they all ran out for their first match in their new football rig, they were greeted with some loud banter by the crowd. The matches were taken very seriously by the men, and everyone wanted to play. Pressure on the three selectors was so intense they were forced to set up a reserve team. So we now had a first team and a reserve team in the camp.

Frank 'Neekie' Henry relaxing on a hot day, waiting for the TV programmes to begin.

Shoemaker Bertie Downey.

There were many matches played in the camp, but one match always sticks out in my mind and in the minds of many ex-campers. I recall the banking was packed and Fox's Corner were the opponents. Both teams had played each other a few weeks previously and that match ended in a bit of acrimony. This, of course, led to a bit of needle in this particular match. Both teams would obviously push the boat out to win this one and obtain bragging rights for the following week. Each team was supposed to field strong sides on the day, with Derry City goalkeeper Willie Ferry expected to keep goal for Fox's Corner.

Word spread around the camp like wildfire that Sunday that Fox's Corner, managed by Paddy Doherty, was bringing out a star-studded side.

The normal Springtown team was:

Jimmy Deery, Neekie Henry, Jim Reilly, Brendan Fleming, Uncle McLaughlin, Artie Morrison, Oliver Brown, Willie Edgar, Stinker Canning, Andy Doherty and Jim Callaghan.

Sid Cooke – an official referee, a Welshman and a camper – was refereeing the match dressed in his full outfit, a sign he gave serious consideration to its importance. When he blew his whistle to start the match, a roar went up from the crowd that could be heard in the Strand Road. Willie Ferry did indeed play in goal that day for Fox's Corner and, in an attempt to unsettle and distract him, dozens of children went behind his nets and roared their heads off. Ferry remained unfazed and the match ended with defeat for the camp team. It was a great match, one of the best ever played in the camp and it has lived long in my memory, especially the scene with the crowd behind Ferry's nets.

Many years later with my mates Stevie and Brendie Wilkinson and Paddy 'Buzzard' McLaughlin, we met Willie Ferry in his fish and chip shop over in Laburnum Terrace. We were coming from St Eugene's Boys Club and were ordering fish and chips. Willie was frying the chips when I mentioned that particular match to him. He turned around swiftly and, laughing loudly, said, 'I remember that match well. There must have been a hundred wains behind my nets.' We told him we were four of those wains! Willie went on to say that when you played in the camp, you knew you had a match on your hands. Afterwards, we all had a good laugh about it; great, never-to-be-forgotten, innocent days, he recalled.

Willie's fish and chip shop became our regular stop off after the club from then on. Actually, one Tuesday night, about six of us were in his shop and we ordered one bag of chips between us. He asked us if we were in training. 'Naw, we're just skint,' we replied. Willie told us to order what we wanted and pay him on Friday. Ever since then, we got tick off Willie and paid him every Friday night. Willie Ferry was a true gentleman.

Chapter 12
Doherty Fire and Women's Protest

Saturday 31 October 1959 was a sad night for the family of Mr and Mrs Hugh Doherty and their five children, along with his brother, wife and child as the hut all ten were living in caught fire and burned to the ground in minutes. Close neighbour Willie Campbell was hailed a hero, as he risked his life when he ran into the blazing hut and rescued some of the children trapped inside. The whole of the camp was furious at this tragedy, which, but for the quick action of Willie Campbell, could have resulted in the death of some of the children. His bravery was acknowledged by all in Derry.

It was terrible that two families were rendered homeless and it was only a matter of time before other huts would go on fire, as the electricity in many huts was in a very dangerous condition. This was compounded by the fact the huts were very cold and damp, leaving the residents with a stark choice: risk a fire or freeze.

The Doherty family's hut after the fire on 31 October 1959. Included in the photograph are Billy McLaughlin, Harry Feeney, Willie McConnell, Stevie Wilkinson, Tommy Rankin, Florrie Divin, Mary Edgar, Philip Killen and a group of young children (see close-up of group on facing page).

Willie Campbell received a bravery award for his actions in saving some young children from a blazing hut. Willie went on to be chairman of the camp housing committee in 1964. Also pictured is his daughter Kate. Getting in on the act are Philip Killen, Brian O'Rourke (Jnr), Eugene McLaughlin and Dennis Campbell, 2 November 1959.

The women of the camp were angry at the worsening conditions of the huts and the overall lack of movement by the Corporation in re-housing them. Deciding something had to be done, they discussed what options were available to them. After a brief discussion, they determined they would go to the Guildhall and confront the powers-that-be, face to face, at their next Corporation meeting.

Tuesday 24 November 1959, the unionist mayor and his councillors of the Corporation filed into the chambers of the Guildhall. Their carefree, relaxed attitude suggested they were expecting the normal whitewash of a meeting. Little did they know that twenty-five resolute housewives from Springtown Camp were in the public gallery ready to confront them. Also in the public gallery to lend his support was Eddie McAteer, Nationalist Party MP. The women were seeking answers to why there was no movement on re-housing the residents of the camp. They were also demanding a commitment from the Corporation to get off their backsides and do something about the condition of the camp until such times as it was closed.

When Alderman Gerald Glover, chairman of the housing sub-committee, had finished speaking, Alderman Hegarty addressed the meeting and said, 'Some years ago, the Ministry passed regulations for the keeping of pigs in proper conditions; these included having their buildings in a state of good repair. The question I ask today is this: why do these conditions not apply to human beings living in Springtown Camp? Are they not entitled to at least the same privileges as the pigs? We have here today some of the residents of Springtown Camp and they have elected a spokeswoman and I ask you to hear her now.'

Lily Jennings, Sadie Campbell, Susan Cullen, Molly Killen, Kathleen Curran, Mary Brolly and Ellen Deane entering the Guildhall to protest about the delay in re-housing families from Springtown Camp, November 1959.

Sadie Campbell had been selected as spokeswoman. She stood up in the public gallery and spoke at the top of her voice. 'I speak on behalf of the citizens of Springtown Camp.'

Before she could ask a question, she was interrupted by Alderman Glover who said, 'I object to you speaking.'

Heated exchanges were to follow between nationalist and unionist councillors and at this point, Mayor Colhoun called for order. One of the women shouted at him, 'My husband served in Korea during the winter and he said the conditions there were much better than we have in Springtown Camp. Is a man who has served all through the war and has a child with TB not entitled to a proper home?'

The mayor and Alderman Glover ignored the woman.

Another woman said she had a child who died in the camp with pneumonia caused by the cold and dampness and she asked, 'Am I not entitled to ask a question?'

She, too, was ignored.

The mayor responded by saying, 'I think this meeting should be adjourned.' A vote was taken and the motion to adjourn was passed by eight votes to five. The women shouted, 'We will be back and we will have our children with us next time.'

True to their word, next week came and back they came. Again there was uproar. This time, the RUC were called by the mayor to evict the women from the public gallery. 'We will be back next week again unless you come out and visit the camp and see the conditions we are forced to live in.'

Drama as it was for the housewives from the camp and the Corporation at the Guildhall, life went on as normal in the city. There was dancing in the Corinthian Ballroom to Jimmy Sturrock and his showband; admission was a hefty 3s 6d (about 17p) while *The Last Train from Gun Hill* starring Kirk Douglas and Anthony Quinn was showing at the City Cinema.

The action taken by the women of the camp, among them Sadie Campbell, Molly Killen, Anna McBrearty, Kathleen Porter, Dolly Sweeney and her daughters, Eileen Deane, Cissie Moore and others had the desired effect. The very next day, Alderman Glover, the housing sub-committee chairman, visited Springtown. He saw the huts for himself for the first time and found the conditions in which 120 families had to live appalling.

The women's action looked like paying off, as at the housing committee's meeting of Thursday 3 December 1959, Springtown Camp was high on the agenda. The chairman of the committee referred to the question of re-housing the residents of the camp. This matter, he said, had been raised at the quarterly meeting of the council held on 24 November 1959, and at the adjourned meeting held on 1 December 1959. Glover advised his committee he had inspected a number of huts in the camp and interviewed some of the tenants, some of whom were at the meetings referred to. After lengthy discussions about the problems in the camp, he proposed the following resolution: the first houses that become available to the Corporation (the twenty-eight then under construction at the Coach Road development) be allocated exclusively to selected families at Springtown Camp. However, spoken words of promises are worthless if deeds fail to match them. This was passed by the housing committee and duly noted in the minutes of their meeting.

The women of the camp forced this unprecedented action and a solid commitment from the hitherto intransigent Corporation. So, to all intents and purposes it was set in stone that the twenty-eight new houses at Coach Road would be going to Springtown residents.

Set in stone? The people of the camp who had heard these promises before from the Corporation urged caution with one long-time resident saying, 'Look, today is Friday and if that lot from the Guildhall told me tomorrow was Saturday, I would still need to consult a calendar.'

If the next new homes that came available at the Coach Road development did go to Springtowners, it would still leave approximately 100 families living in squalor. Nevertheless, it meant that twenty-eight families would be housed within three or four months, and that had to be welcomed.

The women proved the only way to get any action from this Corporation was to fight and confront them every step of the way. That weekend, their actions were lauded when the *Derry Journal*'s headline read: 'Women of Springtown Camp Win First Round'. The report went on to say: 'I take my hat off to the women of Springtown Camp. At the recent Corporation meetings, they demonstrated their ability to make and sustain their case. They made a bit of history by being the first women to speak at a Corporation meeting for as long as I care to remember. Previously, it was not for women to express their views or opinions; opinions were the prerogative of men. Men took their superiority as granted and treated women as more or less necessary nuisances on such occasions. But

The ever-popular Jack McLaughlin holding daughter Brenda, with Briege standing, August 1953.

the debate on Springtown Camp ended that assumption of male superiority. It put men in their place.

'The unionists came to the meeting with all their old bags of tricks, but all fell flat. They found the women of Springtown were not going to be fobbed off. The women knew what they wanted, stated it in plain words and refused to be placated by empty promises and never allowed themselves to lose sight of it. Against their honesty and sincerity, the rehearsed speeches of the unionists were in vain.'

Things went back to normal once again as the people waited to see if they would be among the twenty-eight families re-housed. About four months later, the postman brought good news to some families as he delivered letters of notification of tenancies to new houses at the Coach Road.

Two very happy Springtown campers, Lily Stanley and Noreen Killen, enjoying a night out.

Word swept the camp like wildfire that many families indeed had been re-housed as promised. It was soon determined the Tolands were on the list, as were the McGinleys. The families of Lawrence Bradley and his brother Daniel were also on the list. After about thirty minutes, news filtered through the camp that others were being re-housed: the McShanes, Lynches, Killens, O'Donnells, Smiths and the Browns.

The residents started to ask each other, 'Did you not get a house?' When over an hour had passed, it became clear that indeed ten families in total were re-housed. The general consensus was that the other eighteen would probably be allocated the next week. Over the next couple of weeks, every family waited in anticipation for the postman and that elusive letter; none arrived. With each passing day, the people of the camp became suspicious of the Corporation's intentions.

Their suspicions were well founded, as word reached the residents that the houses at the Coach Road were now fully allocated. Once again, the Corporation had reneged on their promise to allocate the twenty-eight houses at the Coach Road development to Springtown residents. Again no-one in the camp was really surprised at the Corporation's deeds. It had happened many times before and no doubt would happen again.

One of the lucky ten to be re-housed at the Coach Road was the family of Daniel Bradley. Daniel, a very hard-working man, was a chain smoker. Each night after coming home from his day job, he would chop sticks. He never deviated from his routine. First, he would saw the lengths of timber in to 8- or 9-inch-long pieces with a bow saw, then chop them with a very sharp cleaver into sticks; all this work was carried out in his wee room.

Daniel would cut the elastic bands used to bundle the sticks together from old bicycle tubes with a sharp pair of scissors. I remember him telling me he would get about 300 elastic bands from one such tube. He would put about ten sticks to a bundle. Come every Saturday morning, let it be sunshine, hail, rain or snow, Daniel or some of his helpers would be seen pushing a specially designed cart, or even a pram, loaded with bundles of sticks in the Northland Road, all for sale at 1 shilling (5p) per dozen bundles. A good morning's selling would be to sell a gross (144 bundles) which realised the sum of twelve shillings (60p). Daniel gave good value and his sticks were selling like hotcakes around the small terraced streets of the Glen. Now the corner shops started purchasing them also and selling them on to their customers. With this uptake in business, Daniel decided he needed a faster and more efficient means of transport, so he bought himself a horse and cart.

He called his mare Blossom and she was a novelty among the children of the camp. The following year, Blossom had a foal, Beauty. He was now doing a roaring trade as he was delivering a fast, efficient service. I believe he wasn't best pleased when the letter arrived informing him he was being re-housed in the Coach Road. He knew it would be the end of his stick business, as no way would he be allowed to saw and cut sticks in his new house. However, he still kept both his mares and retired them to the nearby fields.

The one consolation for him was that his brother Lawrence and family were also being housed in the Coach Road together with eight other Springtown families. The ten families were the envy of everyone in the camp, as naturally every family hoped they would be re-housed beside some of their former neighbours. The day the ten families moved to their new homes, every man, woman and child wished them well. It was very pleasing and satisfying that all were being re-housed in the same street.

Chapter 13
New Houses and Men's Retreat

Just a few short months previously, in October 1959, a wave of excitement and hope swept through the camp. Parents and children alike hoped this could be the answer to all their problems. Their optimism stemmed from the news that the Corporation had instructed their architect to draw up plans with a view to constructing several hundred houses at Springtown. If this possibility became reality and houses were indeed to be built in the camp, this would mean that the Springtown community would remain intact. The general consensus was this would be the perfect and logical solution to a seemingly never-ending saga. It would have, I think, suited everyone. However, much to their annoyance and frustration, the hopes of the residents were once again to be dashed.

It was late November when the Corporation's architect duly submitted his plans as instructed. The outline plans for the building of several hundred houses at Springtown were now on the board. After studying the plans, inexplicably the powers-that-be binned the idea. They made the following statement on Thursday 3 December 1959.

'Having examined plans submitted by the housing architect showing possible redevelopment of Springtown Camp, and having heard from the city accountant, who tabled figures showing estimated rents of houses in the proposed Springtown Camp, the following tariffs will apply:

2-bedroom-type houses – 32s 6d weekly, inclusive of rates
3-bedroom-type houses – 36s 0d weekly, inclusive of rates
4-bedroom-type houses – 47s 0d weekly, inclusive of rates
5-bedroom-type houses – 53s 0d weekly, inclusive of rates.'

The committee decided not to proceed any further with any scheme for the erection of houses at Springtown Camp at present. The rents quoted were very expensive indeed; for example, take a family who needed a four- or five-bedroom house. With most likely the father unemployed and with no other income apart from the family allowance, it would have been impossible to pay that kind of rent, bearing in mind the dole was approximately £10 per week. Their rent would have jumped from 12s 6d (63p) to 47s 0d (£2.35) or even 53s 0d (£2.65) per week. The Corporation, by estimating the rent so highly, led people to believe that they had no intention of building houses in the camp in the first place.

This was the Corporation's opportunity to lance the boil, but instead they merely irritated it. Once again, the residents were furious and they viewed this as just another devious ploy to keep the people quiet for several months.

Later that week, they announced minor repairs would be carried out to the roads in the camp. With all hopes now dashed as regards building houses in the camp, once again things settled down for a further few months.

The Men's Retreat

Our attention soon turned to the annual Men's Retreat at St Patrick's Church, Pennyburn. All the talk was about the new Retreat Fathers who would be giving the sermons and how they would be pulling no punches from the pulpit. Funnily, the more controversial they were, the more we looked forward to going to the retreat. There was nothing as bad as having to listen to a dull and boring preacher. Each night while attending the retreat, it was customary to give 'silver' money at the collection. I recall on one such night about six of us, all fourteen-year-old teenagers, were attending the retreat. We had a tanner (about 2p) each in our pocket for the collection. While walking to the chapel, we met up with one of the big boys, who conveniently informed us he had a date after the retreat but had no money. After listening to his tale of woe, one of us suggested we give him our tanners; we all agreed. He entered the retreat that night one happy camper.

The main thing for us teenagers was to be seen at the retreat by either the priest or one of our schoolteachers, just to confirm we actually were there.

The early morning football matches between the married men and the single men were a feature of the annual retreats in the camp as they were everywhere in Derry. These were fiercely contested matches with no prisoners taken. It was the norm to see boys limping on their way to school after such matches.

The Women's Retreat was held a week before the men's and was more relaxed. The mothers and sisters gave us the lowdown on the Retreat Fathers and which of them gave the best sermon. The whole camp was up early for those two important weeks. Walking past the old bridge in their droves, the women and girls were a sight to behold, scarf or hat on head, all on their way to Pennyburn Church.

The closing of the retreat was a big occasion, with a white flower a must for the lapel of your suit. Looking back on these mornings, they were happy times as all campers bonded well together walking to and from the retreat.

The Retreat Fathers normally hailed from the south of Ireland and always made a point of visiting the camp several times during their stay. When doing so, they were surrounded and followed all over the camp by children and parents alike. We had so much respect for them and always looked forward to their visits. Many of them made reference to their visit to the camp in their sermons and without fail would pay tribute to the women of the camp for their humility and dignity while living in such conditions.

***

Around August 1960, the people complained bitterly to housing manager Murphy regarding the deterioration of the corrugated huts and the roads in the camp. He promised to report their complaints to his housing sub-committee and would indeed ask them to authorise repainting the huts with bituminous paint (tar). They did agree, but as usual, they were not going to make it easy for the residents as they directed that all such painting of the huts was to be carried out by the two labourers employed at the camp. Given that there were 130 huts in the camp at that time and with only two men to carry out all the painting, it was obvious to everyone that it would take a very long time to tar the tin huts.

Camp manager Bob Hutchman reported to his superiors that

Housing manager Dennis Arthur Murphy in happier times on holiday in Malin Town, County Donegal.

repainting the corrugated huts was continuing but was extremely slow. This was because the two workmen had other duties to perform at the camp. He requested more painters to help carry out this work. The Corporation refused.

The residents of the camp were furious that no real effort was being made to stop their huts being flooded every time it rained. As a last resort, to try to keep the water at bay, the families went to Bob Hutchman with the offer to tar their huts themselves if the Corporation supplied the tar paint. Bob readily agreed that this was the only solution and agreed to supply the tar paint and buckets.

Soon, the fathers and sons of each family set about doing the Corporation's work for them; they had no alternative. It was a simple choice: watch as their huts continuously flooded or take measures to try to solve the problem themselves. With most of the tin huts leaking, every family wanted the tar and buckets and the waiting list grew longer and longer. Some of the huts changed colour overnight from green to black.

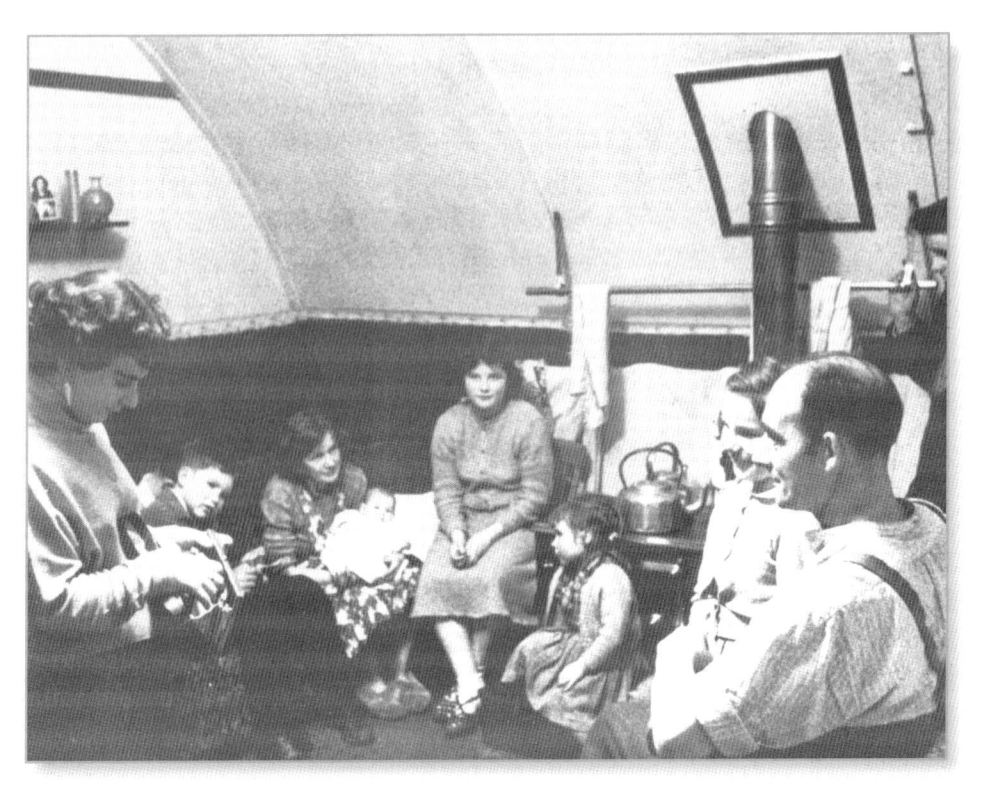

Inside 7 Springtown Camp, the Holden family home. Included: Dolores, Raymond, Sarah (holding Sharon), Vera, Ann, Patricia and Sammy. This photograph appeared in Picture Post *magazine on 17 December 1955.*

Chapter 14
Big Boys and Girls

In the late 1950s, the big boys, like Neil 'Uncle' McLaughlin (his nieces and nephews were around his own age, so they jokingly started calling him Uncle in front of the girls to embarrass him), Seamus and Liam Fleming, John McLaughlin, Snooker Cullen, Kevin McLaughlin, George Lynch and Hugo Henry, and the big girls Kay and Marley Bridge, Maureen Lynch, Mary Divin, Frances Lynch, Margaret Doherty and Ann and Margaret English went dancing every weekend in the Crit or the Corinthian Ballroom.

On a Saturday night, dressed in their best clothes, they would faithfully catch the 9.10 bus to Derry on their way to their chosen dancehall. For some of the lads, first stop would be Jimmy Macari's Café in William Street where they would have a cup of tea or a lemonade while listening to some 1950s hit records on the jukebox. Then they would walk the short distance to the venue of their choice for the night.

Some of the boys were aware of the social stigma attached to the camp so when they asked to leave a girl home from the dances they would tell them they lived somewhere other than Springtown. We joke about it today, but it's proof that we knew it existed way back then. Some people mistakenly associated the character of the people with the conditions of the huts in which we were forced to live.

Frances Lynch, with a smile, tells the story of her being escorted home by a fella who thought she lived in a big house on the Buncrana Road. Technically, Frances was partly telling the truth, as the camp was on the Buncrana Road.

The older teenagers, with their drainpipe trousers, cheap hair oil and suede shoes, would jive the girls outside huts while music blared out of the wireless. The girls wore can-can dresses and had beehive hair styles. They all danced to the music of the '50s, and the sound of Buddy Holly – the new rock'n'roll sensation – was one of the most popular.

The last camp football team, Emeralds FC, managed by George Lynch. Back row: Tony Gormley, Danny McLaughlin, Uncle McLaughlin, Tommy Roberts, Liam Fleming, Seamus Fleming and Seamus Fleming. Front row: Hugo Henry, Hugo Cullen, Eugene McLaughlin, John Brown and Michael Curran.

There was sadness among the teenagers of the camp who frequented the Crit and the Corinthian when the news filtered through that some of their idols had been killed in a plane crash in America. It was 3 February 1959 when Buddy Holly, Ritchie Valens and the Big Bopper, JP Richardson, were killed with their pilot in a tragic plane crash. For weeks after his death, the sound of Holly's hit songs were blasted from the radios in Mary the Hen's and Molly Smith's huts. After the dances, all the boys and girls would walk out home together and they had some great craic on those never-to-be-forgotten Saturday nights.

It was obvious to everyone that some would end up married to each other, and that proved to be the case. Every Sunday night, it was the norm for them to get the bus into Derry and walk up to Carlisle Road, where they would walk up and down the street looking over the local 'talent'.

The boys and girls would separate and walk up different sides of the street. After about two hours of walking, they would meet up again and walk to the bus station to get the last bus out to the camp. By the time they reached the camp, it would be time for the Top Twenty, which was played on the wireless every Sunday night. All would congregate at Molly Smith's hut where Molly would put the radio on top of the open window so all could hear the countdown from the Radio Luxembourg hit parade. They would stay until the No 1 record was played, with some of them doing a bit of jiving to the music.

Monday night was normally Picture Night, when the teenagers would catch the 7.10 bus for Derry. The City and Palace cinemas were the favourite venues around that time. When the film was over, it was straight to the bus station for the last bus home. There were always massive queues for the last buses to everywhere, and while waiting for the buses to arrive, some street entertainers would sing and play instruments to amuse the crowds; they would play accordion, banjo, fiddle or a tin whistle. In turn, the people in the queues would throw a few pennies into their hats or slip a few pennies into their hands. Our own Mickey Jackson was one such street performer who at times would encounter one of his teachers in the bus queues. Undeterred, he kept on entertaining.

The big boys and girls, as we called them, frequented Mary the Hen Doherty's hut, which was just beside McConnell's shop. It was normal to hear the music of the day blaring out with laughter in the background from the likes of Seamus Fleming, Danny Sweeney, Willie Divin, Snooker Cullen, Seamus, Jackie and Liam McConnell. And, of course, where you got the boys, the girls were not too far away, with Kay and Marley Bridge, Maureen Lynch, Frances Lynch and Margaret Doherty.

The Three Amigos, happy and contented with smiles on their faces, are Danny Sweeney, Seamus Fleming and Lornie Burke.

They would meet there most nights for the craic, and it was the main meeting point for them before heading up to the gate to catch a bus when going to the pictures or a dance, or maybe just going to Carlisle Road. It is obvious to anyone who knows them that they consider that period in their lives probably their happiest days spent in Springtown. Whenever they happen to run into each other in the town or wherever, they inevitably talk about their times spent in Mary the Hen's hut.

Mary was a woman full of fun and laughter. She loved and lived life to the full and was a happy-go-lucky person, always up for a joke and she was well loved by all in the camp.

Mary Doherty in her new house in Creggan.

Her popularity was there for all to see at the camp reunion dances as she was danced off her feet for most of the night. Her hut was, as one of the teenagers aptly put it, a place of many happy memories and innocent times. Some of those older boys who enjoyed the craic in Mary's hut had maybe just left school. They fared better than their fathers in getting employment, probably because they cost less to employ. The first-ever job for a lot of the teenagers would have been at the BSR factory at Bligh's Lane. Others took the boat to Scotland to pick spuds.

John McLaughlin was a regular 'taddy hoaker' (spud picker) and he took a lot of the teenagers to Scotland with him. Among those who chose to follow him were Willie Divin, Stanley Colby, Seamus Fleming, Liam McConnell and Mickey Jackson.

John often told how their travelling arrangements were a nightmare, as they could only afford to buy second-class tickets for the boat that sailed from Derry to Glasgow. Their second-class ticket only entitled them to travel on the bottom deck of the 'Scotch Boat'; this meant they had to share the bottom deck with the cattle. The stink of the cattle was awful, he recalls; on a bad crossing, it was sheer hell until you arrived in Scotland. The young lads who were going for the first time thought they were going on a picnic or a working holiday. They soon got a reality check as they boarded the Scotch Boat and had to rough it on the crossing to Scotland and put up with the awful smell of the cows.

When they finally arrived at the quayside in Scotland, they were met by an employee of the farmer who would transport them in the back of an open lorry to his farm. This journey would take about one hour and by the time they reached the farm, they had been travelling for about sixteen hours non-stop. On reaching the farm, they would receive a meal and then be shown to the barn, which would be their living quarters. Each would pick their own individual spot in the barn and would make beds by stuffing straw into big sacks, and that is where they would sleep for the duration of the spud-picking season.

Margaret Doherty, Bridget Moore and Frances Lynch with young Patricia Moore outside Tommy Moore's shop, 1959.

The craic and banter was good and, coming from the camp, they were used to harsh conditions, so they readily adapted and revelled at the thought of earning some money. This would enable them to send some back to their hard-pressed families in the camp and also save a few pounds.

They worked from 8.00 am to 6.00 pm on weekdays and till noon on a Saturday. At the weekend, they would visit the nearest town for a few pints and a bet at the bookie's. Saturday night was dancing night – if you were single – or just a few pints in a bar for the married men.

They did have some great times in Scotland but were glad when the spud season was finally over and they could return home to the camp. When leaving the farms for the boat, they were a happy bunch, as they had saved a few pounds and had bought the latest 'clabber' (modern suits and shoes).

The Three Macs: Joanie McKeever, Mary McMonagle and Kathleen McLaughlin.

Arriving back in the camp, they were greeted enthusiastically by family and friends who were glad to see them back home safe and sound. Their first duty was to give their mothers a few pounds, and all were delighted they were able to do this, as they knew it would be badly needed. After doing this, they looked forward to going to the Crit that night, dressed to kill in their new, modern suits, hoping to impress the girl of their dreams.

While some only went to Scotland once, most were happy to go back year in year out, as it was the only work they could get at that time.

Although not as popular as Bradford, Dundee was a well-liked place for the campers; four local Springtown lads found the girls that were to become their wives while working there. Johnny Divin and his cousin Patsy Moore reside to this day in Dundee. However, both Stanley Colby and Willie Coyle met and married two cousins while in Dundee, but the lure of their hometown on the Foyle was so strong that both returned with their wives to Derry.

One of the most poignant photographs ever to be taken in Springtown Camp. The photographer was the renowned Bert Hardy. In this shot are Bella Carlin and her daughter Moira, December 1955.

Chapter 15
The 10.40 to Springtown

In all, no fewer than fourteen UTA buses travelled to and from Derry, the last bus being the famous 10.40 pm to the camp. Friday night's 10.40 bus was renowned for the banter, which was so good that some young people, me included, used to actually walk in to the bus depot at the Strand Road to get the bus back home again, just to enjoy the craic.

The busmen used to hate being on duty for that particular bus, for no other reason than it took so long for everyone to get off it at the camp gate. At times, the singing and the craic would continue even after the bus had arrived at the camp. The reason was that the bus was full of characters and singers, people like Tipperary, Gander, Danny Sweeney, husband of the legendary Rosie McKay, Jimmy Deery, Jock Brennan and Uncle McLaughlin, a tee-totaller and non-smoker, all singing different songs at the same time.

Among the star attractions on the 10.40 bus were Danny and Rosie Sweeney, who were much loved by all in the camp. They were not only characters in the camp, but like Tip, were well known throughout the entire city.

Danny liked his drink, much to the annoyance of his wife, Rosie. He was, of course, ever-present on that bus and, I might add, an entertaining feature was Rosie, umbrella in hand, waiting for husband Danny to arrive home. She gave him some good-hearted abuse regarding his drinking excesses.

Every once in a while, Tipperary would intervene on Danny's behalf, only for Rosie to turn on him. Tip was soon to learn to mind his own business and to steer clear of Rosie on these particular nights. On the odd occasion Rosie failed to turn up at the gate to greet him, Danny would get so worried that he would head to his hut as quickly as his wobbly legs would take him to see if Rosie was all right!

Danny had only one eye and wore a pink eye patch with an elastic band around his head to keep the patch in place. Sometimes, Rosie would get carried away and the umbrella would find its way to Danny's back, albeit softly. On the not too odd occasion Danny was supposed to come home on an earlier bus, Rosie would be fuming and come the last bus she was even angrier. She'd be waiting at the gate for him, and when Danny appeared, he met the wrath of his loving wife. She would call him every name under the sun. Danny's reply was always, 'I'm drinking no more. I'm taking the pin tomorrow.' But as regards his promise of mending his ways, tomorrow never came.

Rosie was, of course, the sister of that famous Derry character Maggie McKay. Maggie often visited her in the camp and when Danny, Rosie and Maggie got together, the craic was totally amazing. The trio would have the residents of the camp roaring with laughter at their shenanigans. To say the show they put on was worthy of any stage would not be an overstatement.

They threw away the mould when they made this man. Uncle McLaughlin, who was the most popular uncle in Springtown Camp by a country mile. Here, Uncle is singing My Way *his way in a back-to-back competition in Derry's Ulsterbus Club. Believe it or not, he won the competition . . . I kid you not!*

Rosie kept her hut like a palace, glittering from top to bottom. The concrete step outside her door was bright red; she was constantly seen with a cloth and a tin of Cardinal red polish in her hand. Her step glistened in the sunlight and her wee hallway was polished with Mansion polish to a high shine.

Danny and Rosie had some great one liners when arguing with each other. Danny would come off the bus the worse for wear and ask Rosie if his dinner was ready.

'It was ready four hours ago,' would roar Rosie. Danny would then ask if it was now cold and Rosie would reply, 'It's in the hottest place in the hut . . . the dog's belly!'

Deep down, everyone knew all she wanted was Danny home safe and sound and she was happiest when he was back in her hut. In truth, they were a happy couple, liked by all who knew them. They brightened up many a resident's day out in Springtown – and in the Belmont Camp before that. Both departed and long gone now, they are fondly remembered to this day, and will continue to be so for many a day to come.

Happy campers, hair laced with Brylcreem, going out to a dance: George Lynch, Stevie Wilkinson and the camp milkman Charlie Ferry.

When the older family members left school and started work in the shirt factories or the building sites, they contributed to the weekly income of their homes. This eased the burden on parents considerably, because previously, families had struggled on one wage, or, as in most cases, the dole and the family allowance was the only income for many of them.

This change in circumstances was exactly what happened in our hut when my three older sisters began working in the shirt factories. With more money coming, the pawnshop was less frequented and it was then that our parents decided we could now afford to rent our first television, which we duly got around late 1960.

Annie Baldrick and Mary McMonagle, 1955.

Some of the families already had a television in the camp, but the numbers increased dramatically when another new television station, UTV (Ulster Television), started to broadcast on 31 October 1959. It put out some great and very popular programmes, *Rawhide* and *Emergency Ward 10* being two that spring to mind.

On the day we were due to get our first television installed, I ran all the way from school to the camp and when our hut came into view, I immediately looked at the roof for signs of the TV aerial. With no sign of it, I stopped running and, instantly disappointed, I walked slowly to our hut. On entering, I threw my school books on the table and asked what had happened. My mother told me they hadn't arrived yet and suggested that I go up to the gate of the camp and see if the men bringing our television were there looking for our hut.

I ran to the gate and to my delight, Porter's van was just entering the camp. I waved the driver down and asked if he was looking for 89b and he said yes. I told him to follow me and I ran so fast the van couldn't keep up with me on the bad roads.

Our first television had arrived.

It was an 18-inch Ferguson rental from Porter's TV shop in William Street and it looked massive in the corner of our living room as the men placed it on our wee, wobbly wooden table.

Onto the roof they went next to attach the big aerial. They bolted it onto the front of our hut; this big aerial would, they said, enable us to receive UTV and RTÉ. It did to an extent, but the picture was snowy on both stations; however, the reception on the BBC channel was perfect.

If the weather was windy or raining, we would, to a degree, lose the picture on both UTV and RTÉ. When it got really bad, I went onto the roof of our hut and moved the aerial while my brother stood outside our front window shouting instructions to me (given to him by my father, who was watching the television). The conversation would go like this: 'Turn to the right, a bit more, wee bit more, stop, back a bit, hold it there.' This went on until we finally got a half-decent picture.

But in truth, we didn't worry too much about the picture quality as the television brought the world's first superstar, *The Lone Ranger*, to our wee hut. Also beamed into our living room were *Rawhide*, *Bronco Layne*, *Cheyenne*, *Laramie*, *Wagon Train*, *Hancock's Half-Hour* and *Dixon of Dock Green*. The television brought a whole new dimension to our lives; no more would ten of us be huddled around a wee wireless hanging on to every word coming from it. Now a

Molly and Maurice Dunne waiting to meet their friends in the camp.

whole new world via the television was available daily in our home. If I were to choose the one single event that changed our lives in the camp, it would be the arrival of television.

I was completely bowled over by the amazing scenery in the cowboy shows. The names of the Wild West towns – Laramie, Cheyenne, Tombstone and Deadwood – would be etched in my mind and would always be associated with growing up in the camp. Another cowboy film that would also remind me of my boyhood days was the film *Gunfight at the OK Corral*. Six of us went to see it on the occasion of a friend's birthday. Actually, it was the very first time we were allowed to go to Derry on our own. Our parents gave us permission to go unescorted on condition we were on the last bus back to the camp.

We agreed to save up ten shillings (50p) each for the big night and we set about getting this money by going messages, selling sticks, and gathering brock. Every penny became a prisoner, but come the night, we each had our ten-bob note.

After what seemed an eternity, the big night finally arrived. I was so excited I could hardly eat my dinner. Not that it mattered, as it was Friday and, being good Springtown Catholics, it was fish for dinner – no meat allowed on Fridays, even if you had the money to buy it. Tonight was a big step for us; we were going to the pictures on our own. *And rightly so*, I thought to myself – *sure we are all wearing long trousers now.*

Eddie Kelly with wife Mary B and children outside their hut, 1953.

When dinner was over, I bolted out the door like a flash, running about fifty yards before I realised I had forgotten my coat. On turning back to get it, there was my mother standing at the front door with my coat in her hand. Handing it to me, she further warned me to make sure I was on the last bus home – as if I would forget! She also warned me to be quiet in the pictures, otherwise we would be thrown out.

The five of us met at McConnell's shop where we stocked up with penny dainties, lucky dips, bubbly gum, blackjacks, Peggy's legs and clove rock – anything that was good for your teeth, we bought it!

Dessie McGinley with baby Brian, 1959.

We agreed we would get the ice cream in the pictures.

We headed for the gate of the camp and waited for the 7.10 bus to arrive. Our faces were aglow as we caught a glimpse of the bus coming past the aluminium bungalows on the Northland Road on its way to the camp.

Life was wonderful that night. Poverty was now in the distant past as five young, innocent boys were let loose to enjoy themselves for the first time without the constraints of their elders. Tonight we were our own masters and we felt we were embracing the wider human race for the very first time as young men. On the bus and on our way to see this great cowboy film everyone was talking about, *Gunfight at the OK Corral*, we couldn't have been happier. Jim English and Danny Feeney were already stuffing the sweets into them as we waited for the bus.

We got off the bus at the bus station on the Strand Road and went straight to the picture house. On arriving, there was a queue outside and we joined it; everyone of all ages was there to see this film. Soon, the doors opened and we filed our way towards the woman in the pay desk where we duly paid one by one and received our tickets. We handed the tickets to the man standing at the entrance to the cinema hall and, seeing we were on our own, he warned us to be quiet.

The wee picture started and was enjoyed by all, but in truth, we were glad to get it over with, as it was the big picture we came to see. At the interval, we rushed to the girl with the tray around her neck to buy ice cream and returned to our seats with our tubs and wee wooden spoons.

The big picture started and boy, we were not disappointed as we sat glued to our seats, eyes fixed on this gigantic screen showing panoramic views of the American plains. No snowy pictures here like we received on our television screens in the camp. What a difference! It was fantastic; we never spoke a word throughout the entire film. All that was heard was the rustling of our wee sweet bags as we stuffed ourselves, chewing sweets till our hearts were content. What a brilliant film, we all agreed at the end. *If this is what is in store for the grown-ups, then roll on the years*, I thought to myself.

We walked out of the cinema and onto the street, more excited than when we first arrived, and soon we were planning another visit to the flicks on our own.

The City Cinema, the Monday night venue for a lot of Springtown teenagers in the 1950s, finance allowing, of course.

It was 10.25 and we walked the short distance to the bus station to catch the 10.40 bus back to the camp. This was the second part of our treat, as we had heard so much about the banter on this bus and now we could sample the atmosphere for ourselves.

Arriving at the station, a lot of familiar faces were already waiting, some sober as a judge, and some not so sober. Having already heard of the antics of the 10.40 bus crowd, it was just as everyone said. We laughed as we listened to Jock Brennan sing his usual party piece, *Flower Of Scotland*. Sitting beside him was Butcher Carlin reading the *Telegraph*; standing close to him was Johnny O'Hagan, Banty Doherty, Maggie Kelly, Eddie and Mary B Kelly and the ever-present Tipperary and Danny Sweeney. The McConnellogues and the O'Neills, who lived up the Springtown Road, were waiting for the bus also. We heard singing in the background coming from the Strand Road, and all of a sudden appeared some of the big boys from the camp. Among them were Uncle McLaughlin, Seamus Fleming, Lornie and John Burke, Joe and Archie Doherty, Jap McLaughlin and Liam Fleming singing loudly and in great form.

Big Neil roared at me, 'What are you wains doing here? Where were youse?'

'We're no wains now, Uncle. Jim is fourteen today and we were at the flicks on our own. We seen *Gunfight at the OK Corral*,' I replied.

Neil shouted back, 'Well, young Deery, make sure you and your wee pals sit behind us at the back of the bus, because if you think *Gunfight at the OK Corral* was exciting, sit back and watch the ten-forty to Springtown Camp.'

At that, all the big boys laughed their heads off.

Out of the wee office in the bus depot came the conductor and his driver. They walked to a bus and rolled up the sign on the front of it: 151a Springtown. That was the signal for us to run to the bus and, just as Big Neil told us, we headed straight for the back seat and watched as the Springtowners boarded.

Soon, the bus was jam packed and as it wheeled out of the depot, the singing started. Jimmy Deery led the way singing *Mona Lisa*. Someone shouted out, 'Quiet for the singer, please!'

Tipperary shouted back, 'If you worry, you die. If you don't worry, you still die, so why worry?'

Big Uncle McLaughlin really started the banter going by calling out Bingo numbers. 'Clickety click, sixty-six. Legs eleven, number eleven. Two wee ducks, twenty-two.'

It was sheer bedlam as all this racket was going on, but fantastic and innocent fun and great entertainment. The bemused eyes of the pipe-smoking

Elkie Clarke were staring at Jock Brennan, then moving to Tipperary and on to the next character. We laughed our heads off as we observed the antics of the characters on the 10.40 to the camp.

The next morning, I told my mother all about our night's fun on the bus and the great, gigantic screen with magic colour and magnificent scenery in the pictures. I told her that one day I would visit all the places I'd seen in the cowboy pictures. 'Of course you will, son,' she replied, 'but for now just get your homework done or Dickie MacDermott and your master will be visiting me in the camp.'

***

Although by now most people had television and a wireless, some still didn't. It was common to see other children in our hut watching television. In other huts when a big show was on television, some of the living rooms resembled a cinema without seats as children and adults alike sat on the floor to watch. The main reason for this was that some huts had two and sometimes three families living in them – the 'legal tenant', that would have been the mother, father and their family, while the other two families were classed as 'lodgers'. They were, in most cases, the sons and daughters of the parents who'd got married and now had children of their own. With nowhere else to go, they were given a room by their parents. That meant some huts had nineteen people living in them. This was quite a common situation in the camp: the married sons or daughters were now classed as lodgers or sub-tenants as they would become known later on in a phrase first used by Eddie McAteer MP.

Despite the overcrowding and damp huts, the people retained their sense of humour. This was evident in the many nicknames given to the campers because of some physical trait or unusual action associated with them.

Johnny Sweeney was given the nickname Cow Walloper because he was often seen tapping cows on their hind quarters with a stick while directing them into the auction ring at the Brandywell cattle market. The affable John Coyle had the nickname Dootie In bestowed on him by his pals in the camp. When he was playing football as a very young boy, he was often heard saying to his friends, 'I'll go into nets and you dootie in.' What he was trying to say was, 'I'll go into nets and you can shootie in.' Ever since, he was affectionately known as Dootie In.

Eamonn and Hughie Wilkinson were given the nickname The Stoogies. One night while both were in bed, they heard some lads playing football nearby and decided to join them. Slipping on their clothes, they climbed out their bedroom window and joined in playing football with the older boys.

Unfortunately, one of Eamonn's shots went a little astray and found its way to a neighbour's window and the window smashed. The two lads took flight and in a flash were climbing back in their bedroom window. The neighbour went to tell their mother, but their mother advised the neighbour she must be mistaken as they had been in bed for the past hour. Inviting her neighbour to come down and see for herself, the woman, of course, believed Mrs Wilkinson, but their mother insisted on opening their bedroom door to let the woman see them sleeping in bed. When she opened the bedroom door, the neighbour saw the two boys appearing to be fast asleep.

The neighbour said, 'God, I'm wile sorry, I was sure it was them. Shows you how wrong you can be,' and apologised to Martha Wilkinson.

Although they got away with it that night, they were found out at a later date and were nicknamed after the comedy act The Three Stooges.

Patsy 'Quinn' Toland, a very quiet young man, had a very pale complexion and was dubbed by the boys and teenagers of the camp the Ghost.

Tommy Doherty was a merchant sailor and he was dubbed Ship Ahoy.

Tommy Duffy was always telling us tall stories, so we called him Moon Man.

Mary Doherty was given the name Mary the Hen because her husband worked with poultry.

All were given such names affectionately; it was just pure banter and nothing else.

However, as for the other nicknames we called people in the camp, it will take a braver man that me to mention them!

Dolly Breslin at the hut of her sister Mary Duddy, 216 Springtown Camp, 1952.

Chapter 16
Women's Protest Continues

At a Corporation meeting in the Guildhall held on Thursday 3 December 1959, and in direct response to the women of the camp protesting at their previous meetings, the Corporation's housing sub-committee had passed a proposal by Alderman Glover and seconded by Councillor McFarland that the twenty-eight houses nearing completion at Coach Road would be allocated exclusively to Springtown Camp residents.

The motion was passed . . . with not one dissenting voice. That promise, like many other promises in the past, was not kept. This, of course, didn't surprise the people of the camp one little bit. Only ten families were re-housed in that particular development and not the twenty-eight as passed and recorded in the minute book of the Corporation's meeting.

When challenged on this by the residents, chairman of the housing committee Glover, who had himself proposed this motion, simply replied, 'Things have changed since then.' He was correct about that, as the huts were in worse condition now than they had been then! Back again to protest at the Corporation's meetings in the Guildhall went the women of the camp. They wanted a simple answer to a simple question: why did the Corporation go back on their word?

The next meeting was due to be held on 27 September 1960, so the women decided to again occupy the public gallery and seek to ask why only a handful of families got houses and what happened to the twenty-eight houses promised them in December 1959?

Again Eddie McAteer MP sat with the women in the public gallery. There were twelve women and two men from the camp; Sadie Campbell was again spokeswoman. She stood up and asked, 'May I be permitted to speak, please?'

The Mothers of Springtown Camp Confront the Corporation

Last-minute instructions from Susan Cullen to the mothers of Springtown Camp before entering the public gallery in the Guildhall to confront the unionist-controlled Corporation on their abysmal record of re-housing the people of Springtown, November 1959. Included: Molly Killen, Annie McBrearty, Jean McAdams, Lily Jennings, Frances Fox, Eileen Doherty, Ellen Deane, Ellen Brown, Sadie Campbell, Margaret Fisher, Martha Toland, Dorothy Adcock, Susan Crumlish, Kathleen Porter, Mimmie Spratt, Anna Brolly, Kathleen Curran, Florrie Doherty and Susan Cullan.

Women's protest in Guildhall Chambers, 1960. Included are Eddie McAteer, MP; Paddy Doherty; Kathleen Porter; Annie McBrearty; Joanie McKeever; Maggie Mooney; Mary Saunders; Sadie Campbell and Ellen Deane.

'No, you cannot,' replied Glover. Sadie continued speaking anyway, and the meeting was swiftly adjourned for lunch.

The women said, 'We will be back again and again until you agree to meet with us.'

It was the start of scenes never before witnessed in the chambers of Derry's Guildhall when the Springtown women took over the assembly room. The nationalist councillors supplied them with tea and sandwiches brought in by outside caterers. White tablecloths were spread over the councillors' desks and the women proceeded to have their lunch in the chambers. When they finished, they returned to the public gallery to await the afternoon's proceedings.

The mayor and councillors returned for the afternoon session. On seeing the women were still there and had no intention of leaving until they were heard, the powers-that-be agreed to let them address the meeting. Sadie asked for an assurance from the Corporation that early steps would be taken to house all the remaining residents of the camp. She also stated that there was only one street lamp working at the camp and that a considerable amount of rubble remained after the demolition of some huts.

The Corporation promised to house the residents as soon as possible; they also said that the lamps in the camp would be replaced immediately. 'With regards to the rubble, it can be conveniently handled by utilising the services of the two labourers employed at the camp,' they said.

Sadie continued to seek answers, asking why the families of the camp hadn't received the twenty-eight houses that Glover had promised in December past. Glover replied that unexpected emergencies had cropped up and other people had to get the houses instead. But he promised that his committee would do all they could for them when they met the Housing Trust the following week.

The women, although not at all satisfied with the reply they received, decided to wait and see what the outcome of that meeting would be.

The following week, housing manager Murphy submitted a report in response to the women's protest. He stated there were 134 families in Springtown Camp and that the majority of them sought better accommodation. He also said the camp would present a problem until such time as suitable accommodation was found for the residents.

The fact that the Corporation decided to renege on its promise to allocate the houses to the Springtown residents and instead allocated them to other families brought into question the criteria used for the selecting of families to be housed. The unionist-controlled body claimed it was the housing manager who decided who was to receive the houses and it was his decision alone. But this claim is laid bare for all to see from a report sent to the Corporation on 25 February 1953 by Murphy. Opposite is a word-for-word account of this report.

To: The members of the housing sub-committee.

Report on selection of council tenants.

Gentlemen,

As instructed at last meeting, I submit this general report on method of selection of council tenants.

Every salient feature of each case is recorded on application forms, which give details of applicants' family, sex, age, accommodation and other essential information. From the housing register and information supplied by interview or correspondence, files are continually revised, and following investigation, a priority pool is compiled of those cases which are considered to warrant priority. I should point out here that I endeavour to prevent undue weight being given to cases which constantly call at this office or contact members of the council.

When houses become available for letting from the priority pool, I prepare a list from those applicants to whom, in my opinion, allocations can be justified. In drawing up such a list, regard has to be given to the number of bedrooms contained in the dwellings available. While points awarded in accordance with the scheme approved by Corporation are a guiding factor (a most necessary piece of administrative machinery), consideration is given to other aspects, viz number of children in family, sex, age, length of time on waiting list, period of residence in city, and a most important factor – housing need. The prepared list is then discussed at length by the mayor and housing manager, and selections agreed.

Since my appointment, I have inquired from officers in other local authorities as to their methods of allocating houses. I remain convinced that no scheme, however devised, will give satisfaction to those who still await re-housing. I feel that the success of any method must be judged by the extent to which it ensures that the applicants' selection is those in the greatest need of a house.

I am, Gentlemen,
Your obedient servant,

DAS Murphy,
HOUSING MANAGER
Dated this 25th day of February, 1953

It was common knowledge that the mayor decided which families were to be re-housed and it was his decision alone. Murphy, in his report to the Corporation, stated that a points system was used as the main guiding factor in selecting families to be re-housed with the criteria listing the number of children in a family, age, sex, length of time on waiting list and period of residence in the city. Surely it follows if these criteria were implemented without bias, then it would have been impossible to keep Springtown Camp families off the priority-pool list. Which means, of course, if the Corporation and Murphy had carried out selection using their own criteria in a fair and honest manner, then the camp would have been closed about eighteen years before it actually was. Let's examine Murphy's 'own' stated criteria:

OVERCROWDING: In the camp, some huts housed three families, and in many instances, there were as many as nineteen people living in a single hut, with six people expected to sleep in one small room. The case for overcrowding was undeniable.

SEX: With a mixture of male and female, and many of teenage age, again the case could not be refuted.

TIME ON WAITING LIST: Some families were on the waiting list for over ten years. That also could not be contradicted.

DISREPAIR: With the tin huts rusted, leaking water and rodent infested, again it would have been impossible to ignore this.

PERIOD OF RESIDENCE IN CITY: Most of the families were born and reared in Derry, like their parents before them.

HOUSING NEED: With large families with a mixture of male and female living in tin huts with no hot water, no fixed bath, huts leaking water, damp and wet, and rodent infested, how did that not fit their criteria?

So, by the housing manager's own criteria, every family in Springtown met every aspect of his conditions for being re-housed. Yet they were never considered by the Corporation when houses were being allocated up to now. The reason was they were mainly Catholic, poor and mostly unemployed.

The Corporation were solely responsible for the plight the people of Springtown found themselves in. They forced mothers and fathers to bring up their children in such terrible conditions and with the stigma that went with the conditions of the huts.

One member of the Corporation in particular was disliked, to put it mildly, by the residents – the housing manager, Dennis Arthur Murphy. However, was this dislike of him justified? Could it be he was just a scapegoat used by the mayor and his Corporation in their continued gerrymandering and discrimination policy?

It is clear, by his own admission, that it was his brief to draw up a short-list of what he termed a priority pool of who, in his opinion, were in most need of being re-housed. Then he would sit down with the mayor and agree who were to be housed. One thing is certain: it was Murphy who continually had to relay the bad news to the people of Springtown at the behest of the mayor and his Corporation. The nationalist politicians claimed it was the mayor who had sole responsibility for the allocation of the houses and it was Murphy's brief to implement his decisions. If they were correct, it may have been the case that we blamed the messenger. The truth was probably that because Murphy was the public figure put forward to defend the mayor and his Corporation's unjust housing policy, he was so disliked. He also had to personally stand before the people of Springtown, and indeed the television cameras, and try to justify the unjustifiable.

What do we know of the man who was the Corporation's housing manager and so disliked by the campers? He was born Dennis Arthur Spooner Murphy just a mere 200 yards from Springtown Camp in Messines Park, Derry, on 19 March 1921. Known as Daz by his fellow students at university, in 1939 at the age of eighteen, he joined the Royal Ulster Rifles and reached the rank of lieutenant. He was a part of the D-Day landings on 6 June 1944. Unfortunately, however, he was badly injured and was eventually discharged. He returned to Derry with his new English wife and they had four children, sadly losing their first two to illness.

Tragedy was to strike again when his wife Cynthia died of cancer at the very young age of thirty-eight in 1960. He later married a Derry girl in 1963 and they had a daughter and a son. It is ironic that his local bar, the Collon Bar, owned by his close friend Eddie Diggins, was also frequented by some men from the camp.

Murphy and the mayor were the people in the forefront of the people's minds and thoughts in the camp when discussing the possibilities of being re-housed. Still, the lack of action, consideration and the total disregard for the human rights of the people of Springtown to proper homes was not just down to these two men alone. The entire unionist-controlled Corporation, who totally abused their gerrymandered powers, were to blame. They all had their hands in the discrimination against helpless, vulnerable families.

In fairness to Murphy, he consistently through the years brought to the attention of his peers in the Corporation the worsening conditions of the huts at the camp. Indeed, unknown to many people, on Thursday 6 October 1960, he made a strong recommendation to the powers-that-be in Derry's Guildhall. He advised them to consider a specific scheme whereby they would build fifty houses exclusively for the residents of the camp. Included in his recommendation was that they should put pressure on the Rural Council and Housing Trust to fulfil undertakings given some considerable time previously to re-house the families in the camp. He argued that this would effectively solve the problem of Springtown. The Corporation declined to accept Murphy's initiative with the usual fob off that they would do everything they could to re-house the families.

The Housing Trust's response was even more insulting to the people of the camp. They constructed 276 houses at Belmont, a mere 400 yards from Springtown, yet unbelievably, they declined to offer one single house to a family in the camp. The facts of their discrimination against the people of the camp for political reasons were there for all to see. To give one an idea of the blatant nature of this discrimination, let's have a look at the housing allocation around Springtown since the first squatter moved in:

	Catholic Homes	Protestant Homes
Academy Road District: (Corporation Houses)	1	34
Cloughglass District: (Templemore Parish)	34	242
Northland District:	1	101
Rural Areas: (Near to Springtown Camp)		
Belmont (Housing Trust):	37	239

Even though Belmont was a mere 400 yards from the camp, of the 276 families housed there, not one was from Springtown. And the fact that approximately forty RUC men and their families, who incidentally had only been in the city for a short time, were awarded the houses in Belmont came as no surprise at all to the people of Derry. If the powers-that-be had allocated houses to even a small number of families from Springtown in Belmont, that would have dampened the flames of discrimination to some extent.

In the eyes of honest men, these housing allocation figures give conclusive proof, if any were ever needed, of the systematic and unforgivable bias and discrimination against the people of the camp by the Corporation, Rural Council and Housing Trust.

With the passing of each winter, the conditions of the huts worsened. They had now deteriorated to such an extent that water was penetrating the rusty tin at an increasing pace and the floors of the bedrooms were in a really bad state. Keeping wallpaper on the walls became impossible. Some families, fearing for the damage this squalor was doing to their children's health, decided the only way out was to bite the bullet and emigrate to England or Scotland.

And it was understandable why so many families moved from hut to hut. If some family had a 'good' hut and they happened to get re-housed or decided to emigrate, they would tell their best friend and give them first refusal of their hut. Some huts wore better than others and people thought, why let them demolish a better hut than the one they lived in? So they moved into the vacant one and left their own to be demolished. Bob Hutchman, the camp manager, didn't mind as long as a hut was getting demolished, because families who flitted from one hut to another normally kept the same hut number. So as far as everyone was concerned, nothing changed; only the postman was confused!

The remaining families just waited and lived in the hope that their name would be next on the list to be re-housed. They were also hoping that as many families from the camp as possible would be re-housed beside each other, which would make moving to a new area that bit easier. This happened to some extent when the Coach Road houses were allocated to ten families from the camp.

But again, things slowed down badly, as over the next couple of years, only fourteen families were re-housed. At this rate, it was going to take another ten years before every family in the camp would be re-settled.

Chapter 17
First Job and Great Characters

I left school at the Christmas break one week after my fifteenth birthday; it was time to look for my first job in the real world.

After the Christmas holidays, Mickey Curran and I went to the Old City Dairy on the Letterkenny Road. We went to the office in the dairy and knocked on the door. A man's voice shouted, 'Come in.'

'Are you looking for any workers?' we inquired.

'There are a couple of jobs available for helpers on the milk lorries.'

'We'll take them if you want,' we replied excitedly.

'Aye, but wait a minute, let me finish,' said the man. 'It's a five-thirty in the morning start and most lads don't last three days. If you're late one morning, you're sacked.'

'That's okay,' we said. We were told to report the following Monday morning at 5.30 am. We went straight back out to the camp to inform our families. On hearing our starting time, they were less than enthusiastic. 'That means you will have to be up at four in the morning at the latest,' said my father. I didn't care one jot; it was a job and that was all that mattered to me. We both decided to meet at the gate at 4.55 am on the Monday morning.

It was cold, windy and very dark and there was an eerie silence as we set off on our bicycles for the Old City Dairy – and our very first real job. *Welcome to the real world*, I said to myself, the cold wind pelting my face as we cycled in the Northland Road. We made good time and arrived in the dairy yard at 5.15 am, parked our bicycles and reported for work. The night shift were loading the vans with crates of milk.

We were introduced to our bosses, the drivers; mine was called Murphy, a big red-faced countryman.

We were delivering milk around the country roads near Donemana and Strabane, way out in the sticks; I never even knew these places existed. Mickey was the same; his round was in some obscure place in the country and he hadn't a clue where he was – and neither did I.

Our first day went OK. We arrived back in the dairy yard at 12.45, fifteen minutes ahead of schedule. *This is great*, we thought as we cycled out to the camp, *our first day's work done*; it was only 1.00 pm.

The second day, we decided to leave the camp at the same time, 4.55 am. Again it was raining heavily and the wind was at our faces as we cycled in the Northland Road. We arrived in the yard, soaked to the skin and looking like drowned cats at 5.20 am. If we were expecting some sympathy, we certainly didn't get any.

Sitting in the van, wet and cold as we drove out, I thought to myself that school wasn't so bad after all.

My driver expected me to know how many pints of milk to leave at each house on my second day. I hadn't a clue where we were, never mind how many pints to leave at each wee cottage. He got annoyed with me every time I asked him how many bottles for this or that house. I decided there and then that I didn't like him; he wasn't helpful or even civil to me. Sitting in the van after getting scolded for the umpteenth time, I was thinking, *I wish big Neil McLaughlin or Eddie Kelly were here now; they would teach you some manners.* The kindest thing I could say about him was that he was a big, ignorant gulpin. After work, I told Mickey about my experience with him. Mickey didn't have quite as ignorant a boss, but he wasn't too fussed on his either.

The next day, our third on the job, we both fared a little better and we were beginning to think the job might work out all right. However, our fourth day, Thursday, was to be our last. We met at the camp gate as usual, but this wasn't a usual morning. There had been a bad frost overnight and it was dark, but not as dark as normal because the white frost covered the hedges along the first part of the Northland Road. We travelled barely fifty yards when we fell off our bicycles, the bicycles sliding about five yards in front of us. The Northland Road was like a bottle, very slippery with black ice. We mounted our bicycles again and attempted to cycle on. Again we came to grief on the icy roads. It was now 5.10 am and we were only just past the aluminium bungalows; we were beginning to panic. We kept slipping and sliding on our bicycles, but we cheered each other up by saying that everyone would be late in these conditions.

We eventually arrived in the yard at 5.40 am, only ten minutes late. Most of the lorries were still in the yard, but with the country runs being loaded first, both our lorries had left a couple of minutes earlier. The night shift told us they asked the drivers to wait a couple of minutes, telling them we had to cycle a long way and that we would be there soon.

Still, both drivers decided to leave without us, and that was the end of us as far as our jobs were concerned.

The yard staff thought we got a raw deal, but the man in the office was unsympathetic.

I later got talking to Mr Breslin, a milkman at the Old City Dairy, who was delivering milk to Willie McConnell's shop. I told him of our experiences and he said to me, 'You two lads got the two worst men to work with in the dairy.' He also said the yard staff were annoyed at how we were treated, which was nice to hear, as I knew we made every effort to get to the yard on time. In hindsight, they did us a favour; still, it was some experience.

Our pals Brendie Wilkinson and Jim English were at this time working, with Brendie in the BSR factory and Jim doing bar work in Con Bradley's Bar. Some others got message-bike jobs, mostly with the All Cash Stores.

> Save as you Buy . . . . . at
>
> The
> # All Cash Stores
> Limited
>
> 22 STRAND ROAD
> LONDONDERRY
>
> (with 33 City and Country Branches)
>
> •
>
> Best Value in the North-West
>
> STORES AT
>
> | LIMAVADY | CLAUDY |
> | --- | --- |
> | BALLYKELLY | DUNGIVEN |
> | STRABANE | PORTRUSH, ETC. |

Some campers were able to get a job working on the BSR production floor in Creggan.

Kevin 'Jap' McLaughlin, Hugo Henry, George Lynch and Paddy Curran relaxing during a break from work.

The girls who left school around the same time as us had no difficulty in getting employment, as most went to work in one of the many shirt factories; work in the textile industry was buoyant at that particular time.

There was evidence to suggest that social discrimination was practised by some businessmen in Derry with regard to Springtown residents. It is reasonable to say that at times when you gave your address when seeking a job, you were immediately turned down without even being offered an interview. Some parents bitterly expressed this view when interviewed by television and newspaper reporters, with Willie Campbell going as far as suggesting there was social exclusion and social stigma attached to the people of the camp simply because of the conditions in which they were forced to live.

Dolly Sweeney, a much-respected and popular woman, expressed this opinion when interviewed by UTV journalist Charles Witherspoon. Dolly, who had reared a large family in the camp, didn't hold back when she criticised local businessmen and some local firms for their attitude towards the people of the camp. She suggested they should take a good look at themselves and judge people on their ability and not where they lived. This position was echoed by all the parents. It was something that needed to be said, and where better to say it than on national television?

The first time it dawned on me that there was something so very wrong about our situation in Springtown was when I reached the age of fifteen. I had just left school a couple of weeks previously and had had the unpleasant experience of the milk-lorry job.

I was looking through the pages of the *Derry Journal* to see if any shop was advertising for a message boy; there was one advertised. Excitedly, I showed it to my mother – a chemist shop at Dale's Corner in the Waterside was looking for a message boy.

I remember it was raining that morning, but undeterred, I started the three-mile walk to the said chemist shop. On reaching the door, I was a little nervous, as I was thinking to myself this could be my big opportunity to get a good, steady job. So in I went and there was a young girl serving a customer; the pharmacist himself was stacking the shelves with his back to the counter.

He turned around and asked, 'Can I help you?'

'I am over about the message-boy job advertised in the paper today,' I said in a low voice.

He didn't break his momentum as he kept on stacking the shelves, at the same time continuing to ask me questions. 'Can you ride a bicycle well?'

'Yes,' I answered.

'Do you know the Waterside well?' he asked.

'Yes, I do,' I lied, *but sure after a few days I'd know it well enough*, I thought to myself.

'Where are you from?' he inquired.

'Springtown Camp,' I responded. As I said that, he stopped stacking the shelves, the young girl stopped serving the customer and the three of them turned their heads and looked at me. There was an awkward silence for what seemed an eternity, but I'm sure it was only a few seconds in reality.

The chemist broke the silence and said, 'Sorry, the job is already taken, but thanks for coming over.'

I walked out of the shop feeling disappointed. As I made my way back to the camp in the rain, I asked myself why, if the job was already taken, did he ask me all those questions? And why did those other people stare at me?

I was oblivious to the fact that we in the camp maybe did carry a social stigma. The only reason this could be was because we lived in tin huts and the camp was an eyesore. I walked the three-or-so miles back to the camp in the rain and I was thinking so hard to myself that I found myself back in our hut before I knew it. That day was a hard one for me. What did they think I was going to do? Steal from the till, steal the drugs, steal the bicycle? I mean, I wasn't reaching for the stars; it was only a message-boy job I was after. I felt every emotion: I was disillusioned, dejected, frustrated and angry that I had been judged before I had been given a chance. The whole thing drained the youthful, exuberant confidence from me.

I thought long and hard the following day and one question just wouldn't leave my mind: why was where I lived an issue? Surely I as a person was more important than where I lived or in what conditions I lived?

Sleep didn't come easily to me that night.

***

During the next couple of days, and for the first time in my life, I looked at everyone in the camp, including my own family and my closest friends whom I'd known since I uttered my first words. I looked at the dilapidated state of the huts we called home, rotted windows that couldn't close properly, rusted tin at the base of the huts, the rough roads we walked on, the empty, untidy spaces where huts once were, now just slabs of broken concrete. As I gazed around me, there was no getting away from it; the place looked a terrible mess . . . it was a slum, no other word for it.

Yes, the huts were in poor condition and they did look rough, but my friends were as good as anyone in this town, or in the country for that matter. The people here were lovely, genuine people who would never pass you without stopping to ask how you were. To me they were the salt of the earth.

I was starting to feel myself getting angry. I had been angry before, but this was a different anger. Was I angry at the way I was treated in that chemist shop or was I angry with myself because I was thinking the way I was? I wasn't sure how I felt; I was confused.

My mother, sensing I was very quiet for those few days, asked me to go into Derry for some butcher meat, probably just to give me something to do. While walking along William Street, I met Dermot (Dickie) MacDermott, my old headmaster. He stopped and asked me if I'd had any word of a job. I told him I was looking for one and he asked if I'd tried anywhere yet. So I told him about going over to Dale's Corner to the chemist shop looking for the message-boy job. And I told him the reason why I thought I didn't get it. He answered me with a firm voice and a serious look on his face: 'Well, if you are right, son, then he wasn't worth working for. And don't worry, everyone is not like him. Just keep trying. Maybe you should go to some of the building sites and try to get in to serve an apprenticeship. Come down to the school tomorrow and I will give you a reference. It may help you.'

I left my old headmaster that day with renewed faith in people. He instilled a bit of confidence in me to try again; he was that kind of special person.

The next day, I was on my way to him to get the reference that might help me get a job. As I approached the school gates, I observed some men working on the building site next to the school. I decided to take the bull by the horns and I asked one of the workmen who the foreman was. He pointed to a shed and said, 'That's his office, he will be in there.'

I went to the office, knocked on the door and a voice shouted, 'Come on in.' The foreman was Sammy Quigley, a red-faced, sharp-looking man.

'I was wondering if there's any chance of a start as an apprentice?'

'An apprentice what?' he asked.

'Bricklayer,' I replied without thinking.

'Where are you from?' he asked.

I could feel the blood draining from my face. 'Springtown Camp . . . but I can get a reference from my headmaster,' I blurted out, thinking the worst. The chemist shop experience was obviously still embedded in the back of my mind.

'There is no need to get a reference,' he said, looking straight at me. 'Start on Monday.'

'Start on Monday?' I asked him back, just to make sure I heard him right.

'Start on Monday,' he repeated.

'Thanks very much,' I said as I excitedly turned to walk out the door.

'And don't be wearing them shoes on Monday,' he called after me.

What a wonderful feeling! The best feeling I'd ever had in my short young life. I was halfway down Messines Park on my way home when I realised I should have gone into school and told Mr MacDermott I'd got a job as an apprentice. I turned back and headed up to my old headmaster's office with pride and a new-found self-esteem. I told him the good news and he was genuinely delighted for me, and for the first time ever, he shook my hand and, with a smile of contentment on his face, congratulated me. I do believe he was as delighted as I was. I ran like the wind back home to our hut in the camp and as I entered our front door, I shouted to my mother, 'I got a job as an apprentice bricklayer and I'm starting on Monday.' She was delighted for me and the look of relief on her face I can still see to this day.

There was a buzz in our hut that night, but sleep came hard for me, I was so excited.

The next day, my father told me to try Tommy Lynch, an old bricklayer who lived at the top of the camp, to see if he had any tools he could sell me. Tommy had none, but he told me he would ask a man he knew, as he might have some. The following day, I was up again at Tommy's door. He told me the name and address of the man, and yes, he had a few tools to sell, as he was retired. So off I went to this man's house in Derry and I bought a trowel, hammer and level. That night, I was levelling everything in our hut!

Monday morning arrived and I walked the same route I had walked for the past ten years, only this time it was to work and not to school. I was the first man on the site and I was introduced to George 'Spud' Murphy, a bricklayer of some experience and ability. I started my apprenticeship with him and a better teacher you couldn't get.

George was a good union man and he told me to join the bricklayers' union. Every Saturday night, I used to go to the union rooms and pay my union dues as well as taking George's union money up as well. When I got my union card, it held pride of place in my hut, as now I was an 'official' apprentice bricklayer. While working on the scaffold, learning to build bricks, I often glanced at my old school and at my old teachers and it seemed a different world now. I was the youngest on the building site, so I had to make the tea and run to the shop for the men, wash the cups and hang them on a line that was about five feet in the air so the mice couldn't get at them.

It's true to say Sammy Quigley was a no-nonsense, strict boss – strict in the sense that he expected the work to be done in the proper way – but always fair. He was well respected by all who worked under him as a fair and honest foreman. I remember him often keeping men on the payroll on the basis of their need and their families' need above all other consideration; that was the kind of man he was.

It was many years later when I found out that Sammy was an ex-Springtown Camp man himself and indeed was the camp's first-ever committee chairman. He was the main driving force in getting the huts converted at Springtown and was instrumental in bringing a state of normality to the camp in those early few weeks and months of the camp's existence.

After leaving Sammy Quigley's site, I got a job continuing my apprenticeship with Frank Connor Builders. Now I was working steady, as were my neighbours, Brendie Wilkinson, Seamus Fleming and Brendan Fleming, who was working in the BSR factory. Jim English was still a barman in Con Bradley's at the corner of William Street and Rossville Street, and Stevie Wilkinson started in the stores at Kevin McLaughlin's garage on the Buncrana Road after leaving his job as a 'nipper boy' (general tea-maker, message-runner, gofer, get-me boy) on the site of Foyle College.

On Sunday nights, instead of hanging around the camp, we heard about this great 'hop' that was held in the Wolfe Tone Hall in the Brandywell area. We decided we would give it a try and agreed to meet at the top gate of the camp at 6.30. There were about twelve of us and we started to walk to the hop, a distance of about three miles, and the smell of Brylcreem and Old Spice filled the air. Walking to the hall, the craic was great; we decided to stick together in the dancehall and we wouldn't go with any girl who lived far away! As chance would have it, that was not going to be a problem, as all the girls refused to dance with us. I think they just didn't know what to make of us. Undeterred, back we went the next week and slowly but surely, the girls warmed to us and it wasn't long before we were all strutting our stuff on the dance floor at the Wolfe Tone hop.

However, one night Willie Hegarty was dancing with a girl, and a fella, who thought he was her boyfriend, took exception to this and a fight broke out. At one stage, there must have been twenty fighting; well, we did agree to stick together! We were chased out of the Brandywell by a horde of boys baying for our blood – and that was the end of the Wolfe Tone hop for us.

The boys and girls of my age were now going out every weekend to a youth club or a wee dance like the Killea hop, which was on every Monday night. With my mates, I went to every hop that was on, no matter where it was or what night it was on. However, on a Friday night after coming in from work and getting my dinner, I loved going over to 'Seekie' McClelland's hut for a game of cards.

Alphonsus McClelland, or Seekie, as we knew him, had a great card school in his hut every Friday night, and as I liked a game of cards, I was a regular visitor to his hut on those nights. The regular players were the usual suspects: Uncle McLaughlin, Danny Sweeney, Seamus Fleming, Rory Quigley, Liam McConnell, Bap Morrison and, of course, Seekie himself.

Even though the banter was always in full flow, there was still a serious element to each game. One thing that can be said with 100% certainty is that the games were straight, and by that I mean cheating was nonexistent, as we were all friends and neighbours. The money in the pool would range from about £2 in a normal pool to (in a big game with most players standing their ground to the end) about £10 – big money in those days, bearing in mind I was getting about £5 a week as an apprentice. I can remember winning one such game, and not only that, but I remember the exact amount in that particular game. The amount was £12 15s 0d (£12.75), and to make matters more satisfying, as it was the last game of the night, I was certain of leaving the card school with all my winnings intact. The next morning, I was up bright and early, and after getting the buns from Herbie the breadman and having breakfast, I gave my mother £2 15s 0d (£2.75).

To be totally honest, I got skint more often than I won, as I'm sure was the case for most of us. Each game always finished with a discussion about how unlucky each of the losers were. We could always tell if Seekie was in a good mood. When in a good mood, he would always sing a verse of *Liverpool Lou* over and over again, all night long.

Stevie Wilkinson was of the opinion that if we were to get a double-breasted suit each (the very newest style) and went to the wee country hops, we would get 'rushed' and have the pick of the girls there. His thinking was that the country boys wouldn't know what a double-breasted suit was!

Well, after winning the money, I called for Stevie, and that Saturday, we went straight into Burton's tailors and both of us got measured for a double-breasted suit. He got a grey one to match his blonde hair, and I got a black one to match my hair. We had it all sussed out!

The next Saturday, we got our new suits and we couldn't wait until Monday night to hit the Killea hop. Come Monday as usual, John Doherty, a workmate of Stevie and the only one with a car, called for us. Stevie and I had our new suits on, shoes shined, shirts starched and our polka-dot ties with a perfect Windsor knot. Our hair was laced with Brylcreem and we were covered in Old Spice aftershave. We left nothing to chance; we smelled like a perfume factory.

If confidence could make you fly, then we would have been halfway to the moon that Monday night. As we entered the Killea hop, we had a rude awakening, for we expected all eyes to be on us; we nearly fainted when we saw almost every country boy had a double-breasted suit on. We were speechless. Stevie was right about one thing: we got rushed . . . but it was a rush of blood to the head! We stood there looking like two eejits; we struggled to get a dance, never mind getting our pick. It sure knocked the stuffing out of us and taught us a lesson we never forgot; we were a lot more cautious in our approach and thinking in future.

Springtown lads at their first 'hop' in Killea Hall, 1964: Willie Deery, Brendie Wilkinson, John Doherty, Seamus Callaghan and Stevie Wilkinson.

Soon, we progressed to the big 'real' dances in the Stardust, Embassy and Borderland. The showbands were in full flow and we lived for the weekends. We travelled everywhere to hear the big bands like Dickie Rock and the Miami, the Freshmen, the Chessmen, and Joe Dolan and the Drifters. With loads of good dancehalls all over the North West, we would normally try and take them all in. There was a bus to Borderland on Friday and Sunday nights and also one for the Castle in Dungiven. We didn't frequent the Castle a lot because it was nearly always Eileen Reid and the Cadets who played there; we were not big fans of theirs.

Actually, the Castle in Dungiven was one of the first big dances we went to and we nearly came a cropper on the first night. Still being greenhorns and not at all politically aware, at the end of each night the band would play the national anthem, the *Soldier's Song*. This night, the band was going down a storm and the dancers kept calling for more music. After several attempts to get off the stage, the band just went straight into playing the national anthem. Both Brendie Wilkinson and Yours Truly kept on dancing for a few seconds, but luckily we stopped just in time . . . before too many noticed.

The Stardust and Embassy became popular with us, as both were handy to get to and from. Brendan Wilkinson met a girl from the Waterside, Maureen McHugh, and was smitten immediately, and that was the end of Brendie with the boys.

The big boys and girls, like John McLaughlin, Seamus Fleming, Eddie Kelly, Kevin Scanlon and Uncle McLaughlin, Mary Divin, Maureen Lynch, Kay and Marley Bridge, and Ann and Margaret English were by now going steady, some getting engaged and others planning to be married soon. Actually, I was invited to my very first wedding when one of the big girls, Margaret English, married John McCarron from the old Shantallow area. I was a pal of her brother Jim. I remember going in a car to the chapel with Jim; also in the car was Kathleen Curran, a friend of Margaret's, who was soon to be married herself.

With the passage of time, the huts were now in a shocking state and we were of an age where we felt this was just not right or fair on our parents, but there is very little that sixteen-year-old boys or girls can do about it. I remember Brendie Wilkinson and myself were working for Frank Connor Builders, building St Brecan's School in the Waterside. We got a lot of stick about living in tin huts from our workmates, although this was nothing but pure lighthearted banter. Eddie Gallagher from Rossville Street was one of the worst offenders, he and his mate Eddie Conway. However, when we discovered Eddie had no front door to his house in Rossville Street and he had to go through a large wooden gate to gain entry to his home, things changed. 'If you have no front door, you have nothing,' was our answer to Eddie. When an older worker whispered to us that Eddie had no inside toilet, we were in our element. I must say, the older workers enjoyed the banter and I think they were happy when we were able to come back at Eddie.

They were a great bunch of workmates and when our hut was burnt to the ground in Springtown, they all had a whip round and gave the money to the boss, Frank Connor, who handed it over to my shocked but delighted mother.

Brendie Wilkinson later left the building sites and studied for a youth leader's degree and went on to have a very successful career. He is now responsible for the entire leadership and running of Derry's Pennyburn Youth and Community Centre. This centre has received many national and international awards, one of which was presented to Brendie personally by the Queen Mother. Brendie has always maintained that the camp was the best university he could ever have attended because no university could have prepared you for life's ups and downs like the camp. The experience of growing up in the camp taught him the values that spurred him on to dedicating his life to the youth of Derry.

Brendie, the eldest son in a family of ten, came to Springtown in July 1953 when they squatted into a hut with the help of John McBrearty. However, they were evicted by the Corporation and were taken in as lodgers by Frank and Jeannie Harkin, who lived at Hut 135. In November of the same year, they got 'legal' tenancy of the hut when Mr and Mrs Harkin were housed in the Brandywell area. They remained there until September 1967, when they were re-housed at Westway in Creggan. They were one of the last six families to leave the camp.

All the boys in their family were keen sportsmen; Stevie was probably the best known. He was a talented footballer and played for Derry City, Finn Harps and Sligo Rovers at a time when Derry boasted a host of top-class senior footballers. He also was a pivotal member of Shelbourne, a first-rate Summer Cup team.

Unknown to many people, Brendie was a brilliant walker who represented Ireland and won many highly competitive road-walking races. I remember well the night he took up the walking; we were training with the Oak Leaf Athletic Club. Brendie, to be frank, was not among the top runners. Hubert Logue, one of the best walkers in Ireland, was doing his training in the College Field when Brendie decided to walk with him to keep him company. Everyone was astonished when Brendie was able to keep up with Hubert, one of the top three walkers in Ireland. The coaches encouraged him to take up walking (probably because he could walk as fast as he could run); he took their advice and soon he was winning walking races. In a short space of time, he was a match for any top walker in the country.

Champions from the camp. Martin Smith, Brendan Wilkinson, George Lynch (Trainer/Manager), Edward 'Ned' Smith, Eddie Doherty and Hughie Wilkinson displaying their trophies for the season.

Actually, four under-14s from the camp represented the famous Oak Leaf Athletic Club in the Ulster Championships in Newry, County Down. We duly won it, with Mickey Curran coming first. Mickey was an exceptionally talented sportsman, winning under-14 and under-16 Ulster championships with consummate ease. He was also a youth international footballer, playing for Northern Ireland. His brother Willie also played for Derry City and Ballymena United, as did his pal Liam Fleming.

Springtown was home to some great characters and each would merit a complete book on their own; one of my favourites was Uncle McLaughlin, the youngest of a large family. Anyone knowing Neil would know he is not too easily embarrassed, and if there was one man in the camp you didn't want to take on in a slanging match, that man was Neil.

Uncle was a keen footballer, snooker player, card sharp, greyhound trainer and singer – you name it, Big Neil tried it. The only thing he didn't do was to fly Concorde, and that's because no-one asked him!

Neil was one of the people invited by Seán Coyle to record a BBC radio programme about Springtown along with Martha Wilkinson, Mary Deery, John McLaughlin and Yours Truly. Neil had Seán Coyle in stitches as he told him of the times in the camp when he would put on an old World War II soldier's steel helmet going to bed on wet nights to keep the water from dripping on his head! The show was to be repeated by the BBC no fewer than five times at the public's request because it was so popular.

The stories you could tell about Neil would fill a book on their own. One such story keeps doing the rounds: the occasion he travelled to Limerick to buy a greyhound. He was driving, a very scary thing if you were a passenger in his car – trust me, I know – and everything was going fine until he reached Nenagh, County Tipperary. On a bend on the road, Uncle went straight into a tree and wrecked his car. Uncle and Willie Edgar, who was with him, were not hurt, but the car was badly damaged and unfit to drive. Along came a farmer and Uncle and the farmer got talking. At the end of the conversation, he agreed to sell the wrecked car for £20. Part of the deal was the farmer would give them a lift into Limerick.

After getting out of the farmer's car in Limerick, they were walking down the road when all of a sudden, Uncle let a massive roar out of him.

'What's the matter with you?' asked Willie Edgar.

'I sold the car for twenty pounds and I forgot I put twenty pounds of petrol in it five minutes before we crashed!' bellowed Neil. Willie Edgar could only laugh as Uncle shook his head and said, 'What a place to plant a tree!'

Uncle was a decent snooker player, especially if playing for money. Joe Nicholl told me the story of this Englishman who was on holiday in Derry. He was playing snooker in the hall at Sackville Street in the early 1960s and was a little tipsy and he challenged players to a game with a side stake of £1 a time. Joe played him three times and beat him three times. He kept challenging Joe, but Joe refused to play him as he felt the Englishman was useless at snooker.

Joe left the snooker hall and ran into Uncle and a few boys from the camp and he told the story of the Englishman to Uncle. 'Where is he?' Uncle shouted to Joe.

'In the Sackville Street snooker hall,' Joe told him.

Uncle and his mates from the camp emptied their pockets and gave all the money to Uncle and off they went in search of the Englishman and some easy pickings. 'We'll soon get the dance money now,' Uncle assured his mates. They arrived in the snooker hall and indeed, as Joe Nicholl had told them, the Englishman was challenging everyone around him.

'He hasn't won a match all day,' Ding Cassidy told Uncle.

Uncle smiled and said to the tipsy player, 'I'll play you.'

'How much for?' asked the Englishman.

'Two pounds,' said Uncle. The Englishman agreed and set the balls up. Uncle played his worst game of snooker ever and the Englishman beat him in a black-ball decider. The news swept around the snooker halls of Derry and big Uncle was to receive some stick for weeks to come.

However, only a few short years ago, Jamesie Nicholl and I went down to Shantallow House looking for Uncle, as we had a back-to-back singing team who were performing the next night in Strabane. On arriving in Shantallow House, we went up the stairs to the snooker hall and there was a young man challenging Uncle. Uncle couldn't take him up on his challenge because he had no money. The young man was going a bit over the top at this stage, and when a gentleman turned to Jamesie and asked him if Uncle could beat him, Jamesie replied, 'It could be close, but Neil has nerves of steel when playing for money and he may just beat him.'

The young man then made the mistake of saying he would beat Uncle even if he gave him twenty points up. The gentleman intervened because he, too, thought the young man was going over the top.

'How much do you want to play Neil for?' he asked.

'Whatever amount he wants,' replied the young man, 'but sure he's skint anyway.'

The gentleman pulled from his wallet several £20 notes and told the young man, 'You can play Uncle for as much as you want now.'

The young man suddenly became very quiet, but as he couldn't be seen to back down, he agreed to give Uncle twenty points up. Uncle proceeded to give the young man a lesson in 'pressure' snooker and beat him easily.

Some say there are only two things certain in life: taxes and death. Yet I would say there was maybe a third: if there was loud banter and craic at a greyhound track, a card school, a snooker hall or a bookie's, it's a fair bet big Uncle would be at the centre of it.

He was a larger-than-life character, and those places are a lot duller and less inviting today because of his absence.

One of Neil's great friends, Willie Edgar, a man as tough as nails, a great footballer and ultra-keen greyhound enthusiast, married Mary Scanlon and came to live in the camp in 1952; they raised a family of nineteen. Willie, a member of the camp football team, played for Derry City Reserves and he was a greyhound and pigeon enthusiast all his life. He loved to have a bet, be it on the horses, dogs or football; he also liked a game of cards and was a frequent visitor to the many card schools in the camp.

Mary, his wife, also played cards with other women in the camp, but mostly just for pennies and to pass the time on a summer's night. It was common to see some women playing cards at their doorsteps while the children played near them in the 1950s.

Willie Edgar, who was known simply as Edgar, was an ever-present feature at the greyhound tracks with Uncle, or Big Neil, as he would call him. I will never forget a conversation Edgar had with Jack McLaughlin. I was standing petting Edgar's greyhound; I was a very young boy wearing short trousers and water boots. Jack came along and the conversation with Edgar went like this.

Jack: 'Edgar, that dog has no legs.'

Edgar: 'Oh, he has legs all right, don't you worry about that.'

Jack: 'I'm telling you, Edgar, he can't run. He's a grub destroyer.'

Edgar: 'Wait till I take the boots off him.'

Jack: 'He'll end up taking the boots off you, Edgar.'

Willie Edgar enjoying the sunshine with three of his children in the summer of 1955.

There was me, standing bemused, not understanding what they were talking about, my head and eyes moving from the greyhound to Jack to Edgar and back to the greyhound again. I left them, scratching my head and thinking they were nuts. Edgar was looking at Jack with a solemn face, so it was a serious conversation.

It was much later that I realised what the conversation was all about. Jack was telling Edgar the dog was useless and Edgar was telling him that when he wanted the dog to win, it would win. Normal everyday greyhound language, but I sure was confused that day.

Willie was always on the batter, walking everywhere with two or three dogs on leashes. He stayed very fit right up to his death at the age of eighty-two. Even when he was diagnosed with a serious illness, he still never left the roads with his dogs. He remarked to me one day, 'I'll stay on my feet for as long as I possibly can.' It was to his eternal credit that he did just that. I often saw him coming in from walking his dogs as I was going to work at 7:45 on a cold winter's morning, and him with a serious illness. As I said, a man as tough as nails, a man who never complained. His motto was, get up, get on with it and stop moaning.

That is how he lived his life to the end.

Sammy Porter, Hugh McMonagle and Jack McLaughlin walking their dogs out the Buncrana Road, 1954.

Paddy Parsons

As you would expect, there were a lot of love stories in the camp, with many a neighbour's daughter marrying a neighbour's son. I stopped counting when I reached sixty people who lived in the camp and who married a person from the camp.

One young, happy camper travelled a little further to find the woman of his dreams. Paddy Parsons, a born and bred Springtowner and a quiet and very popular lad, caught sight of his wife to be while browsing through a magazine. Liking what he saw and was reading, he decided to put pen to paper and write to this pretty young woman who just happened to live at the other side of the world in far-off Malaysia. She responded and wrote back to Paddy.

The irrepressible Paddy Parsons looks the camera straight in the eye at the tender age of three years, September 1953.

After months of writing to each other, Paddy decided to take the bull by the horns and go out and meet her in person in her home city of Ipoh in Malaysia. Paddy takes up the story.

'I went into the Foyle Taxis office in Foyle Street and booked a taxi to take me to Belfast the next day. The office man, who was drinking a cup of tea, asked where I was going. I told him Malaysia. He nearly choked! As I had a few drinks taken, I don't think he believed me.

'The next day he called to see me to make sure I was for real. I told him of course I was and to call for me at three. Shortly after three, I set off in a taxi for Belfast airport.'

Paddy flew to London's Heathrow airport where he boarded a plane for the long-haul flight to Malaysia. As Paddy stepped on to the tarmac at the airport in Malaysia, he considered that he was a long, long way from Springtown Camp and his first love, Bridget Hegarty. As Paddy weaved his way through the busy airport, he thought to himself, *won't I look a right eejit if she doesn't like me?*

Casting such thoughts from his head, he booked in to the Mandarin Hotel beside the airport for an overnight stay. The following day, he boarded a coach for a three-hour journey to the city of Ipoh where Helen, his bride to be, was anxiously waiting for him.

'Before I knew it, I was standing at her doorstep with a large suitcase in my hand. Helen's mother opened the door and nearly fainted when she saw this born-and-bred Springtown Camp man who had travelled halfway around the world to meet her daughter standing on her doorstep.'

Paddy recalls he had arranged to stay at a hotel close by, but Helen's family demanded that he stay with them. 'They made a spare room just for me and made me feel very welcome.'

He went on: 'When I was taking Helen out to a restaurant while in Malaysia, it was their custom to have a chaperone accompany us. Not once were we allowed to go out on our own without being escorted by another member of the family.'

After coming home, Paddy knew Helen was the girl for him and further visits took place. Just ten months later, Paddy walked Helen down the aisle in Our Lady of Lourdes Church in Ipoh, Malaysia. Two weeks later, he brought his new bride back to his home town of Derry.

Helen fell in love with Derry and her family are frequent visitors. Paddy and Helen have two children, a boy and a girl, and are as happy and contented now as when they first met.

Paddy said while in Malaysia he saw a camp exactly like Springtown, but it was now a tourist attraction, so he decided to take a trip round it. 'It was uncanny. It was just like Springtown. As I wandered round it, I was half-expecting to hear Francie Brandon shouting "Fresh herring, fresh herring",' he laughed.

Like most of the young lads, myself included, Paddy would often collect the *Belfast Telegraph* bundles from the bus and bring them down to Butcher and Bella Carlin's hut.

Butcher, his wife Bella and children, were one of the many families who came to Springtown after being evicted from Belmont Camp in 1947. He was known as the 'Tillie' man, as his hut is where you bought the *Belfast Telegraph* and *Ireland's Saturday Night*.

Someone always collected them off the bus for Butcher and without fail, there were always a few people waiting outside his hut for them to arrive. It's funny: my father would tell me to go over to Butcher's for the *Tillie*, whereas my mother would always say go over to Bella's.

On arriving at the Carlin hut, you would stick your head inside the door and shout, 'Is the *Tillie* in yet?' and the answer was always the same: either, 'Aye, come on in' or 'Be here in five minutes'. When you paid Butcher or Bella, they would throw the money into a wee tin box.

When collecting the paper, you might be lucky enough to get a penny for going and if so, it was over to Donnelly's hut to buy a wee bit of icing or a toffee apple – that is, if there wasn't a toss pit on the way and you were lured into it in the hope of making a few bob. More times than not, I lost the *Tillie* money as well, so it was back to the hut to tell my parents a wee white lie – that I tripped and the money fell out of my hand and was lost.

In the warm weather, my favourite choice would be a nice pineapple ice-pop from the fridges of Willie McConnell's shop. McConnell's and Moore's shops always had such a great variety of sweets and ice cream and ice-pops that we were spoiled for choice. When getting messages for your mother, you would just say, 'Put it in the book.' Sweets or ice-pops were not allowed on tick, because they could not be sure if your mother had sanctioned them. So it was cash only for ice-pops or sweets. Sometimes, that rule would be relaxed, especially if Jackie McConnell was serving behind the counter. Jackie was always a soft touch for a sad story.

I have often wondered what Willie McConnell did with all those 'little red books' when he swapped his wee green tin hut for the splendour of a three-bedroom house in Osborne Street in 1966. I have a feeling they would be of great enlightenment and make great reading, and I have no doubt they would bring a smile to many an ex-Springtowner's face today. The shop owners of Springtown provided a lifeline to most of the people in the camp in the days of hardship and poverty.

Not to be outdone by the boys, the girls' walking team – captained by Annie Wilkinson and managed by George Lynch – were also very successful. Included: Patricia Grey, Mary Doherty, Maura Rafferty, Joan Doherty, Roisin Mallet and Annie Wilkinson.

Chapter 18
Protests Intensify

Thursday 4 May 1961 was to prove to be another infamous day as far as the Corporation were concerned. They sought and were granted in Derry Court, eviction decrees against five families from the camp. The families, with nowhere to go, had moved into vacant huts. The residents of the camp were warned that if they took any of the families in as lodgers, then they as legal tenants would be in danger of being struck off the housing waiting list.

This vindictive stance by the Corporation was typical of their policy towards the people of the camp and few doubted they would indeed carry out their threat. Two of the five families left the camp within days of the eviction notices being served on them. It was a very wet morning on Wednesday 31 May 1961 as bailiffs arrived in the camp to evict the other families. The families of Edward and Kathleen McCarron, Willie and Margaret Morrin and Philip and Claire Green were evicted from their huts. The people of the camp were very angry and deeply frustrated, as they were rendered powerless by the threat made to them by the Corporation.

Eddie McAteer MP said on the issue: 'Someday, the public conscience in Derry may wake up to this.' He added, 'The neighbours of the three families evicted are prevented from performing an act of charity by taking in the homeless, under threat from the Corporation that if they take any of these unfortunate families in as sub-lets, they themselves will be struck off the housing waiting list.'

Edward McCarron, who had a child of one month, said he had to split his family up, with his wife and youngest child going to stay with his wife's sister while he and his other child stayed with his mother. He stated, 'We are now back where we started when we took over the hut last March.'

Willie Morrin, whose children ranged from one year to four years, said two of his children had to stay with his wife's mother while the other two stayed with his mother. He said both he and his wife Margaret had to sleep in a chair 'and it looks as if we will have to do the same again tonight'.

Philip Green said that despite the Corporation's threat to his neighbours, they 'offered our four children, whose ages are from ten months to five years, sleeping accommodation. Both my wife and I had to stay up all night and it will be the same arrangements tonight as well.'

The families met with Mayor Glover, but he said he was unable to assist them. Later, a petition was signed by the people of the camp supporting all three families and the Morrin family were let a hut by the Corporation.

By September 1962, the huts had dwindled to ninety-two from their peak of 302 in 1946. However, although there were ninety-two huts, these housed 116 families, many with young children as young as three months. The additional twenty-four families were sons and daughters who'd married and now had children of their own. They were living with their parents or with some kind neighbour who let a room to them.

***

Nevertheless, what was very clear was that the people of the camp laid the blame for their situation on the mayor, his Corporation, housing manager Murphy and his housing officials. As far as the Springtowners were concerned, all had played a part in the injustice meted out to them.

Murphy was always the first port of call for the campers when inquiring about getting re-housed. On many occasions, actually getting a mere meeting with him was extremely difficult and, as one irate resident said, 'It would be easier to get a meeting with the Queen of England than with Mr Murphy.'

George 'Buzzard' McLaughlin talking to a television crew outside his Springtown hut.

Then again, the reason for that was very clear: he was unable to defend the Corporation's discrimination against the people of Springtown. It was patently obvious they were not on the Corporation's radar as far as getting re-housed was concerned.

When interviewed by Charles Witherspoon of UTV on the matter of the camp, Murphy appeared unsure and very uncomfortable during the discussion. He had very little to say by way of a defence as to why the people of Springtown had not been re-housed and why they had to live in such conditions. However, to his credit, he finally admitted he found it hard to defend the Corporation's position regarding the camp. This was the first time in almost twenty years that the Corporation publicly admitted any culpability on the issue of the camp. His only semblance of a defence was to say that the issue of Springtown might have to be decided in court. The fact that the people of the camp paid rent for almost twenty years to the Corporation didn't seem to matter. Of course, the dogs in the street knew the Corporation and the Rural Council were never going to face each other in court over the issue of Springtown Camp.

A picture says a thousand words! Housing manager DAS Murphy has no answers to the questions of UTV interviewer Charles Witherspoon about the Corporation's policy towards the people of Springtown Camp.

1964 Protests

With the huts now crumbling before their very eyes, dampness was the least of the residents' worries as now the water was actually seeping in through the rusted corrugated tin. The concrete floor was wet and the huts became infested with rodents. The residents' position was dire, the feeling of despair and hopelessness increasing by the week. Emigration was now looking the only option out of their desperate situation. Some families decided they had had enough and moved to England and Scotland in search of a decent home.

I remember standing in the camp, watching people I had known all my young life, suitcase in hand, walking through the camp for the last time. They were on their way to catch the bus to Derry, to catch a train to Belfast and board the boat to England or Scotland, some never to return to the city of their birth. They believed they would be treated better in a foreign land, surely a shocking indictment on their own city. Most of the families got a house and a job within several weeks in their adopted towns and cities throughout England, Wales and Scotland.

Left: Jean Adams (née McCloskey) who, with her husband and children, were lodgers in the camp. Jean is photographed eloquently putting the lodgers' case to UTV's Charles Witherspoon, 1964. Right: Johnny Doherty and Dorothy Adcock about to be interviewed on television, January 1964.

From the late 1950s, the people of the camp watched in disbelief as their close-knit community was being ripped apart. This enforced emigration was exactly what the Corporation had hoped would happen: by denying the people houses, they were forcing Derry people to leave their own city.

The residents of the camp didn't want a repetition of the '50s, which had seen scores of young families forced to catch the emigration boat. This spurred the men of the camp on to action; why should they stand by and watch families born and bred in Derry, as were their fathers and grandfathers before them, having to emigrate in order to get a proper home?

Now realising they would have to do something about this awful situation to achieve the right to rear their children in a proper house, they determined to take control of their own destiny and take the battle to the Corporation. It was obvious that no matter how hard the nationalist politicians worked on their behalf, and work hard they did, with the unionist-gerrymandered majority they were fighting seemingly impossible odds.

The facts were there for all to see and were irrefutable. Some 276 houses had recently been built in Belmont by the Housing Trust, of which 239 went to Protestant families. With over 120 families in Springtown living in squalor in tin huts only 400 yards away, not one single house was allocated to the people of the camp.

In the eyes of honest men, it was a complete and utter scandal perpetrated by little men with little minds with little or no conscience in the Corporation, Rural Council and Housing Trust, men who themselves were prisoners to their own bigoted way of thinking. Such injustice against a long-suffering community was disgraceful. The residents knew it was time to fight back against those who had denied them their basic right to a proper home for nearly twenty years.

Willie Campbell handing out leaflets to highlight conditions in the camp. The women of the camp helped him to distribute them throughout Derry on 15 January 1964. Included with Willie: Cissie Moore, Mary Edgar, Mary Jane Moore, Annie McBrearty, Maureen Harkin and Bridget Moore.

As the people of the camp were ringing in the new year of 1964, some men decided that they had had enough of living in deplorable conditions and decided to do something about it. They decided to form a committee to agitate for everyone in the camp to be re-housed without delay. They were tired of the petty squabbling between politicians of different affiliations in the Guildhall while they were forced to live in terrible conditions. After a stormy yet productive first meeting in Rory Quigley's hut, a committee was elected. Willie Campbell and Willie Edgar were elected joint-chairmen, with Rory Quigley, Jimmy Deery, John McBrearty, John McLaughlin, Hughie Harkin, Buzzard McLaughlin, Eddie Moran, Johnny Doherty and Charlie O'Hagan making up the rest of the committee. The whole camp was behind the committee, with the exception of between ten and fifteen families who did not wish to be housed at that particular time.

Two things were agreed at the outset: they would fight for houses for everyone in the camp – the eighty-four 'legal' tenants and lodgers; they would also take their fight for proper houses all the way to Stormont, thus making it a government matter.

The Corporation had a policy of refusing to re-house families who had been legal tenants since 1946, simply because they now had living with them a married son or daughter, themselves with children of their own. They wanted them to throw their married sons and daughters onto the streets before they could be considered for re-housing. This, of course, was never going to happen.

Sadie Campbell, who was re-housed at Quarry Street, joins her former neighbours in distributing leaflets in the city centre to highlight conditions in the camp. Included: Sadie Campbell, Annie McBrearty, Mary Edgar, Lily Jennings, Maggie Campbell and Maureen Harkin, 15 January 1964.

The committee's opening shot was on Wednesday 15 December 1964 when over eighty residents of the camp converged on Derry's city centre and distributed over 5,000 leaflets. The leaflets bore the headline 'An Appeal to the People of Derry' and added: 'We address this appeal to everybody, members of parliament, aldermen and councillors, clergymen, trade unionists and businessmen, and to all those who are, or should be, concerned in conscience about the conditions under which we are forced to live.' The leaflets also refuted a charge that heavy drinking was breaking up homes in the camp. The leaflets were simply signed: The Men, Women and Children of Springtown Camp.

AN APPEAL TO THE PEOPLE OF DERRY

1—The residents of Springtown Camp are not drunkards.

2—Six hundred of us, men, women and children, live in 20-year-old wartime American Nissen huts. These huts were totally unfit for human habitation some ten years ago.

3—We appeal to you, our fellow-citizens, to help bring pressure on the housing authority, the Derry Corporation, to provide us with houses.

Time and again over a period of years, we have asked the Corporation to do this but without success.

4—We address this appeal to everybody, Members of Parliament, Aldermen and Councillors, Clergymen, Trade Unionists and Businessmen; to all those who are, or should be, concerned in conscience about the conditions under which we are forced to live.

Signed:

THE MEN, WOMEN AND CHILDREN, SPRINGTOWN CAMP.

JANUARY, 1964.

They had a great response from the Derry people, who pledged to support them. A further meeting was held by the committee to formulate plans for further protests. In the knowledge that their cause was a just one, they would campaign and protest in an organised, dignified manner at all times. With this in mind, they enlisted the help of the women, who would assist in many ways. No longer were they going to allow themselves to be pushed onto the emigration boat by the unjust local unionist authorities who controlled the allocation of houses in Derry. They would be stronger together, speaking with one united voice. They left the meeting, focused and determined, and vowed that they would not stop until the camp was cleared and everyone re-housed.

It was a battle they had to win; the alternative was the boat.

The people of Derry were now awakening to the plight of the Springtown people. On Tuesday 21 January 1964, in response to Sir Basil McFarland's statement the previous week when he stated 'the people of Derry have never had it so good', Ursula Gillespie of 1 Alexandra Place had published an open letter in the *Derry Journal* to the powers-that-be in Derry's Guildhall.

In her letter she asked them: 'Are you all the smug, indifferent, individuals that you appear to be? Why are over 600 citizens of this community living in wartime evacuation conditions? I cannot believe that these people do not merit decent housing conditions in this, their own city. Surely, you cannot, in all conscience, imagine that these unfortunate people are being unreasonable in their demand for better living conditions? I call your attention to the word "camp", which is defined as follows: "temporary quarters of nomads". The inhabitants of Springtown Camp cannot be classified under the above title. Does Sir Basil McFarland imagine these people have something to be grateful for? Can you, in all decency, tell them they have never had it so good?'

That same week, new light appeared out of an old window when, at their monthly meeting, the Middle Liberties Young Unionist Association (the Middle Liberties being the electoral area of which Springtown Camp was a part) passed a resolution condemning the Corporation and Rural Council's handling of the Springtown Camp housing situation.

The resolution also urged these bodies to honour their obligations to these unfortunate people and to devote thought to immediately re-housing them. Their spokesman said, 'These hutments should have been cleared long ago. They are an eyesore on one of the main roads leading out of the city or into the city from Donegal; they are a bad advertisement for this city. How would any member of either council like to live in one of these huts?'

The camp committee, now determined to apply as much pressure on the Corporation as possible, organised a march from the camp to the Guildhall for Tuesday 28 January 1964 to coincide with the Corporation meeting.

On the night before the march, the RUC visited the committee and warned that if there was the slightest hint of trouble they would stop the march.

The committee came up with the idea that the march would be a silent protest march. They instructed the people that they should not talk to the public walking on the footpath or shopping or just looking on. All agreed: this would give no-one an excuse to halt their protest march.

The marchers assembled at the bottom gate of the camp; there were around 200 men and women. Some carried placards which read: 'Derry's Little Rock', 'Nobody's Child', 'Our Lives In Your Hands', and 'Man's Inhumanity'.

One particular placard on the march summed up the situation with a lot of the families. It read:

When I was a lad,
I lived with my dad
In Springtown Camp.
Now I'm a dad
With a few lads,
Still in Springtown Camp.

Springtown Camp residents on the march for fair treatment led by Willie Campbell and Willie Edgar. Included: Tommy McLaughlin, Rita Duffy, John McLaughlin, Hughie Harkin, Lily Jennings, Kathleen McLaughlin, Mary Edgar, Dolly Sweeney and Johnnie McKeever.

The marchers walked along the Buncrana Road, past Pennyburn Church and turned right up the Strand Road. As the march was approaching Waterloo Place, a strange but welcome thing happened: the shoppers, who didn't have a clue what was happening, came out of the shops and for a moment just looked on in bewilderment. Then, on reading the placards, some started clapping and the rest of the shoppers joined in the applause. The people in William Street, hearing the clapping, rushed down to Waterloo Place to see what was going on and on seeing the marchers, they, too, joined in the clapping.

The march proceeded right up to the Guildhall steps, some of the protesters going into the public gallery to observe the meeting taking place. The Corporation had no alternative but to agree to meet with the joint-chairmen of the committee, Willie Campbell and Willie Edgar.

Willie Edgar told them that the camp was a complete eyesore, the sanitation was terrible, the roads were in a dangerous state and the huts were in an awful condition. It was impossible to decorate the huts, as putting wallpaper on the walls was a waste of time – it just peeled off in a matter of days because the walls were so damp.

Willie Campbell told the Corporation that there were 600 men, women and children living in terrible conditions and he appealed to them to put aside their political differences and work together in the interest of the health and welfare of the people in the camp.

Alderman Hegarty said the Corporation would prosecute private landlords if they let houses like these huts. He also called on the Corporation to put aside all political and religious differences and quarrelling with the Rural Council and work together to finish off Springtown Camp. He concluded by saying, 'These people are human beings and deserve better that this. The only way to do this is to house all the residents of the camp as soon as possible.'

Willie Edgar and Willie Campbell, January 1964.

Alderman Glover told the meeting that they would get priority for ten houses to be let at Creggan soon. He said the people of the camp would get a 'fair proportion' of homes to be built by the Northern Ireland Housing Trust at Shantallow.

With that assurance, the two men left the meeting, still determined to keep up the protests. They had heard these promises before, remembering the twenty-eight houses at Coach Road they had been promised by the same man. The families had received ten houses and not the twenty-eight they had been promised.

There followed a heated debate between the nationalist and unionist councillors on the Corporation's record and policy of housing in the city.

The protesters returned to the camp a little happier, as they now believed the people of Derry had finally woken up to their plight and were now supporting them. The television cameras captured the mood of the marchers and the pictures were shown on every TV in every home across the country that night. The nation was now aware of the plight of the residents of Springtown Camp.

Another camper, young Willie Curran from Hut 176, had every reason to be very happy that weekend also as he made his debut for Derry City at the Brandywell. Playing at left-back, Willie made a very promising debut in Derry City's 5–2 win over Glenavon.

The *Derry Journal*, in their Friday edition that week, printed a letter from prominent businessman Frank Guckian. I quote his letter in full.

Tuesday was surely Derry's day of shame.

On that day, a group of our residents suffering injustice for so many years asked for our help. We could only offer them vague promises.

On that day, a debate on the problems of Springtown Camp took place in Derry's Guildhall and many of our representatives remained silent.

On that day, television recorded our apathy and pointed an accusing finger.

On that day, I was ashamed to call myself a Derryman.

Mindful of the fact that members of the Corporation are elected to represent the people of the city and are aware of the widespread feelings of sympathy for the residents of Springtown Camp, I would ask our representatives to take immediate action to house all the people of Springtown within the next few months. I would ask them to call a special meeting of the council to take this decision, and if they are in any doubt about the feelings of the people of the city, representatives of every creed and class from all parts of the city would be present to reassure them.

No longer can delay be tolerated. Let's act now.

The Corporation went to great lengths to keep any news about the Springtown Camp situation under wraps. In January 1964, BBC television news editor Cecil Taylor sent Alan Reid and a film crew to do a substantive story on the situation in the camp. Reid reported back to Taylor that they had received no co-operation whatsoever from the Corporation. Taylor, who later became head of programmes at the BBC, had this to say about the non-co-operation of the Corporation.

'If there was one story that confirmed the BBC's editorial independence, it was the coverage in January 1964 of Springtown Camp in Derry. The people there were living in poor conditions, and when Alan Reid told me he received no co-operation from the unionists, I decided I would travel to Derry and see if I could help. One of the most influential unionists there was Gerald Glover. He told me he would make sure that nothing about Springtown would be broadcast.

'I told him we would cover the story with or without his co-operation.

'I took the precaution of phoning the BBC head of programmes to tell him what was happening. He duly got a call from Glover and rejected any suggestion that the story of Springtown Camp should not be covered.'

The unionists on the Corporation then did a U-turn and decided to co-operate, and a twelve-minute film was shown in due course. It included an interview with Eddie McAteer MP. When he was approached for the interview, his comment was, 'Good God, miracles will never cease!'

The Corporation, Rural Council and Housing Trust were now faced with a determined, well-organised campaign by the people of the camp. Now with their backs to the wall, the Corporation had nowhere else to run, no more excuses to offer, no more lies to tell.

Their normal excuses were no longer an option.

None of their stalling tactics would ever be tolerated again by the long-suffering people of Springtown. Public opinion was now firmly against the housing authorities for their inactivity over this issue of re-housing the people of the camp. The Corporation and the Rural Council knew they would be facing an onslaught of protests and media attention on the issue of Springtown in the near future.

With this in mind, they devised a ploy to try to weaken the residents' position. They were to employ a strategy of offering to selected residents of the camp houses situated miles out in the country. This was done in the full knowledge that the residents would obviously refuse such offers. Why would families born and reared in Derry want to go and live miles out in the country? It was, in effect, a defensive policy: in the face of searching questions being asked by the media, they could claim they had offered families houses and that the families had refused the offers.

Their first throw of the dice came on Thursday 16 January 1964, just two short weeks after the protests by the residents had started. The Rural Council sent a letter offering a house in Strathfoyle to Willie Edgar, who just happened to be a joint-chairman of the camp committee. The entire Edgar family, all nineteen of them, were born and reared in Derry, as were Willie and his wife Mary. Why would they want to go and live miles away from their families to a place they'd barely heard tell off?

The offer was, of course, refused as both the Rural Council and Corporation knew it would be.

The camp committee knew now what their ploy was going to be and they gave warning to the residents of this. The municipal bodies continued to offer the residents similar houses miles away out in the country. The residents, with a few exceptions, continued to reject such offers.

Derry Trades Council at their monthly meeting called for the immediate closure of the camp. Their statement said this camp was an affront to the entire city. Frank Bradley said he'd seen cattle living in better conditions than these people. 'It is an outrage to any man's conscience that people should be forced to live in these huts.'

The Corporation were now under pressure to act, and in response to the march by the Springtown people the week before, they announced that ten maisonettes nearing completion would all go to Springtown Camp families.

However, once again, all was not as it seemed as the all-electric maisonettes, at a rent of £2 9s 5d (£2.47), were the most expensive new homes in Creggan. On Wednesday 4 March 1964, five families were offered these maisonettes; three accepted them under protest and two refused them on the grounds they just couldn't afford them. This was way beyond the means of most of the families in the camp, but, of course, the Corporation knew this.

Margaret (Maggie) Campbell, wife of camp committee joint-chairman Willie, pointed out that in addition to the £2 9s 5d (£2.47) weekly rent, there was also £1 for central heating and a whopping £13 4s 5d (£13.22) deposit and stamp duty. Mrs Campbell asked how many families in Derry could afford these maisonettes. She concluded by saying, 'Only people with a lot of money coming into their home every week can afford these.'

Willie and Maggie Campbell decided to accept one of the maisonettes under protest. However, a family at 43 Creggan Heights offered to swap them their house for the maisonette. Willie and Maggie agreed and the family moved into Creggan Heights that week. Their close neighbours in the camp, Francie and Maisie Brandon, were housed close by at 47 Creggan Heights.

The rent for the houses in Northland Avenue, Northland Crescent, Northland Parade and Northland Way ranged from 17s 6d (87p) to 21s 5d (£1.02).

The Springtown families just wanted an ordinary three- or four-bedroom house like other people in Derry were getting at the time, as the rent for this standard house was much less than the maisonettes.

The camp committee continued to exert pressure on the powers-that-be, with their secretary writing to everyone and anyone who could put pressure on the Corporation and Rural Council to have them re-housed and the camp closed.

When joint-chairman Willie Campbell was re-housed in Creggan, everyone was delighted for Willie and Maggie and their children, but Willie was going to be a hard act to follow. It was a huge setback for the committee. It has to be recognised that Willie Campbell, a very articulate, charismatic and determined man, was the main driving force behind the committee. He was their leader, a man who made things happen, and undoubtedly, without him the committee would probably not have existed.

Willie Campbell had led the people of Springtown through the streets of Derry in protest at the terrible conditions in which they were forced to live. He'd brought the plight of the Springtown people to the television screens, to the front pages of every local newspaper and to the attention of the Stormont Government. His strategy left the Corporation with nowhere to hide, their outdated excuses no longer an option for them. He'd led the camp people on what is now widely recognised as a prototype of the civil rights marches that were to follow throughout the island of Ireland. But above all, he awakened the people of Springtown to their right to a proper house in which to live and rear their children. That is his legacy.

Jimmy Deery was to take over as chairman.

As was expected by the residents, the Corporation didn't keep their word on their pledge at their meeting on 28 January when they said that the camp residents would receive priority on future re-let of housing. Apart from the expensive, all-electric maisonettes, no other houses were offered. The Corporation were still carrying out their policy of discrimination against the Springtown people.

John McLaughlin, who went to work in Northampton, wrote to the editor of the *Derry Journal* on this point; the *Journal* carried his letter in its St Patrick's Day edition of 1964. John said he had been living with his wife Mary and four children with Mary's grandmother for the past several years. He went on to say:

'I understand that lodgers were to be re-housed as well as the tenants, or to be found alternative accommodation. Since I have come to England, my wife and children have been evicted by the Corporation. My wife has had to move in with her mother in another hut in the camp, but as she has a family of eight, it leaves them overcrowded. What I want to know is, will my wife and children be put on the street again once my wife's mother is re-housed? What will happen to the other lodgers in the camp? Will they be treated in the same way?'

John had to leave his work in England and return to the camp, where he rejoined the camp committee in their fight to be re-housed.

On 9 April 1964, the camp committee had another meeting with the Corporation. Jimmy Deery, Willie Morrin and Charlie O'Hagan represented the people of Springtown; also in attendance was Mayor Albert Anderson, Alderman Glover, who chaired the meeting, DAS Murphy, housing manager, and town clerk, R Henderson.

Given that all of the Corporation's top personnel were present, it indicated that the Corporation were in no doubt as to the determination of the camp committee. The camp's representatives submitted the following statement:

1. We, the members of the above committee, wish to appeal on behalf of the residents of Springtown in respect of the housing allocation. We wish to inquire into the following circumstances concerning the remaining residents. First, we would like to have a few questions answered. Having been promised a certain percentage of re-lets, we have not received any of these.

2. We would like to ask the housing sub-committee of their intentions concerning the future of the sub-tenants of Springtown Camp. The Corporation have victimised tenants owing to the fact that their relatives are sharing these huts as sub-tenants.

3. The residents of Springtown Camp want to know how long they will have to endure living under these appalling and primitive conditions and a definite answer given as to when this camp will no longer exist.

John McBrearty, Jimmy Deery and Johnny Doherty of the Springtown Camp committee posting a letter to the powers-that-be at Stormont, April 1964.

During discussions, the camp's representatives agreed that about ten to fifteen tenants in the camp had no wish to be re-housed at the present time. The mayor informed them that the various points they had raised would be considered and a reply given to them as soon as possible. The camp representatives withdrew from the meeting, determined to keep up the protest until all were housed.

The Corporation's reply was received the following week and, as expected, it was the usual standard one that 'reasonable preference in the allocation of new houses and re-lets would be given to eligible families occupying huts at Springtown Camp'. So, all of a sudden, the word 'priority' was replaced by 'reasonable' as regards the housing allocation to them. The camp committee's secretary, Rory Quigley, wrote to Stormont Prime Minister Terence O'Neill in May 1964 asking him to come and visit the camp and see the conditions in which the residents had to live.

The prime minister replied the following week, telling Rory that his request was being considered. He further stated that he had summoned the Corporation and the Rural Council to a meeting with his health minister on the subject of Springtown. This was movement as far as the committee was concerned.

Rory Quigley, who was a lodger with his mother-in-law in the camp, wrote directly to the then Prime Minister Lord Brookeborough in 1959, telling him of his plight. Brookeborough replied to his letter, telling Rory he would do what he could for him. The following week, Rory and his wife and children were given a hut of their own.

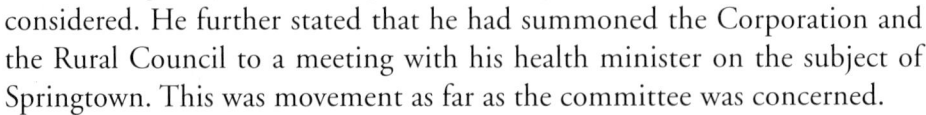

Rory had done sterling work on the camp committee and indeed was the perfect person to carry out these duties. A quiet and intelligent man, he also loved a game of cards and was one of the regulars at the table in Seekie's hut. He was a roof tiler by trade and worked on most of the building sites in and around Derry. Rory was always pushed forward by the people of the camp when the television cameras visited Springtown, as he was a fluent and articulate person, an ideal choice as spokesman for the residents, as had been Willie Campbell and Willie Edgar. His many press releases during that time kept the Springtown housing protest in the public eye and he certainly was one of the key members who hastened the closure of the camp. Another man who played his part in the campaign was a young John McLaughlin; John, who had married at a tender age, was a lodger in the camp with wife Mary and their young children.

The lodgers, who were regarded by the Corporation as illegal tenants, were fearful of being left on the streets. However, the camp committee made it one of their main priorities that all tenants were housed without delay. John, being a lodger, was the ideal man to be spokesman for these tenants.

The teenagers in the camp, although aware of their mothers' and fathers' campaign to be re-housed, were more interested in the news that pop/skiffle star Lonnie Donegan and his band the Dustmen were due to appear in the Stardust on Tuesday 26 May 1964. I can recall the excitement in our hut about this news, and indeed the whole town was talking about this big star coming to Derry. At least the dress style of the big boys and girls improved; can-can dresses were now a thing of the past, as were the nylon scarves they wore around their necks to match the bands on their hair. The big boys dispensed with the drainpipe trousers and blue suede shoes and replaced the cheap hair oil with the nice-smelling Brylcreem.

Lonnie Donegan, I suppose, earned the right to be classed a star because he entered the charts at No 1 with *My Old Man's A Dustman*, a feat only equalled by Elvis Presley and the Beatles at that particular time. His other No 1 hits were *Cumberland Gap* and *Putting On The Style* and it was a chance to see this 'massive' star in the flesh.

It was an occasion not to be missed for the dance-crazy teenagers of the camp.

People queuing to sign the petition to close Springtown Camp. At the table are Springtown Camp committee workers John McBrearty and Leo Fitzpatrick.

Johnny McLaughlin and George 'Buzzard' McLaughlin adding their names to the petition demanding the closure of the camp in May 1964. Seated: Johnny Doherty and John McLaughlin.

The camp committee continued with further protests. They organised a petition, residents collecting signatures at factory doors, building sites, street corners, in Guildhall Square . . . The people of Derry queued to sign this petition and in the end the Springtowners collected a staggering 21,428 signatures, all calling for the camp to be closed. A minibus was hired and the entire committee travelled to Stormont on 16 June 1964 where they were met by Eddie McAteer MP. He accompanied them inside the building, where they presented the petition to Mr J Malley, private secretary to Prime Minister O'Neill.

That week, several MPs visited the camp to see the conditions for themselves. One of them, leading British MP Shelia Murnaghan, was visibly moved by the conditions she saw there. She had this to say: 'In all my years of public life, I have never, ever seen conditions like this anywhere in the world. The conditions here at Springtown Camp are on a par with the slums of Johannesburg. I must pay tribute to the women of this camp, who have reared families and managed to keep their dignity in the most difficult circumstances imaginable.'

George Lynch, Mickey and Hugo Henry get ready to catch the 7.10 bus from the camp to Derry on their way to the pictures in 1960.

Following her remarks, the BBC and RTÉ sought interviews with Corporation officials. They refused to be interviewed, fearing further bad publicity; the television cameras were now visiting the camp at regular intervals. That fortnight, no fewer than seven sitting Stormont and Westminster MPs visited the camp to see conditions for themselves. They included Eddie McAteer, Nationalist, Edward Jones, Unionist, Shelia Murnaghan, Liberal, Charles Stewart, Independent, Tom Boyd, Labour, Harry Diamond, Republican Labour and Frank Hanna, Independent.

On Thursday 11 June 1964, local businessman Frank Guckian chaired a meeting of businessmen, teachers, doctors, trade unionists and a cross-section of politicians. One subject was on the agenda: Springtown Camp. The meeting was held in the Guildhall and it was decided to ask the Minister of Health and Local Government to attend a meeting in the city soon to discuss the re-housing of the remaining families at the camp.

Alderman Glover said the Corporation had made a good contribution by reducing the numbers there from 302 to eighty-one. Alderman Hegarty said he blamed the Corporation for the situation they now found themselves in. Frank Guckian said the camp was a pretty bad example of housing in the district, one which could bring disease. He went on to say that this eyesore in the city should be removed very quickly.

With the wave of support for their plight, coupled with the considerable pressure being heaped on the Corporation and the Rural Council, the Springtowners thought 1964 would be the last year they would have to endure living in the camp. It was not to be. Nevertheless, light did begin to appear at the end of the tunnel when five families were re-housed in Shantallow just before the end of the year.

A surprise Christmas present was delivered to James and Minnie Brown, who were living with Minnie's mother and father at 30c Springtown Camp. They became the first lodgers to be re-housed when they were moved to 45 Drumleck Gardens in Shantallow on 22 December 1964. That same day, Bella Lewis and her family moved to 47 Drumleck Gardens. On the move also that very same day were Benny and Bridget McLaughlin and family, the Craigs and the Killen family, all moving to Shantallow.

In late 1964 and early '65, movement was swift as several families were re-housed every couple of months, mainly in Shantallow. This was good news for those families, as they were being housed close by each other. Of course, this made settling into their new surroundings easier by virtue of the numbers of ex-campers re-housed there. Plus the fact that many old friends from Pennyburn School had already moved there from the ageing terraced houses in the old Shantallow. Many more families were also soon on the move to 'Little Springtown' in Shantallow.

In June of 1965, the camp was a changed place; many had been re-housed. As well as the huts decaying, the old concrete footbridge at the camp, built over the old railway line, was now in a dangerous condition. The estimated cost of demolition and removal was put at £110. The bridge, our old and trusted friend, was now on death row.

While the old bridge was now doomed, one sprightly pensioner was getting a new lease of life. Mick Power, one of the two caretakers who worked in the camp for most of the camp's existence, had reached the retirement age of sixty-five in August 1965.

Housing manager Murphy requested the Corporation's permission to extend Mick's employment in view of his experience of working in the camp;

with the camp's intended clearance, Mick's services would be of great assistance to all concerned. The Corporation agreed; providing Mick was willing, they would agree to his employment being extended until such times as the huts were demolished.

The old bridge with its iron handrails was a landmark as far as the camp was concerned. It had been passed a million times by the men, women and children of the camp over a period of almost twenty years. The first camp residents would stand on top of the bridge and watch as the train passed under it, smoke billowing out of its funnel. When the trains ceased to run, the bridge was only used when the old railway line was flooded. Other times, it was used mainly as a play area for the children.

We also met there if we were going 'out the line' to catch tadpoles or just to have a swim in the burn in summertime. It evoked many fond memories of many happy times during our childhood days in the camp. Now it was the end of the line, and it was finally demolished on Thursday 21 October 1965.

By September 1965, the number of huts in the camp had dwindled significantly. Although there were now only forty, they still were home to fifty-six families, with four families living in one hut alone.

On Thursday 4 November 1965, a deputation from the families at the camp led by Mrs E McCarron sought a meeting with the Corporation, which refused to meet with them.

Nonetheless, this move by the remaining residents had the desired effect, as a further thirty families were re-housed in the next few months. This left only nineteen huts standing, housing twenty-six families.

The huts that were left were spread all over the camp and were in terrible condition, thus making it a depressing sight. By August 1966, only twenty families were left in the camp. These remaining families felt isolated and anxious about what lay ahead for them. Every day, they waited on the postman to see if he would bring them news of a house.

When eventually the postman did bring the letter a family were praying for, there was elation in that particular hut and their neighbours in the camp were delighted for them. The remaining families were left feeling increasingly frustrated and wondering when it was going to be their turn.

With most of the residents now gone, the ever-popular Paddy Moore, who had seen many a child grow from boy to man and girl to woman in the camp, decided he, too, would call it a day. Paddy, a larger-than-life character who had worked in the camp since its very early days, retired on Monday 29 November 1965.

Chapter 19
Mothers of the Camp

When mentioning the Wilkinsons, it would be impossible not to include Martha, their mother. Martha, who hailed from Killea in County Donegal, was a woman of great humour and she made light of anything difficult which may have crossed her path. She was a very fit woman and would cycle into Derry to do her shopping. It was a common sight to see her cycling at full speed out the Northland Road to the camp with her shopping bags hanging from each side of the handlebars and her basket full of messages.

Martha Wilkinson, who raised a family of eleven in the camp and was one of the last to leave in September 1967.

Most times, she cycled the second half of the journey from Derry, from Eden Terrace to the camp, faster than the old buses. Her husband, Willie, was from the Brandywell area and a well-known musician. Willie played in many bands, but he particularly liked playing in the marching bands popular at that time. He worked part time as a docker down the quay.

The Wilkinsons were one of the last families to leave the camp, being housed at Westway in Creggan in September 1967.

Another woman who was well known in the camp and who was actually the last to leave Springtown was Kitty Lynch. She and her daughter Frances were the last two mothers to leave. Kitty and her husband Eddie and family lived in one hut, with her sister-in-law Sarah, brother-in-law Charlie, Mary, Frances and her two children in the other hut.

Both families had to endure a lot of trauma as they battled with the Corporation, who wanted to house them miles away from Derry. Kitty and her family displayed great courage and resolution, steadfastly refusing to be bullied by the discredited Corporation. They had lived in Derry for over twenty years and most of their children were born in Derry, so they were entitled to be housed in Derry.

The Springtown people, their neighbours of almost twenty years now spread all over Derry, were delighted when the news reached them that the two Lynch families were to be re-housed in Derry.

Kitty, Eddie and family were re-housed in Creggan Street in the Rosemount area, while Sarah, Charlie, Mary, Frances and her two young children were re-housed in Pitt Street.

Kitty Lynch, who reared a large family in the camp. Kitty was the last mother to leave the camp in October 1967.

Kitty was another mother never seen without her apron on, except when going to Mass. She reared a large family and was always busy cleaning, washing and cooking, working day and night in her hut to make it as comfortable as possible for her family. She always had a smile on her face and was always happy and contented. She enjoyed the craic and banter with her friends and neighbours. Like other mothers, Kitty could be seen arms folded, yarning and joking with her neighbours the Brollys, Stewarts and the Crumlish family at her or her neighbours' doorsteps. Her front door was open from morning to late at night, as were all the front doors in this tightly knit Nissen-hut village. A closed front door during the day was a sight I've never witnessed in my life in Springtown.

Kitty later moved to Little Springtown in Shantallow after her house in Rosemount was demolished for redevelopment. Speaking to Kitty and her daughter Sarah many years later, she told me she was contented living there among some of her old neighbours from the camp. Like everyone else, Kitty reminisced about her never-to-be-forgotten days in the camp.

Frances Lynch was one of the big girls, as we called the older girls in the camp, and a close pal of Margaret Doherty, who was the daughter of the popular Mary the Hen. Both were keen dancers and, with the rest of the big boys and girls, frequented the dancehalls of Derry every weekend. Both she and Margaret remained friends after the camp closed and both always maintained their Springtown days were among the best times of their lives. The two girls attended and supported every function held in connection with the camp over the years. Frances's twins George and Margaret were the youngest children to leave the camp when it closed.

A woman close to Frances's heart was Mary Edgar. Mary was a woman who liked to play a hand of cards, and it was common to see her with Rita Duffy and Maggie Campbell and other women playing at the front door of their huts. The women, unlike the men, played cards for pennies and only played to pass the time on a summer's night.

Margaret (Maggie) Campbell talking to a television interviewer in the camp, January 1964.

Talking about women working hard, Mary was one of those women. I remember being a young boy gathering spuds for local farmers. The farmers collected us at 7.45 am in their tractors and big trailers at the top gate of the camp. Mary Edgar, Jenny McBride, Angela McCloskey and many other teenage girls were aboard the trailers on their way to a hard day's work in a spud field. Mary at that time was mother to six or seven children, but to make ends meet, she was prepared to work in the spud fields when her children were at school. She was a great worker, and as it was normal to select your partner to pick the spuds with you, Mary was the one everyone would have gladly chosen.

I also recall Mrs McCloskey enjoyed the craic playing in whist drives, while Kathleen McLaughlin loved to dance ballroom-style with her husband Jack.

Margaret Brennan (left) and Bridget Fleming (right) being interviewed in 1964.

Bridget Costello, Mary McMonagle and May 'Siberie' Sweeney enjoying the summer sun on the Buncrana Road.

Mothers of the Camp

In her pram the infant slumbers peacefully, blissfully unaware
While mother silently weeps in her chair so close, so close to despair.
Is it not enough you're inhuman and unkind?
Can you not see the suffering you place in my mind?
Oh, you nestle at the foot of mountains of green,
But your human misery is clear to be seen.
Bright buttercups and daisies surround rusty tin.
Still, four paces inside, you're dark, cold, and grim.
Seeking a job, the very mention of your name
Sends employers scuttling, to their eternal shame.
Helplessly, we watch our sons with suitcase in hand
Leave home to seek employment in a foreign land.
After eight children and almost twenty years,
You have caused me to shed many, many tears.
Now, you may think my spirit you will break,
But determined and strong I'll be for my children's sake.
So once again I will dry your moisture and damp.
Sure what am I? Just a mother out in Springtown Camp.

Charles Stewart MP, visiting the camp in June 1964. He is accompanied by camp chairman Jimmy Deery and is pictured talking to residents Elizabeth Collett (née Parke), Kitty Lynch and Phyllis Doherty. Kitty Lynch was the last woman to leave Springtown Camp on Wednesday 11 October 1967.

It is, of course, impossible to mention all the mothers of the camp, but each and every one deserves the utmost credit for their unstinting devotion to rearing us, their children, in the most difficult of circumstances. It is often we think back and wonder just how they did it, given the things they had to overcome. Hindsight is a wonderful thing, but we children can now identify times when our parents often went without to make sure we got what we needed. Their days seldom varied as the same obstacles had to be overcome on a daily basis; still, they kept smiling and met each day as it came.

***

One thing that was obvious in the camp was the fact that most families were of the same social standing, therefore there was never any family trying to outshine the other. That in itself was a good thing and, I believe, the reason why the camp was such a close-knit community.

It was also a fact that very few of the teenagers in the camp drank alcohol or smoked cigarettes. I can think of Georgie Lynch, Brendie Wilkinson, Eamonn Wilkinson, Danny Feeney, Alex Parsons, Robert Armstrong, Paddy McLaughlin, Eugene Bradley and Yours Truly, to name but a few. And the same can be said of the teenage girls around the same age: Briege and Brenda McLaughlin, Kathleen and Sally Bradley, Sally Parsons, Angela and Pat McCloskey, Rosaleen Doherty, Molly and Christine Dunne, and my sisters, never drank or smoked. Innocent days.

Enjoying the good weather in the camp in 1960. Back: Tony Gormley, Danny McLaughlin, Hugo O'Neill and Seamus Fleming. Front: Hugo Henry, George Lynch and Steven Canavan.

Another young man who neither drank nor smoked was Seamus McConnell. Seamus was one of the gifted musicians in the camp; he started to learn the guitar as a young teenager. He played with Jimmy and Johnny Jennings, Charlie O'Hagan, Hugo Lewis, Paddy Walsh, George O'Hagan and Harry Feeney in skiffle and rock'n'roll groups. They were doing so well together that they decided to take a few bookings and named themselves the Starlighters. They were, by all accounts, very good, as they played on a few occasions at the famed Sunday night concerts in St Columb's Hall, and just to show their impartiality, also played to packed crowds at the Friday night dances in the British Legion hall in the Collon Lane.

Seamus, as we know, went on to play in the Johnny and the Jokers showband. The Jokers were one of the better showbands in Derry and toured England and Germany as well as playing in every county and every hall in Ireland. Seamus was then to join the famed Plattermen and again travelled every road in the country with them. He later formed a very successful group, Blues Etcetera, with his brothers Jackie and Danny, both unfortunately and sadly no longer with us.

Seamus McConnell with the Jokers Showband from Derry who toured Ireland and Germany in the early 1960s.

Music class: Georgie O'Hagan, Hughie Harkin, Eddie O'Hagan, Paddy Harkin and Bernie McGinley.

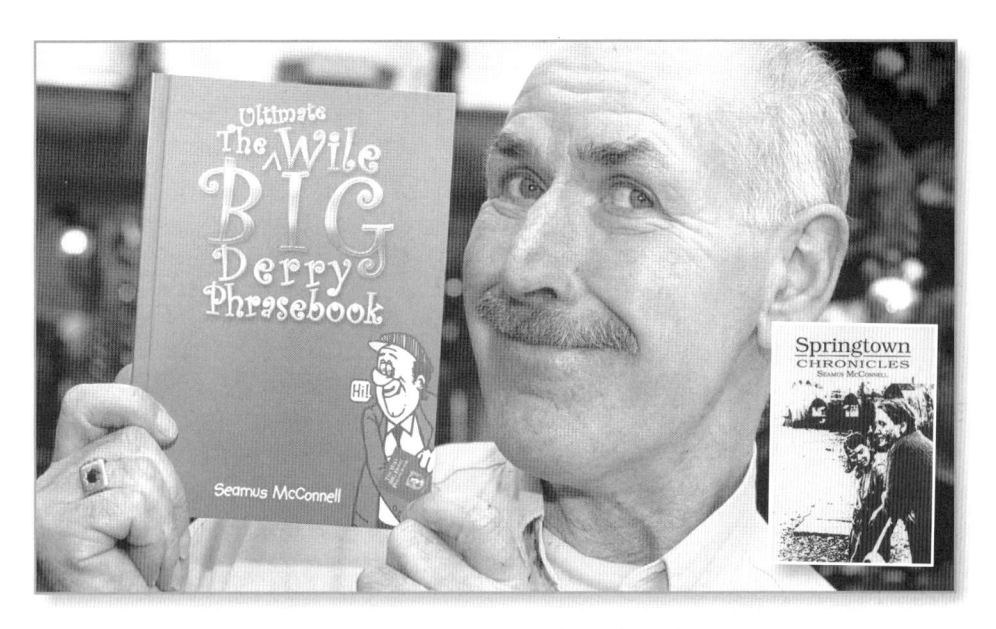

Seamus McConnell, one of many multi-talented Springtowners.

The McConnells were a fine musical family, as Hugo, Paddy and Martin also play instruments, while their sister Liz sang in some bands. Blues Etcetera were extremely popular and drew large crowds to all the venues they played; actually, some notable musicians were of the opinion they were a band ahead of their time. Seamus was not only a talented musician, but also a very good songwriter; he wrote many songs that featured in finals of major song contests, including the world-famous Castlebar Song Festival. He is also the author of two books: *The Wile Big Derry Phrase Book* was a smashing success, outselling any book in Northern Ireland at that time; and *Springtown Chronicles*, a book of verse about the camp, also sold very well and was a hit with all the ex-Springtowners.

Myles Sweeney was another gentleman who excelled in his chosen pastime of Irish dancing; fleet-of-foot Myles was a regular winner in competitions. He, like many others before him, found employment in a foreign land where he also met his wife and reared a family. His son was a successful young actor, appearing in such films as *The Elephant Man*, and went on to direct some short films.

Alex 'Toby' Stewart, an accomplished accordion player, who toured with Jimmy Shand.

Another Springtown man, Robert Armstrong (now known as Rob Strong), was also to make an impact in the music world. Rob had a son, Andrew, who became an actor who hit the big time on the big screen when he starred in the smash-hit film *The Commitments*. Andrew, who possesses the same quality voice as his father, became an overnight success after *The Commitments*, a story about a young soul band from a working-class area of Dublin attempting to make it into the big time. (Also appearing in that film was Derry actress Bronagh Gallagher from Creggan Estate.) Andrew was the lead singer of the band in the film and toured with the same band, playing to capacity audiences in cities and towns throughout Europe. The natural progression for him was to go into the recording studio, which he duly did, recording several successful albums.

Rob Strong as he is today, still strutting his stuff on stage all over the continent.

Rob, a top-class musician, was, like most musicians in the camp, self-taught, and the many nights practising in Alex Parson's hut with Alex and Bernie and Patsy McGinley certainly paid dividends. He joined the Plattermen, whose lead singer was the enduring Brian Coll, arguably Ireland's best country singer of that era. Rob was then the main back-up singer to Coll and he proved very popular with dancers. His style of singing and choice of songs were completely different to Coll's, so it was inevitable something would have to change. Coll left the Plattermen and formed his own band, the Buckaroos.

When Rob took over the mantle as lead singer and took the Plattermen in a different direction music-wise, he added more pop material to the band's repertoire. They then became known as Rob Strong and the Plattermen and continued to attract a large following and were in demand by every dancehall promoter in the country during those halcyon days of the Irish showbands.

Rob went on to make numerous television and radio appearances, including Ireland's top television show, *The Late Late Show*. A class vocalist by any standard, he has recorded many albums and is still today treading the boards and strutting his stuff with his own band, playing mainly blues and soul music. They are so entertaining they can command fees of between £1,500 and £2,000 per show.

He still keeps in touch with his old mates from his boyhood days in the camp. When playing anywhere near Derry, Rob always makes a point of calling to the Coshquin area to meet with his old musical buddies, Alex Parsons and Bernie McGinley. It was also pleasing to see Alex Parsons cutting a CD to commemorate his sixtieth birthday, and I have enjoyed many a pleasant hour listening to it.

It would be remiss of me when talking about musicians and singers who came from the camp not to mention Stan 'Elvis' Colby. Stanley, with his glamorous Elvis suits, strutting his stuff on stage in every pub, hall and club in and around Derry, was a sight to behold. His performances gave joy to everyone who saw him perform and he will always be remembered as an inoffensive man who loved being on stage and belting out Elvis numbers.

Danny Feeney is another man who gave his life to music and entertaining people over the years. Danny gave his time to organising and conducting cross-community choirs. His choirs perform mainly at old people's homes in Derry and its surrounding areas. He was also music director on many charity CDs and lends his expertise to many other projects.

Danny is regularly accompanied on such projects by fellow ex-campers Bernie McGinley, Tony Nash, and one 'Whitey' O'Neill, no stranger to the people of Springtown.

Danny and his team are an inspiration to all and the sheer joy they have given to the public over the years is inestimable. The enjoyment they get from playing to live audiences is infectious and the crowds love them. After finishing one of their many CDs, Whitey, who was narrating, hit the nail on the head when he signed off with, 'No-one was killed or injured in the making of this CD.'

Some liked to use their free time playing music, but the majority of the young men and boys would, after work, normally walk through the plantin' and over to the BSR field in the Northland to play a game of football. These matches were not for the faint hearted, as the tackling was rough, to say the least. Still, they were very enjoyable and a great way to keep fit.

The routine was always the same: Uncle McLaughlin and Liam Fleming would be the captains; they in turn would select a man from the squad of players assembled until everyone was picked. Some would be kitted out in a football rig while others would simply tuck their trousers inside their socks and that was them ready to play.

'Whitey' O'Neill.

At times, Willie McConnell would referee the match, and at times some players from the Collon area or Governor Road came along to play in those matches. Fred McKinney was a notable regular, an absolute gentleman and true sportsman. He was so good a footballer he went on to play for Southend United in the English League. Tragically, he lost his life in a car accident while home on holiday at the tender age of twenty-one.

Margaret Doherty, Willie McConnell and Andy Doherty outside Willie's shop, 1955.

The matches would normally be six goals each half and lasted about two hours or so. After such matches, on the way back to the camp, it was always the usual, good-humoured banter with Kevin 'Jap' McLaughlin, Uncle, Seamus, Sean and Liam Fleming, Georgie Lynch, Danny McLaughlin, Mickey Curran, Stevie Wilkinson and Yours Truly.

Mostly, all the banter was in the direction of Uncle, and if truth be told, we simply were no match for him on that front.

Georgie Lynch was later to form Emeralds FC. All the players were from the camp with the exception of, I think, goalkeeper Tommy Roberts and Hughie Kelly. They played in the Derry and District league and held their own in most matches. When they disbanded, Georgie became a referee and officiated at his first Derry and District match on Sunday 10 September 1967 between Foyle Harps and Rosemount. He was to referee at many important matches, including top Summer Cup competitions, for several years afterwards.

Brendan Fleming, a regular in the old Springtown team, handed down his football flair to his sons John 'Flea' and Gary. Gary made a great career in football, playing week-in week-out under arguably the greatest football manager ever, Brian Clough, at Nottingham Forest. Gary was also a regular on the Northern Ireland International team and played in the World Cup.

Brendan's brother Seamus, a keen footballer himself, also had a son who played regularly in the Irish League.

There were many fine footballers in the camp, a host of them playing senior football: Liam Fleming, Stevie Wilkinson, Willie Curran, and probably the most talented of them all, Mickey Curran. I have no doubt Mickey could have played for any senior team in Ireland, north or south, had he so wished.

John McGinley, Hughie Brown, Eugene McLaughlin and John Brown played with distinction in many Summer Cups.

Charlie Nash (below), who first saw the light of day in the camp, fought for the World Lightweight title against Jim Watt. He was unquestionably Derry's most successful boxer and one of two British Champions who came from the camp – John Doherty also won a British title. John is the son of Sarah Bridge and John Doherty, both Springtown campers.

Charlie came very close to winning the world title as he'd had Watt in trouble when he floored him in the first round. However, cruel fortune was to strike as after a clash of heads, Nash was left with a badly cut eye and the referee had no option but to stop the fight. The most relieved man that night was World Champion Jim Watt, because lady luck was certainly in his corner. One wonders what would have happened if Nash had turned professional a couple of years earlier. Yours Truly is of the belief that Derry, Springtown Camp and Creggan would have had a World Champion to cheer.

Our Hut Going On Fire

Monday 1 March 1965 was a bitterly cold night as I got off the bus with my mate Brendie Wilkinson after finishing our day's work on the building site of St Brecan's School in the Waterside. Unknown to me at that time, I was about to enter our hut at 89b Springtown Camp for the last time. I had my dinner as normal, and after sitting down for a while to watch the television, I got up to go down to the bedroom to change into clean clothes before calling on my friends.

It was 7.45 pm; I was to meet my friends at 8.00 pm.

As I approached the room, I smelled smoke and felt heat coming from the bedroom. I opened the bedroom door and was met with fierce flames. I closed the door instantly, ran to the living room and alerted the rest of the family. At first, they thought I was joking. My young brother Gerald, who was eight years old, ran to the door of our living room and the look on his face made everyone jump up and see for themselves. Within a minute, the fire caught hold of the hut and we literally just had seconds to flee through the front door before the hut was completely engulfed in flames. With only one door, the hut was a death trap. A minute later, we would have been trapped in our small living room, the only escape being one small window. We hadn't even the time to grab our clothes, as when a fire strikes a hut, it does so like lightning. Within a few minutes, the flames were bursting through the roof and could be seen all over the camp.

It was not the first fire in the camp (many huts had gone on fire before) and the cause was identified as an electrical fault. This came as no surprise, as the electrical fittings in most huts were broken and lying bare and in a dangerous state.

We had only been in the hut for a few months (the previous occupiers, John McBrearty and family, were now housed in the new housing estate at Shantallow). We'd moved from our former tin hut, about fifty yards away and which we'd occupied for eighteen years, as it was falling down around us and leaking like a sieve.

When a fire happens in a wooden hut, it burns as fast as a bale of straw. By the time the fire brigade arrived, and they arrived on the scene very swiftly, it was just a matter of saving the adjoining huts as ours had already burned to the ground. We had a little pet Collie dog and we were worried he didn't make it out of the hut, but to our delight we heard him barking as the fire brigade engines approached.

With nowhere to stay, many families offered us accommodation for the night. We ended up staying in Mrs McCloskey's hut. She kindly let us have her big room, with two big beds in it.

Luckily for us, my uncle heard the news and arrived out in the camp the next morning. He lived with just one son in Westway, Creggan, so he was able to offer us accommodation until such times as we were allocated a house of our own.

Chapter 20
End of the Camp

In early 1967, only eleven huts remained in Springtown. The Rural Council offered the families houses miles from Derry. Naturally, the offers were refused. The Corporation sought to evict the remaining eleven families and summonsed them to appear in court: they received a 'notice to quit' from the Corporation on Friday 6 January 1967. The court date was set for Thursday 2 February 1967 at Bishop Street courthouse. I attended the court on that day with my friend Brendie Wilkinson, whose family was one of those summonsed to appear. There was tension in the courtroom as the case against the residents began. Patrick Maxwell, solicitor for the residents, outlined the history of the camp, but after several hours, the magistrate granted decrees in 'ejectment' against all the residents.

I remember to this day the scene at the courthouse as Frances Lynch immediately instructed Patrick Maxwell to appeal.

Despite decrees being awarded in favour of the Corporation, the residents' determination to continue the struggle for proper and reasonable treatment from the housing authorities caused considerable panic in local-government and Stormont circles.

A high-powered meeting was hastily scheduled for Wednesday 8 February 1967 at Dundonald House, Belfast. There was only one topic on the agenda: the residents of Springtown Camp.

The old bridge over the railway track looking abandoned as the camp nears the end, 1965.

Attending that meeting were representatives of: The Ministry of Health and Social Services, The Ministry of Home Affairs, The Ministry of Development, The Derry County Council, The Derry Corporation, The Derry Rural Council and The Northern Ireland Housing Trust.

Throughout the meeting, the Corporation's housing committee was under very considerable pressure to agree to re-house some, if not all, of the remaining residents of the camp. The Corporation refused. It was suggested, in view of the greater facilities available to the Housing Trust and the refusal of the Rural Council to make fresh offers to the tenants, that the Housing Trust might agree to house the residents of the camp. In return, the Rural Council might re-house tenants from the Housing Trust list. Both bodies agreed to consider this suggestion.

The Ministry of Health and Social Services urged that a fresh, concerted effort be made at local level to find a solution to this problem.

The appeal was heard at Bishop Street courthouse on Thursday 8 June 1967. Presiding was Recorder of Derry, Judge Little.

Again I went to the court with Brendie Wilkinson and this time, Liam McConnell accompanied us. Liam and his family had been re-housed in Osborne Street, a few doors from me. Paddy Maxwell argued the Corporation and Rural Council were being awkward and unreasonable in their dealings with the residents. However, after almost three hours of legal arguments by both sides, the judge came down on the side of the Corporation.

Judge Little gave an order for possession of the huts with a stay until 1 August 1967. Paddy Maxwell gave the judge notice that he intended to have a case stated at the High Court in Belfast. Within a short space of time, the majority of the remaining residents were re-housed. In September 1967, Willie and Martha Wilkinson and family were re-housed at Westway, Creggan.

From the time the very first squatter moved into the camp, Springtown had become the focal point in housing discrimination in Derry. The discredited Corporation's systematic policy of discrimination against defenceless people whose 'crime' was they were poor, mostly unemployed and mainly Catholic, had lasted over twenty-one years.

Above: The Last Goodbye. Mick Power and workmen moving furniture from Charlie and Sarah Lynch's hut on Wednesday 11 October 1967. They were the last family to leave Springtown Camp. Also in photograph: Sarah Lynch, Frances Lynch's twins George and Margaret, and Mary Lynch.

Left: Young George Lynch standing at his front door at 29b Springtown Camp for the last time on Wednesday 11 October 1967. George and his twin sister Margaret were the last children to leave the camp.

In October 1967, out of over 500 families who had resided in Springtown Camp, just two remained. Both families, to their credit, steadfastly refused to be re-housed miles out in the country, and rightly so. They had been living in the camp since 1947 and most of their children had been born there also. Even though they were on their own, they unflinchingly stood their ground. They demanded to be re-housed in Derry, and after a prolonged struggle with the Corporation, both families were eventually re-housed in the city.

In the eyes of honest men, the Corporation and the Rural District Council were devoid of any courageous or moral leadership. They were, in essence, prisoners to their own bigoted thinking and their every action was controlled by this mindset. Disliked by many and remembered by few, it obviously never occurred to them – or if it did, they were not too worried – that their deeds would be judged by future generations of this city and that history may not judge them too kindly.

On Wednesday 11 October 1967, the Bee Gees hit the No 1 spot with their massive hit song *Massachusetts*. It was just a normal day in Derry, and life went on as usual in every work place and school in the city.

However, for the men, women and children who lived and were born and reared in Springtown since that very first day when the first squatter moved in on Thursday 22 August 1946, this day had great significance. It was to be the day that the place of their birth and childhood days would no longer exist.

Kitty Lynch, who epitomised the mothers of Springtown, after a titanic struggle with the powers-that-be, was on her way with husband Eddie and family to a house in Creggan Street. Her daughter Frances with her twins, George and Margaret, her Aunt Sarah, Uncle Charlie, and sister Mary, were on their way on the same day to a house in Pitt Street.

It had been twenty-one years, one month and twenty-one days, thousands of births, scores of marriages, poverty, frustration, sadness, but most of all, as far as we, the children of Springtown Camp were concerned, years of childhood innocence and happiness.

Kitty Lynch switched the lights out in her hut for the last time, closed the door behind her and walked away.

The story of Springtown Camp had ended.

***

Chapter 21

After the Camp

The still fleet-of-foot Mick Power was to continue to work well into his sixty-eighth year; he didn't retire from his duties until 3 November 1967, a few weeks after the camp closed.

The Corporation's housing manager, Dennis Arthur Murphy, resigned from his post a few weeks later on 31 December 1967.

The discredited Corporation was disbanded in April 1969. It was replaced by the Derry Development Commission, a move that was welcomed by the vast majority of Derry people.

We were eventually re-housed in Osborne Street in Rosemount. Our whole family were particularly happy to be located there because five other Springtown families were already living there. They were the Andersons, Callaghans, Flemings, Moores and McConnells. The Wilkinsons, McLaughlins and Dohertys were housed in nearby Westway and the Lynch family were housed in Creggan Road. So we were surrounded by old neighbours and friends.

Springtown Camp's popular manager and rent man Bob Hutchman (right) at a presentation to mark his retirement in 1967.

There was great excitement when we got the letter confirming we were to be housed in Osborne Street. At last, we were in a house of our own. Of course, we were grateful to my Uncle Johnny and his son John for accommodating us, but we were still glad to be in our own house. We set about the task of painting and decorating it and getting acquainted with our new neighbours. The excitement of moving into a new home was short lived as my mother died suddenly a few short months later. She didn't get much time to enjoy her new surroundings.

Heartbreak And Sadness

Sadness and heartbreak were to follow for some former Springtown families. On Britain's day of shame, Sunday 30 January 1972, at a civil rights march from Creggan to the Bogside, thirteen innocent men were gunned down on the streets of Derry by British Paratroopers. A further man died of his injuries a few weeks later. Dozens of other innocent people were also injured that day.

Four of the teenage boys who were killed on that day had close ties with Springtown. Three of them had been born in the camp, and one of them was born in Creggan a couple of years after his family left the camp. They were Jackie Duddy, Hugh Gilmore, John Young and William Nash. Alex Nash, father of William, also shot and injured, had lived with his wife and family for several years in the camp.

Michael Bridge, a well-known Springtown man, was shot and badly wounded on that fateful Sunday.

The search for justice goes on to this day.

In December 1972, Springtown Camp man Frank Doherty was one of five men murdered by loyalists as they sat watching a football match in Annie's Bar in the Top of the Hill, Gobnascale.

Michael Devine, who was born in the camp, died after sixty days on hunger strike in Long Kesh.

Christopher Hegarty, born and reared in Springtown, was shot during Operation Motorman, the British Army drive to remove the barricades surrounding the No Go areas. The search for justice for Christopher also goes on.

Thomas Friel was shot dead by the British Army; he was also born in Springtown.

Neil McMonagle was shot dead by undercover SAS men at Carnhill; his family had lived in Springtown for years before moving to Creggan.

A book could be written about any of these young men; however, it would take a much more talented writer than me to do them justice.

Jackie Duddy's family lived at 216 Springtown Camp.

Hugh Gilmore, born at 16 Springtown Camp.

John Young, born at 190 Springtown Camp.

William Nash, born at 98l Springtown Camp.

Alex Nash lived at 98l Springtown Camp.

Mickey Bridge lived at 54 Springtown Camp.

Christopher Hegarty, born at 98h Springtown Camp.

Thomas Friel, born at 230 Springtown Camp.

Neil McMonagle's family lived at 11 Springtown Camp.

Frank Doherty lived at 156 Springtown Camp.

254

Mickey Devine

Hut 63 Springtown Camp had been the home of Patrick and Elizabeth Devine since they'd moved from Ardmore, where they'd lived with Elizabeth's mother. They had one daughter, Margaret. On Wednesday 26 May 1954, their hut was filled with laughter, joy and happiness when their only son, Michael, was born. Michael, or Mickey as he was known to his childhood friends in the camp, enjoyed all the usual Cowboys and Indians games and was a happy-go-lucky child. When he reached the age of five, he was sent to St Patrick's Primary School, Pennyburn, but stayed only one year there as in 1960 his family got re-housed in Circular Road, Creggan.

Mickey Devine.

With the Troubles now raging all over the North, the British Army shot dead two unarmed civilians on the streets of Derry. This led to many young men joining the republican movements; Mickey was one of them. He was arrested on Monday 20 September 1976 when he was stopped in a car on Central Drive, Creggan, and later charged, convicted and sent to the H-Blocks in Long Kesh.

It was a very tough time to be in prison, as the prisoners were refusing to wear prison clothes and had only a blanket wrapped around them in their cells. This protest was to escalate to a hunger strike.

On 1 March 1981, Bobby Sands refused breakfast; Mickey joined the strike on 22 June.

Sands died on 5 May 1981 after sixty-six days on hunger strike, aged twenty-seven. These were Ireland's darkest days, with Francis Hughes, Raymond McCreesh, Derryman Patsy O'Hara, Joe McDonnell, Martin Hurson, Kevin Lynch, Tom McElwee and Kieran Doherty all dying on hunger strike.

Michael Devine, a quiet, inoffensive lad, died on Thursday 20 August 1981 after sixty days on hunger strike, aged twenty-seven. Mickey was the last of ten hunger strikers to die.

Lornie McMonagle

When meeting ex-campers in Derry on holiday from their homes throughout the world, I found they had interesting stories to tell, as some had travelled extensively while others had chosen to just settle somewhere in England, Scotland or the USA. It was, of course, nice to listen to them recalling their experiences since leaving the camp.

However, it's fair to say none could match the story of stay-at-home ex-camper Lornie McMonagle. In fact, Hollywood's finest script writers couldn't have come up with an amazing story like his.

Lornie McMonagle.

Born in Belmont Camp, he was a nephew of Uncle McLaughlin's, his mother Mona being Neil's sister. Lornie, a charismatic man, was a keen boxer in his younger days in Springtown; later on, he was to follow in his father's footsteps as a devoted greyhound man. He worked mostly as a docker at the quay throughout his early years. It was while playing a game of snooker that he suddenly became ill and was taken to hospital as a precaution. To everyone's surprise, it was diagnosed as a heart attack. After ten days in hospital, Lornie returned home, made a good recovery and carried on his life as normal.

Several years later, he became ill once more and it was confirmed that he had suffered another heart attack. He battled on and made light of his ill health, saying, 'Sure, there are people worse off than me.'

As he lay in Altnagelvin Hospital, his condition didn't improve; in fact his heart was to grow weaker. He was later moved to the City Hospital in Belfast. Lornie, who by now had been in hospital for three months, was told the dreadful news that there was little or nothing the doctors could do for him. They confirmed what Lornie had been thinking: he needed a heart transplant and needed one soon. As he lay in his hospital bed, his life ebbing away, Lornie never gave up hope. After consultations with the doctors, his family, who were constantly at his bedside, feared the worst. What was to happen next was to make news all over Ireland and Britain.

With Lornie now dangerously ill, he received more very bad news when told his young nephew, Mark Robinson, was critically ill and on a life-support machine in the nearby Royal Victoria Hospital after being brutally beaten by a group of men in the Collon Lane area.

The next day, Lornie was told the tragic news that Mark was brain dead and there was no alternative but to turn off his life-support machine.

The doctors visited him and told him that Mark's heart could be a match for him. Lornie was naturally feeling very bad about young Mark's death and told the doctors he wanted to speak to his family in private. The doctors left the room and his family gathered around his bed. His family told Lornie his sister Marian and her husband Jim would dearly love him to have Mark's heart, as then something good would come out of young Mark's death. This was an unbelievable, heart-wrenching, sad time for the entire family circle. Marian had to watch her young son lose his fight for life, while at the same time her brother lay gravely ill across the city in another hospital. Unbelievable suffering for any mother to endure. The heartfelt sympathy of the Derry people went out to her at that time.

Within a matter of hours, the family were told the news: tests confirmed young Mark's heart was a perfect match for Lornie. The wheels were immediately set in motion and Lornie was within hours on his way by air ambulance to the world-renowned Freeman's Hospital in Newcastle, England.

Lornie takes up the story. 'I remember being wheeled through the doors of Freeman's Hospital. The next thing I can remember was waking up in hospital, the operation over and me with a new heart. The next few weeks I was asleep most of the time, but gradually I began to get stronger and soon I was walking, albeit gingerly. It was a great day when I was transferred back home, a new man. I think about Mark each and every day, and will do so for the rest of my life.'

Lornie made a fantastic recovery and lives life to the full. He often recalls the day young Mark Robinson came to visit him in hospital. On his way out, Mark grabbed a handful of donor cards from the ward and signed a card himself and gave the rest to his mates, who in turn signed them and posted them off.

While in Freeman's Hospital, another amazing thing happened. Beside Lornie in the next bed lay an unknown gentleman. It later transpired the unknown gentleman had just received the most precious gift of all, the gift of life, from Lornie's young nephew Mark Robinson, as he had been the recipient of Mark's lungs.

This grateful gentleman and his family wrote to Marian and Jim Robinson and relayed to them their heartfelt gratitude.

Lornie and Marian's mother, Mona, was a quiet, unassuming woman and was a golden nugget regarding information about Belmont Camp. She told me, word for word, what actually happened during the short history of the camp at Belmont and the evictions that took place there.

After listening to Mona, I delved into the story of the camp in Belmont and it soon became clear to me that Mona's recollections of events there were spot on and her account of the happenings at Belmont Camp was a major source of information to me.

Mona, husband Charlie and their children were evicted from Belmont along with the other residents and they moved immediately to the camp at Springtown in May 1947.

Fr James Clerkin was one of the best-known priests in Pennyburn Church, which served the complete Pennyburn parish of which Springtown Camp was a part, and was a frequent visitor to the camp, calling on many families there. Father Clerkin had this to say a few years after the camp was finally cleared.

'I was associated with Springtown Camp as a curate; my first impression of the camp was it was something that one would not have seen in many parishes in the country. Even though the conditions were dreadful, I found the people very patient with their lot. They had a very happy and close relationship with their priests and as the camp housed over nine hundred people, we were constant visitors there.

'I found the huts were mainly neat and clean, although some huts were of better quality than others, and it has to be said that some huts were better looked after than others. The children were a very happy bunch and the people as a whole lived as a happy community, this mainly being because they were all in the same position and had the same social standing. This was the principal factor in creating the type of community spirit that was evident in Springtown. The entire population of the camp looked forward to the day when they would be housed. Some people were genuinely sorry at leaving the camp and the close-knit spirit that was there. I would say the vast majority were glad to get a new, modern house.'

To the question of whether the community in Springtown was a better community than the one in which we now live, I would have to say no, simply because they lacked so many basic amenities in the huts. There were no recreational facilities, but there was peace and a general lack of trouble of any kind, and in that sense, it was a happy community for the residents to live in.

The people regarded Springtown as just another part of the parish, although they were, I suppose, cut off from the rest of the parish and a bit isolated. I don't think the people outside adopted a prejudiced attitude towards the people of the camp because of who they were, but perhaps more because of what the camp stood for. In general, the people I am in contact with now, who lived in the camp, liked their time there. They still have many a laugh about some of the things that happened there.

However, I wouldn't think that if by some sort of magic wand the camp could be set up again there would be too many people who would want to go back there and live in it.

Reunion Dances And Play

Every once in a while as we listen to a song or tune played on the wireless or television, or we hear someone just whistling or singing a few bars of a melody, it instantaneously reminds us of some one, some place or some thing. For instance, every time I hear Petula Clark singing *Sailor*, it reminds me of my time in Springtown Camp. At times, I try to fathom why. Maybe, I thought to myself, that was the era in which sailors docked with their ships at Derry Quay. The dancehalls and bars were frequented by many sailors and they were a big hit with the local girls, much to the annoyance of some local boys, who were jealous of their smart uniforms and 'exotic' accents; this led to many a fight between the sailors and the local 'James Deans'. Plus, the sight of a sailor in uniform walking through the camp with a girl would stand out in a young boy's mind.

My first recollection of our wee wireless in the camp was when I was playing with a toy bus on our range and listening to Guy Mitchell singing *She Wore Red Feathers*; that is as far back as I can remember. It was while I was at work and we were listening to Seán Coyle on the wireless. He played both those songs back to back. Hearing the songs again started me thinking about the camp and all the people who lived there.

That night, I met Willie Edgar and told him I was thinking of holding a Springtown Camp reunion dance, as it would be nice to see all the old ex-campers again. He agreed it was a good idea. So with this encouragement, I decided to go and talk to Raymond Rogan, the manager of the Stardust (St Eugene's Parish Hall). He told me the hall was available, so I booked it there and then.

I called on Willie Edgar, Jackie McConnell, John McLaughlin, Stevie Wilkinson and Uncle McLaughlin. All agreed to help me organise the re-union. The first reunion dances coincided with the twentieth anniversary of the camp's closure. They were a fantastic success, with ex-campers coming from every part of Europe to reminisce about days gone by. The first reunion was held on Saturday 27 January 1986; the last to leave the hall that night was Snooker Cullen and Yours Truly. I glanced at my watch; it was 4.05 am. Other reunions followed and all were sold out and enjoyed by everyone.

Marley Deery (née Bridge), Mary McLaughlin (née Divin), Tina Smith, Maureen Lynch, Betty Smith and Kay Fleming (née Bridge) in jovial mood at the Springtown Camp reunion dance in the Stardust, 1987.

Anthony McGowan and Andy Doherty, who travelled from Bradford for the first reunion in 1986.

The King lives on . . . Stanley 'Elvis' Colby strutting his stuff on stage.

Large group of Springtowners pictured in the Stardust at the reunion dance in 1987. Included: Sandy McDermott, Stanley 'Elvis' Colby, Don Duffy, Rosie Jennings, Stevie Wilkinson, Willie Campbell, Patricia Moore, Willie Deery, Margaret Fleming, Mary McLaughlin, Lily Jennings, Hughie Harkin, Mary 'the Hen' Doherty, 'Snooker' Cullen, Frances Lynch, Seamus Fleming, Kay Fleming, Marley Deery, Pearse Deery and Liam Fleming.

A packed Stardust bursting at the seams with hundreds of happy campers all enjoying the reunion dance in 1988. Included: Charlie Smith, Maureen Lynch, Seamus Fleming, Kay Fleming, Mary Edgar, Raymond Holden, Vera Holden, Tina Smith, 'Junior' O'Rourke, Willie Deery, Sammy Porter, Jim Boyle, Bridget Boyle (née Jennings), Peter Divin, Neilly Divin, Sammy Holden, Mary Holden, Jackie McConnell and Paddy Deery.

The Divin, McLaughlin, Colby and Moore families enjoying the craic at the Springtown reunion dance in the Stardust, 1986. Included: Peter Divin, James Moore (all the way from Dundee), Stanley Colby, Johnny Divin, Jim Delaney, Neil Divin, John McLaughlin, Willie Divin, Betty Divin and Mary McLaughlin, with Colm Wilkinson in background. Also in background is Jack McLaughlin in deep conversation with Willie Deery.

Fifteen years after the last reunion, I met John McLaughlin in McBride's bookmaker's office. 'Do you know what I think would be good?' he said to me.

'What?' I asked.

'If we had a play about the camp.'

I looked at him and said, 'Okay, let's do it.'

The play opened at the Millennium Theatre on 23 January 2007 and was a great success. Both nights had packed houses, and the young cast received a standing ovation for their performances.

A second play was a must now, so it opened at the same theatre on 20 February 2008. Again the play went down very well to a very appreciative packed theatre; the cast received loud and sustained applause.

Frances Lynch with Rachel McGinley, one of the actresses in the Springtown Camp play, 2007.

Hugo McConnell, a well-known camper, was one of the actors in the play. Hugo was such a hit that he later was successful in getting major parts in nationally acclaimed plays.

Brendie 'Smilie' Wilkinson, who played the part of Tipperary, brought the house down and he had the audiences in stitches of laughter on all four nights. He was a revelation.

Stevie Wilkinson came over to me at the end of the first play and said, 'Willie, it was uncanny. I thought I was sitting in our living room in the camp tonight. You all got it perfect, the stage was brilliant.'

I personally was very pleased at all the positive reaction we got from the people of the camp about the set on stage, as I know how much effort Sean, my son, put into getting it right.

***

Hugo McConnell and Sadie Campbell, the oldest living resident of Springtown Camp, meet President Mary McAleese at the Guildhall in Derry, 2009.

Springtown Camp Website

Hugo McConnell had the foresight and the knowledge to set up the magnificent website www.springtowncamp.com. It is probably the first of its kind in Ireland and gives great pleasure to ex-campers throughout the world. At the press of a button, you can see hundreds of photographs of former residents of Springtown and the camp is brought back to life instantly. I personally know how much effort and money Hugo invested in this project. People who would never have dreamt of going on a computer do so now to see the Springtown site. The site was designed to keep the Springtown Camp story alive for generations to come. It will be a wonderful research source for future grandchildren and great-grandchildren whose relatives came from the camp. People from all over the world have visited the site; exiles from Derry who never lived in the camp enjoy it also, as they remember people who had lived there.

The children of Springtown are spread all over the globe but now can keep in contact through this website. People who lived in the camp in bygone days, folk like the Clingans, now living in Ohio, USA, the Dunnes in Manchester and Liverpool, McNairs in Quebec, Canada, Lynches in Melbourne, Australia, Divins and Moores in Dundee, Scotland, Shields in New Zealand, McGinleys in Dublin, Rankins in London, Kellys, Dohertys, Scanlons, Burkes, Cannings, Greens, Moores in Bradford . . . the list is endless.

As the years roll on and younger generations emerge, they will, of course, be more conversant with computer technology. Using the web will be like reading a newspaper to past generations. To these future generations, the story of Springtown Camp and its people will be there for all to see, simply by pressing a few keys on their laptop. Then websites like our own will be more commonly used, not only by people at home, but by everyone around the globe.

So take a look at our past and visit **www.springtowncamp.com**.

Hundreds of ex-campers, especially the children of Springtown, have always talked and reminisced about growing up in the camp and I am sure their children and grandchildren have heard their stories of the camp a hundred times or more, me being no exception.

I'd often told my children about the promise I made to my mother all those years ago as a boy growing up in Springtown to one day visit the places made famous in the cowboy shows on television and in the movies.

So on a cold January night in 2003, and with much encouragement from my family, I told myself it was time I kept that promise. There and then, I grabbed my laptop and started planning my boyhood dream trip.

The day came on a sunny July morning in 2003 when I boarded a plane at Derry airport for Dublin on the first leg of my long journey. There, I caught a plane bound for Chicago, USA, where I stayed for two nights before flying on to Rapid City in South Dakota. On arrival at Rapid City, I hired an open-top car and drove the thirty or so miles to my hotel in Deadwood, home of Wild Bill Hickok and Calamity Jane. While visiting their graves and saying a wee prayer at their graveside, my mind slipped back to the camp and the day I went to see the film *Calamity Jane*. I also saw the famous Deadwood Stage and toured the Black Hills of Dakota. *What a beautiful 'Indian Country'*, I thought, as I stood on top of the Black Hills looking down on Deadwood.

Five days later, I drove through Sundance in Wyoming and on to Montana to the Little Bighorn mountains, where the most famous of US Cavalry generals, George Armstrong Custer, met his fate at the hands of Sioux and Cheyenne warriors.

On my way back to Wyoming, I stopped at a Sioux reservation, where there was a small shopping mall selling genuine Sioux handmade items. I bought my new-born grandson, Ethan, a pair of soft moccasin shoes as a souvenir of my trip. Then it was on to Laramie and a visit to the place where the Laramie stagecoach arrived and departed. Next stop was Cheyenne, just forty miles away; I didn't see Cheyenne Bodie, but the very name of the place held fond and romantic memories for me.

I crossed the Mississippi and Missouri rivers, took in El Paso and drove through the Texas Plains before boarding a plane bound for Phoenix, Arizona. From there, I journeyed to and crossed the Rio Grande and over the Mexican border. Then it was on to my top 'dream place' – Tombstone, Arizona, which was now close by. This was where the gunfight at the OK Corral took place: Wyatt Earp, his brothers and Doc Holliday against the Clanton brothers way back on 26 October 1881. Then I took in the sights around Tombstone, which, I was told, were unchanged since that famous shoot out and are still to this day maintained as a major tourist attraction.

The promise I made to my mother as a boy in our wee hut in Springtown Camp many years ago was fulfilled in totality on that hot August day in 2003 – standing on the exact spot where the most famous gunfight in Wild West history took place. My thoughts slipped back to that cold Friday night in November 1962 when five innocent young boys from the camp were sitting in the flicks, chewing our halfpenny chews and dainties, watching this gunfight on the big screen in the pictures.

Great though it was, standing on that famous spot, I was thinking, *big Uncle McLaughlin was right.* It was nothing compared to the pure excitement and craic of big Uncle, Paddy Banty Doherty, Maggie Kelly, Tipperary, Gander Scanlon, Mary B Kelly, Jock Brennan, Jimmy Deery, Rosie and Danny Sweeney and the rest of the characters on the 10.40 to Springtown Camp.

No Room at the Camp

> 6238
> Walkers Place
> Londonderry
> N.9.
> 18 3 55
>
> Dear Mr Murphy
> I am writing to ask you if you will give me a Hut in Springtown as there is one empty as I am in a awful Fix my Husband cont get on with my mother so he has left the house and my Husband is not living me this last 4 weeks so my Husband me we would be better with Place off our own my File no is 6238 I hope you will give me a Hut as I would be very thankful to you
> from Mrs
> Walkers Place
> Londonderry

23rd March, 1955.

Walker's Place,
LONDONDERRY.
Ref. HA/6238.

Dear Madam,

    I have your letter of 18th instant and have to inform you that it is not the policy of the Corporation to re-let huts becoming vacant at Springtown Camp.

Yours faithfully,

[signature]

HOUSING MANAGER.   DASM/JC.

Appendix A
Springtown Camp Milestones

July 1941
American 'civilian workers' moved heavy machinery and plant onto a green-field site 200 yards past the city boundary on the Northland Road. They began to build roads, sewers, and hutments. The site was heavily guarded during construction.

December 1941
Hundreds of huts were now completed with roads throughout the camp. The camp was surrounded by an 8ft-high fence. Canteen cooking facilities were installed; beds, lockers and other furniture were moved into the huts. The compound was now known as Springtown Camp.

Sunday 18 January 1942
First group of US Naval personnel from Headquarters and Service Company under Major James J Dugan, and B Company under Captain Frank A Martincheck, moved into Springtown Camp. The camp was guarded round the clock by US Marines.

Friday 18 August 1944
All US personnel left Springtown Camp with the exception of the radiomen, who continued their duties there.

Monday 12 November 1945
The naval base at Springtown Camp was disbanded and the radiomen vacated the huts. The camp was closed and the gates locked.

Wednesday 21 August 1946
Adam Smith and four families from Limewood Street decided they'd had enough of living cooped up in one-bedroom homes with as many as fifteen people using one outside toilet. They squatted into huts at Bligh's Lane Camp.

Thursday 22 August 1946
The first squatters moved into Springtown Camp. Three days later, over 100 huts were occupied in Springtown.

Sunday 25 August 1946
Hundreds of spectators lined the roads leading to both entrances to the camp, watching as families moved their belongings by van, horse-drawn carts or push carts on their way to the camp, most of the families flitting from run-down, overcrowded tenement buildings in the city. The spectators were of such vast numbers that they blocked roads and traffic came to a standstill.

September 1946
By now, the unionist-controlled Corporation knew they had a major problem on their hands. If at first they thought this would peter out and the families would return to their former homes, they knew otherwise now. The long-suffering families of Derry had made their move, deciding they had had enough and were not going to live in squalor any longer. A total of five camps which had been used to billet US military personnel were taken over by squatters. Despite the fact that the huts were without electricity, running water or toilet facilities, they were still regarded as much better than the conditions they had previously been living in. The numbers of families from the city who took possession of War Department camps and other huts situated mostly outside the city boundary on that date were as follows:

1. Springtown: 101 families representing 454 persons
2. Clooney: 24 families representing 102 persons
3. Belmont: 40 families representing 191 persons
4. Bishop Street: 3 families representing 17 persons
5. Bligh's Lane: 6 families representing 29 persons
TOTAL: 174 families representing 793 persons.

In addition, some outlaying camps, like Mabuoy, had also been taken over.
The Ministry of Health and Local Government instructed the Corporation to take action in regards to the camps as follows:

Springtown Camp. Water supply to be turned on; also to request the naval officer-in-charge to permit the electricity supply to continue. Make arrangements to clear at regular intervals the sewerage. That a charge of 5s 0d (25p) per week per hut be levied on the occupants of Springtown Camp from 30 September 1946 for water, scavenging and sanitation.

Letter received from naval officer-in-charge, RN Barracks, Derry, conveying approval for the continuation of electricity supply to the above camp, subject to the Corporation maintaining the overheads from the Navy Yard Transformer to the camp. The Corporation also to pay a proportion of the Navy Yard supply costs.

Clooney Camp. Water to be turned on, refuse bins to be supplied. To connect the electricity after the occupants have lodged a deposit.

Belmont Camp. Water to be turned on, make sure the sewer which occupants are using is clear. Apply for electricity to be switched on.

Bishop Street. Turn on water supply.

Bligh's Lane. Water to be turned on, refuse bins to be supplied and electricity supplied on payment of deposit.

2 September 1946
Work to convert the huts at Springtown began; 150 huts were now occupied and work started on the other 152 vacant huts. When these were completed, the families moved into the converted huts and the remaining huts were converted. The Ministry of Health and Local Government met the bill for the conversions. When this work was completed, there were a total of 302 huts in the camp, housing over 2,000 people. The speed at which the Stormont Government and the Corporation moved on the issue of converting the huts at Springtown suggested it was to ease their considerable embarrassment on their poor housing performance in Derry rather than a desire to help the beleaguered people.

17 September 1946
The Ministry of Health and Local Government offered the Corporation ownership of Belmont Camp. The Corporation declined. Springtown residents elected a committee to look after the interests of the squatters. Samuel Quigley was elected chairman.

26 September 1946
A meeting of all the camps' representatives was held at Springtown; Sammy Quigley chaired the meeting. Also in attendance was Councillor Paddy Fox, Derry Labour Party. Discussions included the levy of 5s 0d (25p) put on every hut. Belmont Camp residents received a summons from the War Department to quit the camp.

9 October 1946
Belmont Camp residents appeared in court and were fined 1s 0d (5p) for squatting into huts there and had eviction notices served on them. The judge remarked: 'I gather this camp was lying idle for almost two years while people of this city were dying from TB, diphtheria and other diseases due to overcrowding.' He concluded: 'Why the sudden urgency now by the War Department?'

2 December 1946
Margaret Mary Doherty became the first baby born in the camp and was baptised in St Patrick's Church, Pennyburn.

1 May 1947
A resolution passed by the education committee urging the transport committee of the Corporation to use all influence to secure an adequate and effective bus service to enable the children to be conveyed from Springtown Camp to the city was submitted. The Corporation left the matter in the hands of the mayor and GS Madden, NIRTB (Northern Ireland Road Transport Board), to look into and see what effective steps could be taken.

Monday 12 May 1947
After months of negotiations failed to resolve any of the issues, bailiffs arrived at Belmont Camp with British soldiers and four RUC policemen in tow. The first families of Belmont Camp were evicted shortly after 10.00 am after bailiffs moved their furniture and the rest of their belongings onto the street. British soldiers were on the roofs of the huts within seconds and began to demolish them at speed. They dismantled the gables first, rendering the huts useless in minutes; not a normal soldier's duty, but they carried out the task with some relish.

The RUC, who were there to protect the bailiffs, looked on but refused to assist them in their work. All other camps were soon to face the same fate. Ninety-nine per cent of the families at Belmont Camp and the families in the other camps were housed at Springtown.

July 1948
Ulster Transport Authority (UTA) agreed to run a limited bus service to the camp after representation from the Springtown committee. The route proved a major success and soon a full service was in operation. The children of the camp now had a bus to take them to the city to attend various schools there. The families settled into the camp and were happy with their lot in their newly converted huts.

7 January 1952
The huts started to show signs of serious dampness and condensation. The housing architect inspected them and reported back to the Corporation. He recommended that alterations be carried out on the huts and they be treated for dampness. He also said many huts needed immediate work to improve conditions if the Corporation intended occupation to continue. He submitted plans showing the huts affected with condensation and dampness.

The Corporation responded to his report by instructing that all future vacant huts be sold. They instructed their town clerk to invite the Ministry of Health and Local Government to discuss with them the future policy regarding the camp. They declined to take any action on the architect's recommendations.

21 January 1952
The mayor and Corporation met with Ronald Green and JL Donaldson, Ministry of Health and Local Government. They discussed with the Ministry officials the various

matters regarding Springtown. Ministry of Health officials intimated that closure of Springtown should now be considered. The mayor requested the decision be deferred pending consideration of a financial scheme whereby the Corporation might acquire and manage the property for a further temporary period.

1 May 1953
Housing manager DAS Murphy reported that huts which had been vacant and scheduled for demolition had been unlawfully occupied. He was instructed by the mayor and the sub-committee to negotiate completion of a licence agreement with the families concerned. The mayor also instructed Murphy to discontinue the demolition of huts until such times as families were not prepared to reside in them.

8 July 1953
The Derry to Buncrana train ceased to operate when the Londonderry and Lough Swilly Railway, which incorporated the Pennyburn crossing, closed its railway stations in Derry. The railway operated three different single-class fares of 2s 0d (10p), 1s 3d (6p) and 10d (4p). The railway had been in existence since 1863.

16 July 1953
Margaret Hasson of 139 Springtown Camp, through her solicitor Claude Wilton, sought permission to open a shop in the camp. The Corporation refused her request but suggested they would let her a site to erect a temporary shop. They also refused permission to the cleansing department, who wished to garage a tractor in one of the vacant huts.

Councillor James Doherty was asked by some residents to seek a meeting with the mayor. The people of the camp selected a five-man deputation to represent them. Councillor Doherty informed the mayor and his committee that he understood the deputation were requesting assurance that the proposed renovation scheme would not delay transfer to permanent houses of genuine housing applicants in Springtown. They refused to meet with the deputation but assured them that they intended to allocate 10% of all houses that became available to 'genuine' residents of the camp.

23 July 1953
Housing manager Murphy reported that huts 71 and 135 had been entered and were unlawfully occupied. The mayor and his committee instructed him to institute legal proceedings against the families to have them evicted. A month later, they decided to desist from this action and instead instructed Murphy to give legal occupancy to the two families concerned.

24 September 1953
The roads in the camp were starting to cause concern to all residents and many children were cut and bruised on them. They were potholed and large chunks of stone were a hazard and difficult to walk on. The Corporation once again were reluctant

to spend any money on the camp and demanded that the Rural Council pay for the upkeep of the roads there. The Rural Council refused to pay. Margaret Hasson wasn't taking no for an answer and was back again with her solicitor Claude Wilton, only this time she had plans drawn up herself for a new temporary shop in the camp. This time, she forced the Corporation's hand and they said they would send out their own architect to draw up their own set of plans for the shop. She returned to the camp, confident that they would have no legal reason to deny her this time.

Meanwhile, the Corporation contacted The Honourable the Irish Society, the owners of the land at Springtown. The Corporation requested a meeting with them in London to discuss the purchase of the camp. The mayor and his senior officials offered to travel to London to facilitate the meeting. The meeting was agreed and pencilled in for 6 October 1953. The mayor, the town clerk and two unionist aldermen travelled to London for the meeting.

20 October 1953
Report of the conference between representatives of The Honourable the Irish Society and of the Corporation regarding the proposed purchase of lands at Springtown was discussed. The report intimated that the society representatives had stated that they could not recommend a figure lower that £150 per acre for a plot measuring 31 acres, 1 rood and 32 perches, while on the other hand, the Corporation representatives declared that they could not recommend a price in excess of £130 per acre. The housing architect suggested it would be possible to build permanent houses on the Springtown site. He was of the opinion that eighteen acres could be earmarked for such development. The plans of the architect were forwarded to The Honourable the Irish Society for their comments. The Corporation continued to haggle over the price wanted by the Society for the purchase of the camp.

27 November 1953
Margaret Hasson's official application for a temporary shop in the camp had set the cat among the pigeons. It was the first official application ever made by anyone in the camp, and as it was conveyed through her solicitor Claude Wilton, the Corporation had to be careful how they managed this application. Mrs Hasson was effectively playing the Corporation at their own game. The need for a shop at the camp had sound legal claims, which the Corporation had no legal grounds to deny. With their backs against the wall on this issue, they said they had no objections in principle to erecting a block of five temporary shops in the camp. They informed Mrs Hasson they would consult with their architect on the matter. All they were doing was delaying the inevitable.

22 January 1954
The majority of huts were now suffering from dampness and after a visit to the camp by the secretary of the County Borough health committee, he called on the Corporation to close the camp as soon as possible. The Corporation ignored his call, instead

informing him that they had instructed their architect to purchase anti-damp seculate paint and treat one hut, as an experiment. What they didn't tell the health inspector was that they ordered their architect not to exceed the value of £5 in this experiment. The experiment failed miserably, having no effect whatsoever. The architect again advised that the huts needed major renovations if they were to succeed in combating the damp and condensation problem. His advice brought no action from the Corporation.

8 February 1954
Back again came Margaret Hasson, with the help of her solicitor, determined not to let the Corporation off the hook. Claude Wilton told the Corporation Mrs Hasson was prepared to erect a temporary shop at the camp in accordance with the Corporation's architect's plans. The Corporation had no option but to agree to Mrs Hasson's application and finally gave her permission to have her shop. The rent would be charged at 3s 0d (15p) per foot frontage. With that, Mrs Hasson signed a legal tenancy agreement for her shop, becoming the first official shop in Springtown Camp.

That same day, the Corporation gave notice of their intention to keep the families in the camp for another few years, as James Doherty & Co, electrical firm, started work rewiring twelve huts in the camp at a cost of £158 14s 0d (£158.70).

8 July 1954
Some families were now starting to emigrate to England, Bradford in particular, and five huts became vacant. The Corporation let them stay vacant for a few weeks to see if any family would squat into them. With no takers this time, they ordered them to be sold by public auction. The farmers arrived with their men and lorries and proceeded to demolish the huts. They were re-erected days later in some remote fields and became shelters for their animals. This was to become the first of many auctions held in the camp.

27 July 1954
The saga of purchasing the camp was still ongoing with the Corporation meeting to consider the town clerk's report on negotiations with The Honourable the Irish Society. They finally agreed on a price of £4,000 and approved the purchase of the thirty-seven and a half acres at Springtown, subject, of course, to the approval of the Ministry of Health and Local Government. Finally, the Corporation became owners of the camp. However, the Irish Society was to make a condition to the sale. They demanded the Corporation would, with all speed, proceed to the clearance of the present unsuitable hutments upon the lands to be sold. This condition worried the Corporation and they decided to write to the Society to query it.

27 August 1954
The Corporation advertised in local newspapers and the *Belfast Telegraph* seeking tenders for the demolition of vacant huts when they became available. This advert

brought farmers, churchmen, and youth clubs from as far as Galway and Belfast, all seeking to buy a hut. The Ministry of Health and Local Government gave approval to the Corporation to purchase Springtown Camp for a sum not exceeding £4,000, full ownership to take effect from 1 January 1953. The Corporation also intimated they would be prepared to purchase the old disused railway line at the bottom of the camp from the Lough Swilly Railway Company.

4 November 1954
Minor repairs continued to be carried out with re-felting of the roofs of the wooden huts, which were leaking badly. The huts' numbers were 63a, 63b, 63c and 63d. The total cost of the works was £76 13s 4d (£76.67). Offers to buy vacant huts were rolling in with J Warnock & Sons, Maghera, RJ Stevenson, Portstewart and Spendlove Jebb, Belfast, all seeking to purchase units.

3 February 1955
Moving about in the camp in the dark nights was proving difficult for the people, as few lights were installed there and the ones that were had bulbs fused. The Corporation agreed to add another pole with lamps; to carry out this work, they needed to demolish two huts that were in the direct line of the wiring. They demolished huts 98n and 98o and instructed housing manager Murphy not to re-let vacant huts 98d, 110, 130, 152a and 160, which were vacant portions of double huts. He was further instructed to find alternative accommodation for the families in the adjoining portions so that demolition and removal could be carried out at the earliest opportunity.

The Corporation were doing the usual: giving with one hand and taking away with the other. They ordered the council's electricity department to downsize the 150-watt bulbs to 100 watts. In all, there were seventeen 150-watt bulbs in Springtown, an area of over twenty acres. With half of the bulbs either fused or broken, this left the camp a very dark place in the winter nights.

3 March 1955
No fewer than four families squatted into vacant huts in the camp. They received a letter threatening them with legal action within fourteen days if they did not vacate the huts. No such action was taken and the families got legal tenancies in due course.

5 April 1955
Mr Jackson from Springtown House, owner of the lovely orchard, was seeking financial help towards more fencing to block off his property. He was of the opinion the Corporation had responsibility to pay for the fence. The Corporation refused Mr Jackson any financial help towards a fence. That was probably the only decision the campers agreed with. They would have been seeking a walkway to the orchard, but I suppose that would have been refused also!

9 June 1955
The solicitor acting on behalf of The Honourable the Irish Society notified the Corporation that if they would not agree to enclosure of the lands in question from adjoining Society lands and undertake early removal of hutments at Springtown Camp, the Society were unwilling to proceed further with the matter. They also expressed concern that a report of the proceedings had appeared in the public press while the terms of an intended contract were still being considered. The Corporation decided that the mayor and chairman would go and discuss the position with representatives of the Society. Another six huts were sold by public auction and removed by farmers, leaving the usual mess behind them.

18 August 1955
Margaret Hasson's husband Alex approached the Corporation with a view to them letting him Hut 160, which was the adjoining hut beside his business. Alex wanted to garage his car in the hut. His request was refused. He decided to open a bookie's shop in his hut but this time didn't seek permission; it was to do a roaring trade.

5 September 1955
The roads were once again causing many problems; wheeling a baby in a pram was a major task. Bob Hutchman was consulted by several women on the subject and he said he would report it to his superiors. The county sanitary officer complained to the Corporation that four licensees at the camp were using their dwellings to sell foodstuffs. The Corporation, fearing a flood of applications from shop owners in the camp, declined to take any action.

6 October 1955
The saga of purchasing the camp continued, the sticking point being the condition that the huts should be closed soon. A report by the town clerk was submitted with a draft agreement of sale of Springtown Camp, which had been forwarded by PW Dickson, solicitor on behalf of The Honourable the Irish Society. In his report, the town clerk stated that neither he nor the city solicitors could advise the committee to accept the terms in their present form. The mayor and Councillor James Doherty were selected to negotiate.

3 November 1955
The roads in the camp were getting worse by the week and it was obvious to everyone that they required resurfacing and that extra gullies were necessary to alleviate flooding. The Corporation received an estimate that the work recommended would involve an outlay of approximately £2,300. The housing sub-committee authorised the city surveyor to execute limited repairs to the roads but not to exceed £300. The committee banned the UTA from using the roads inside the camp as a bus stop. They pledged to further reduce the number of huts in the camp by re-housing families as soon as houses became available.

5 January 1956
The committee were displeased when they found out that the city surveyor authorised the roads contractor to spend an additional £108 12s 8d (£108.63). In his defence, the city surveyor said to do the job properly he would have needed to spend £2,000. The committee approved the extra cost but stated that he was not permitted to proceed with any further repairs to the camp at present. The disused foot bridge at the bottom of the camp was now considered to be in a dangerous condition; some steel handrail bars were missing. The committee refused to demolish it, as they were not sure who the legal owners of the bridge were.

8 May 1956
A motion was put before the Corporation by Councillor James Doherty that the town clerk, city surveyor and housing manager be instructed to prepare a joint-report on the means of initiating the construction of 500 houses in the city, and in particular, the possibility of a comprehensive redevelopment of the Springtown Camp site. There were many people in the public gallery and the meeting was continually interrupted. There followed several attempts to proceed with the meeting, but the chairman proposed the meeting be adjourned; the proposal was passed with a show of hands.

31 May 1956
The Ministry of Health and Local Government wrote to the Corporation proposing that Springtown Camp be included under the Statutory Slum Clearance Scheme (SSCS). The Corporation complained that as Springtown was outside their boundary, there was no legal obligation for them to include the camp in the SSCS. The Ministry, while agreeing with the Corporation on a legal point, intimated that payment of a proposed higher rate of subsidy in respect of houses to accommodate persons displaced from Springtown would not be ruled out merely on the grounds that the area to be cleared lay outside the city boundary. That fact that the camp lay outside the city limits was now irrelevant, as the Northern Ireland Government were now prepared to allocate additional funds to house the camp residents. This carrot of additional money to house the residents was spurned by the Corporation.

4 February 1957
Vermin were now a serious problem in the camp; most huts were affected. The Corporation authorised the sum of £8 2s 7d (£8.13) for rodent control at the camp that month.

7 February 1957
The city accountant submitted a statement showing that £750 10s 2d (£750.51) was lodged to the accounts of the council as a result of the recent public auction of seventeen hutments and fourteen old ranges at the camp. The ranges made more than the huts.

1 March 1957
A letter dated 1 March 1957 from PW Dickson, solicitor for The Honourable the Irish Society, was submitted with a revised draft agreement relating to the purchase by the Corporation of certain lands at Springtown Camp. A report from the city solicitor to the town clerk dated 4 March 1957 was also submitted in which the city solicitor re-iterated his objection to the Corporation accepting certain restrictions by the Society. A report was also submitted by the housing manager intimating that he had examined the revised draft agreement and was satisfied that it complied with the expressed requirements of the committee. It was agreed that the committee approved the endorsement of the revised draft agreement. The city solicitor advised the Corporation against agreeing to the contract, but the Corporation decided to accept the contract in its present form. Springtown Camp was purchased for the sum of £4,000.

5 December 1957
It would seem the Corporation wanted the camp to survive. They again changed the goalposts and now decided that they would re-let vacant huts once more, citing the problem of finding homes for the homeless. These families, they said, would be glad to have temporary accommodation of any kind. They again instructed the housing manager to suspend forthwith the demolishing of vacant huts, and to once again let huts to families who wanted them.

9 January 1958
With the huts steadily deteriorating, the Corporation architect reported on the possibility of reconditioning a sample hut in the camp. The Corporation adjourned consideration of this idea pending further investigation.

6 February 1958
Homeless families occupied three huts: numbers 115, 177 and 196. William Cavanagh, who occupied Hut 115, left after a couple of days. The Corporation threatened legal action to recover the other two huts, which they considered uninhabitable. The residents of the camp from September 1946 had only signed licences for temporary occupancy and it was advised by solicitors for the Corporation that they should now be granted tenancies.

6 March 1958
Pursuant to the minutes of 9 January 1958, the housing architect reported on possible reconditioning of a sample hut. In this connection, the observation of the housing architect to the effect that many tenants had installed various types of flue pipes through the corrugated tin roofs, thus occasioning damage, was noted, and housing manager Murphy and camp supervisor Hutchman were directed to submit explanations. They both reported that the flue pipes were for additional heating by means of potbelly stoves in the main bedroom. They also said the huts were very cold and

damp and that this wasn't unreasonable, all things considered. There was no further mention of the potbelly stoves.

3 April 1958
The Honourable the Irish Society gave approval to the housing sub-committee to let huts for a period of twelve months, subject to each case first being referred to them.

1 May 1958
Derry's district traffic manager of the UTA requested that the Corporation allow them use of a small portion of road inside the camp for a bus terminal in the interest of safety. The Corporation refused their request on the grounds that they believed the buses would cause undue wear and tear to the roads in the camp.

The war of words between the Corporation and the Rural District Council reared its ugly head again. When the city architect once again reported that the huts were now in a very serious state of disrepair, it prompted a visit to the camp by the sanitary officer. They both suggested that because the huts were in such bad condition, the housing committee should now reconsider its policy of re-letting vacant huts in the camp. It was proposed by Alderman Glover and seconded by Councillor Cochrane that 'this committee decline to make any change in its present policy of re-letting the huts at Springtown Camp but direct that the Derry Rural District Council and the Northern Ireland Housing Trust be requested to accept a bigger share of the burden of re-housing existing tenants'.

The motion was carried, Councillor Doherty dissenting.

5 June 1958
Letters dated 19 May 1958 from the Northern Ireland Housing Trust and 16 May from the Derry Rural District Council were submitted regarding the Corporation's request for assistance in re-housing the camp's remaining families. The committee noted with regret that the Rural Council had decided to take no action regarding the problem, as it considered that the tenants were originally city dwellers. The committee directed the housing manager to prepare a list of the families remaining in the camp for submission to the next meeting.

3 July 1958
A split appeared between Corporation officers as a memo dated 24 June 1958 from the town clerk was submitted intimating that the council, having noted that the housing sub-committee had declined to make any changes in their policy of re-letting huts at Springtown Camp, again requested that the matter be given further consideration. Once again, the housing committee declined their request, stating:

1. The committee adheres to its earlier decision to re-let huts which may from time to time become available.

2. The committee notes a report by the housing manager giving particulars of census recently taken of the remaining 160 tenants of hutments at Springtown Camp.

10 December 1958
As only one hut was let in the past twelve months, the council requested the housing committee should once more reconsider its policy of re-letting huts at the camp. The committee said they retained the right to re-let huts if circumstances so dictated.

2 April 1959
Getting curved tin to repair damaged and rusted tin on the huts was proving difficult, so vacant Hut 154e was demolished and the corrugated tin was re-used for repairs to existing huts.

4 June 1959
Another report by housing manager Murphy was submitted regarding the state of deterioration of hutment corrugations and roads at the camp. This time, the committee agreed to authorise the repainting of corrugated-tin huts using bituminous paint, but again there was a sting in the tail as they declared all painting of the huts and other such works were to be carried out by the two labourers employed at the camp, namely Mick Power and Paddy Moore. The committee directed the housing architect to confer with the city surveyor and submit an estimate for road repairs to the camp.

3 September 1959
The committee notes the statement submitted by the city accountant dated 1 September 1959 showing the sale of three huts at Springtown had realised the sum of £97 less advertising expenses of £6 9s 0d (£6.45).

1 October 1959
Housing manager Murphy once again informed the committee that the deteriorating state of the huts at Springtown continued to give concern in spite of the patch repairs. He also stated that the repainting of the huts' exteriors continued but was extremely slow as the two workmen concerned also had other duties to perform in the camp. The committee agreed in view of the uncertain future of the huts not to engage additional painters.

During discussion of the several problems allied to the present conditions of the camp, the view was expressed that some action should be taken at an early date to improve at least the principal roads running through the camp. The housing architect was directed to bring before the committee a report on the desirability and estimated cost of making good the said road to a standard acceptable to the county surveyor, bearing in mind the possibility of attracting unemployment-relief grants.

The people of the camp realised that if they wanted to stop the rain from flooding their huts they would have to re-paint the tin with tar themselves. The Corporation agreed to supply the tar.

5 November 1959
The housing manager submitted a report intimating that on Saturday 31 October 1959, Hut 33b was destroyed by fire and that the occupants thereof, Hugh Doherty, his wife and five children together with his brother, his wife and child, were rendered homeless. The chairman informed the committee of a conference he had with the county welfare officer and housing manager regarding possible re-housing of tenant Hugh Doherty. The committee agreed to offer Hugh Doherty the tenancy of a house at Brandywell at the earliest possible date.

24 November 1959
The women of Springtown Camp protested about conditions in the camp. Twenty-five women packed the public gallery of Derry's Guildhall for the quarterly meeting of the Corporation; also in the public gallery with the women was MP Eddie McAteer. The meeting was adjourned. As a direct result of the protest, the housing committee's Alderman Glover visited the camp to see the conditions for himself the following week.

3 December 1959
The committee noted a report submitted by the city accountant intimating that payment of £130 had been received from insurers in respect of a hut at Springtown in a recent fire, and for damage caused to an adjoining hut. The committee noted also the housing manager's statement that the remains of the destroyed hut had been demolished and repairs carried out to the adjoining hut.

The chairman referred to the question of re-housing the families from the camp, which matter had been raised at the quarterly meeting of the council held on 24 November 1959 and at an adjourned meeting held on 1 December 1959. He intimated that he had inspected a number of huts on 2 December and had interviewed some of the residents who had been in attendance at the meeting referred to. After lengthy discussion of the problem, the following resolution was unanimously adopted:
Proposer – Alderman Glover
Seconder – Councillor McFarland

'That the first houses becoming available to the Corporation of the twenty-eight dwellings presently under construction at Coach Road be allocated exclusively to selected families of huts at Springtown Camp.'

The Corporation didn't keep their word on this, housing only ten families in the Coach Road development.

At the same meeting, they examined plans submitted by the housing architect showing possible redevelopment of the camp and heard from the city accountant, who tabled figures showing that estimates of rent of houses in the proposed Springtown scheme:

  2-bedroom-type houses: £1 12s 6d (£1.63) weekly, inclusive of rates
  3-bedroom-type houses: £1 16s 0d (£1.80) weekly, inclusive of rates
  4-bedroom-type houses: £2 7s 0d (£2.35) weekly, inclusive of rates
  5-bedroom-type houses: £2 13s 0d (£2.65) weekly, inclusive of rates

The committee decided not to proceed further with any scheme for the erection of houses at Springtown Camp at present.

3 March 1960
Letter dated 13 February 1960 from Mrs M Bond, leader of the Arellian Senior Youth Club, Belfast, was submitted asking if the Corporation would be prepared to sell a vacant hut at Springtown Camp. The committee noted that three vacant huts would be offered for sale by public auction on 16 March 1960 and directed Mrs Bond be so informed.

5 May 1960
The sale of huts continued as people emigrated or got housed, the Corporation noting a report from the city accountant intimating that the sale of huts 39, 114 and 154c by public auction on 16 March 1960 had realised a net sum of £56 4s 6d (£56.23).

3 June 1960
Housing manager Murphy and the city solicitor report the unauthorised occupation of Hut 58 by Mr and Mrs Pollard. The committee direct the city solicitor to take all possible steps to obtain from the court a warrant for possession of the hut.

8 July 1960
The housing manager reported that in response to an advertisement, only one offer had been received for the purchase of vacant huts at the camp; the committee declined to accept the said offer from James McCormack, 399 Carnanbane, Dungiven, amounting to £15 for one hut. The committee directed the housing manager to arrange for the vacant huts to be sold by public auction.

19 July 1960
Letter dated 28 June 1960 from PW Dickson, general agent for The Honourable the Irish Society, was submitted with reports therein from the town clerk. The town clerk in his report pointed out that the committee on 5 April 1955, following consideration of the city solicitor's report dated 19 March 1955, decided as follows:

'That the sum of £40 be offered to Londonderry and Lough Swilly Railway Company for the strip of land at Springtown Camp known as the disused railway track; the company to pay its own legal expenses.'

  PW Dickson in his letter referred to the above sought payment from the Corporation of a total sum of £95. The report further pointed out that the draft deed submitted by Dickson contained a number of covenants to be undertaken by the Corporation, and that bearing this in mind, together with his price asked for the strip of land, neither the town clerk nor the city solicitor could recommend acceptance of the draft deed. The committee agreed that the town clerk and the city solicitor should consult with Dickson and report regarding this matter.

1 September 1960
More huts are sold by public auction, the main attraction being the ranges in the huts. They were coming from every corner of Ireland to purchase the ranges. At this auction, fourteen huts and five ranges were sold; nine ranges had been sold separately at a previous auction.

6 October 1960
Housing manager Murphy submitted a report dated 29 September 1960 regarding a statement made by the spokeswoman for the deputation which occupied the public gallery at the council meeting on Tuesday 27 September 1960.

In his report, the housing manager stated that there were 134 families occupying huts as tenants in Springtown Camp; the majority of them sought better accommodation. It was also stated that the camp would present a problem until such time as more suitable accommodation was found for the camp residents, over those considered unsuitable as occupants of post-war council houses. The housing manager said about twenty-five of the 134 families in the camp could not be recommended for any of the post-war houses, and that if the Rural Council would fulfil its undertaking to re-house those families who were genuine rural residents, say, thirty-three, and the Housing Trust re-house, say, twenty-five families, fifty houses provided by the Corporation would go a long way towards solving the problem presented by the camp.

The housing manager recommended:

1. That a specific scheme of, say, fifty houses be considered by the committee and
2. That strong representation be made by the Corporation to both the Housing Trust and to the Rural Council to fulfil undertakings given some considerable time ago.

The committee agreed to defer consideration of the housing manager's recommendations to the next meeting.

25 October 1960
The protest by the camp's women paid off as the Corporation met with twelve women to discuss the re-housing of the remaining tenants at Springtown. Sadie Campbell was elected spokeswoman. She asked the Corporation to give assurances that early steps would be taken to find alternative accommodation for the remaining residents of the camp. Sadie also stated that only one street lamp was working in the entire camp and that considerable rubble remained on the sites of demolished huts. The

Corporation pledged to rectify the lighting in the camp speedily and instructed camp manager Hutchman to have the rubble cleared by the two workmen in the camp.

The committee declined housing manager Murphy's suggestion that fifty houses should be built at the camp. The housing manager also asked that strong representation be made to both the Housing Trust and the Rural Council to take radical steps to house some of the residents in the camp within a reasonable period. The committee agreed to do this.

3 November 1960
The following offer (the only one) was received in response to a public advertisement for purchase of vacant hut at Springtown Camp: PJ Brown, Glenona, Draperstown – £25. The committee agreed to accept the offer subject to the structure, including the brick walls, being demolished and removed from the site.

1 December 1960
The Corporation noted a report submitted by the city electrical engineer, which stated that lamps at the camp were damaged maliciously, practically every night, and that during the month of October, sixteen bulbs out of the thirteen lamps were smashed. It was his policy to keep as many lights as possible in operation.

Letter dated 9 November 1960 from the Northern Ireland Housing Trust and a letter dated 28 November 1960 from the Rural District Council were submitted relative to the re-housing of families from the camp. The Trust intimated that they had given the matter consideration for some considerable time and would continue to do so. In its letter, the Rural Council stated it was very mindful of its decision to endeavour to re-house families from the camp who were genuine rural residents. While difficulty was experienced in obtaining suitable sites for the re-housing of such families, the matter was presently being investigated with a view to re-housing of such families in the area in which they originally resided.

The committee directed the town clerk to thank the trust for its assistance to date, and request that further efforts be made to house more families as soon as possible.

The committee further directed that the Rural Council be informed of the committee's disappointment that as far as it could be traced, no Springtown Camp families had at any time been re-housed by the Rural Council and that the matter should be treated as one of great urgency. The Rural Council should bear its fair share of the burden of re-housing families from Springtown Camp.

5 January 1961
The committee approved a report dated 6 December 1960 submitted by the city accountant setting out particulars of prices realised from the sale of eleven huts at Springtown by public auction on 30 November 1960 totalling £320 after paying expenses, with the exception of the *Coleraine Constitution* account, for advertising.

Letter dated 13 December 1960 from the Rural District Council was submitted relative to re-housing families from the camp. It stated in the letter that every effort was being made to re-house, in the areas from which they originally came, genuine 'rural' families presently occupying huts at Springtown. It was further stated in the letter that negotiations were at present taking place for the purchase of a plot of land at Coshquin on which it was proposed to build between thirty and thirty-six houses wherein it was the intention of the Rural Council to re-house certain families from Springtown.

The committee directed the town clerk to inquire from the Rural Council the approximate date when it expected to have the proposed houses at Coshquin ready for occupation.

10 January 1961
The old railway line down by the burn was purchased by the Corporation when the Corporation agreed in principle to pay to The Honourable the Irish Society the sum of £95 for the disused trench at Springtown.

3 March 1961
The argument about housing responsibility continued between the Corporation and the Rural District Council. When a letter dated 21 February 1961 from the secretary of the Rural District Council was submitted regarding the Corporation's request for assistance by the Rural Council in re-housing Springtown Camp residents, the committee directed the town clerk to convey to the Rural Council its disappointment and regret that the council had not found it possible to proceed more quickly in co-operating with the Corporation in the re-housing operations necessary for the ultimate clearance of Springtown Camp.

The housing manager intimated that he had received a call from Patrick Gibbons, 'Mount Carmel', Devon Park, Galway, offering £40 for Hut 210 at the camp. The committee agreed to accept the offer.

The committee adjourned consideration of a petition sent by a number of tenants of huts at Springtown, stating they would have no objections should William Morrin be given possession of vacant Hut 168d.

21 March 1961
Families were still desperate for any sort of housing as squatting into huts in the camp continued. A report dated 15 March 1961 from housing manager Murphy was submitted setting out details of squatters who had unlawfully broken into and occupied four huts at the camp. The committee agreed that the circumstances of the squatters were distressing, but were unanimous in their decision that their present policy relating to the clearance of huts at Springtown remained unchanged.

4 May 1961
There was much anger in the camp when evictions were sought and granted in court against five families at the camp. The Corporation directed their solicitor to proceed with his steps to recover the said huts. The people of the camp signed petitions condemning the evictions of families with young children.

Wednesday 31 May 1961
Terrible scenes took place in the camp as bailiffs evicted Charles McCarron, wife Kathleen and children, the youngest just two weeks old, William Morrin, his wife Margaret and their children, and the family of Philip and Claire Green and their children.

6 July 1961
Huts were now disappearing at a steadier rate as nine more were demolished; some families were re-housed while others took the boat to England. Once again, the Corporation condemned the Rural District Council for their lack of action in housing families at the camp. They blamed them for the delay in closing the camp.

Wednesday 15 January 1964
Willie Campbell, the Springtown Camp committee chairman, together with eighty women from the camp, kicked off the protest campaign by distributing leaflets in Derry's city centre, protesting about conditions in the camp.

Thursday 16 January 1964
The Rural District Council and the Corporation began their policy of offering houses out in the country to residents. Willie Edgar, joint-chairman of the Springtown Camp Housing Committee, was offered a house in Strathfoyle. The offer was refused.

Tuesday 28 January 1964
Willie Campbell and Willie Edgar, joint-chairmen of the camp committee, led a protest march of 200 people from Springtown Camp to Derry's Guildhall, demanding the housing of all families from the camp and closure of the camp as soon as possible. The Corporation received Campbell and Edgar. Both men called for the Corporation to put aside their political and religious differences and work together to end the nightmare of the camp's families. The Corporation said they noted a handbill dated January 1964 signed: The Men, Women and Children of Springtown Camp.

February 1964
The Presbytery of Derry called on the Corporation to house all the families of Springtown Camp without delay. The Young Unionists condemned the Corporation for their handling of the Springtown situation. They asked the members of the Corporation how they would like to live in such deplorable conditions. They concluded by saying all the residents should have been housed years ago.

March 1964
A proposal by Councillor James Doherty was seconded by Councillor P Friel that the Derry Rural Council be urged to issue a slum-clearance order for Springtown Camp. The proposal was carried.

Thursday 9 April 1964
Members of the camp committee met with the Corporation in the Guildhall. Mayor Albert Anderson, housing manager DAS Murphy, town clerk RH Henderson, and councillors A McGowan, J Doherty, JT McFarland and P Friel were in attendance.

Representing the families of Springtown Camp were Jimmy Deery, Willie Morrin and Charles O'Hagan; it was stated that the fourth member, Willie Edgar, was unable to attend the meeting.

The camp deputation questioned the Corporation members on why the families in the camp hadn't received the allocation of re-lets that had been promised two months earlier. Furthermore, they asked the housing sub-committee about their intentions concerning the future of the sub-tenants of the camp. They stated that some tenants were being victimised because relatives were sharing their huts. They called for all tenants to be housed. They also said all the residents of the camp wished to know how long they would have to endure living in such deplorable and primitive conditions. They also demanded a definite answer to when the camp would be closed. During discussions, the Springtown deputation agreed with the Corporation that between ten and fifteen tenants in the camp did not wish to be re-housed at that time.

6 May 1964
Rory Quigley, camp committee secretary, received an answer to his letter from Stormont Prime Minister Terence O'Neill. The prime minister was asked to visit the camp and see the conditions for himself. The PM replied he was considering their request.

23 May 1964
The Minister of Health summoned Derry Corporation and Rural District Council to a meeting in Stormont on the deteriorating situation at Springtown Camp.

4 June 1964
Camp committee secretary Rory Quigley, 99a Springtown Camp, wrote to the Corporation asking them to meet a deputation from the committee. They accordingly met Jimmy Deery and Johnny Doherty, who asked the Corporation to attend a meeting at the camp with the residents, the medical profession, the Unionist Party, Nationalist Party and the Rural Council. The Corporation declined the invitation.

16 June 1964
A petition signed by 21,428 people was presented to Stormont prime minister's private secretary J Malley by the camp committee. Meeting the committee at Stormont steps was Derry MP Eddie McAteer.

2 July 1964
Another eight huts were sold at a public auction held in the camp, along with a quantity of scrap iron. It realised an amount of £258 6s 6d (£258.33).

22 July 1964
With the entire population, medical practitioners, politicians and health authorities now demanding that the camp be closed without delay, the Minister of Health and Local Government called a meeting with the mayor, the chairman and vice-chairman of the Rural Council, the chairman of the Housing Trust and officials from all four bodies. The following was agreed by all in attendance:

1. The Housing Trust, the Corporation and the Rural Council agree to be responsible for re-housing one third of the remaining families

2. A detailed list of families at present be compiled by the Corporation and agreed by the three authorities

3. Any family who squats into a vacant hut after this list is compiled will be evicted by the Corporation

4. Each hut will be rendered unfit for habitation by the Corporation immediately it becomes vacant

5. Families will be offered a substantial proportion of houses as they become available and also of new houses being constructed

6. The three authorities will consult with each other on families to be housed

7. Any family refusing to accept suitable accommodation when offered will be evicted from Springtown Camp.

The minister drew each authority's attention to paragraph five. He concluded by saying he was most anxious that the re-housing of the residents of the camp should commence at the earliest possible date.

27 July 1964
The above public statement on an agreement by the three housing authorities accepting responsibility for the re-housing of all the residents of Springtown seemed conclusive. No further statements, meetings or correspondence could be traced from the Springtown Camp Housing Committee from that date. Some of the committee were re-housed a few months later. It is without doubt that the emergence of the camp committee greatly hastened the closure of the camp. Despite this statement of intent, it was to take more than another three years before the last residents were re-housed.

3 September 1964
At a meeting convened by the Ministry of Health and Local Government, the Housing Trust, the Rural District Council and the Corporation agreed to work together to close the camp within a reasonable time.

March 1965
Lester Jackson complained to the Corporation of trespass on his property through the fence dividing his property with the camp. He demanded through his solicitor that the Corporation repair the fence. They agreed to do this.

1 July 1965
Housing manager Murphy reported that the bridge that covered the old railway line was in a dangerous condition and needed to be demolished. The cost of such demolition and clearance of rubble was £110.

3 September 1965
The Corporation agreed to sell Springtown Camp to the Ministry of Commerce as soon as the huts were demolished. Housing manager Murphy recommended that the services of Mick Power – a labourer employed at the camp who was due to retire on 2 August 1965, having reached the age of sixty-five – be retained in view of the work pending for clearance of the camp. The Corporation agreed.

21 October 1965
Old bridge over the railway line demolished.

4 November 1965
The Corporation agreed to sell Springtown Camp to the Ministry of Commerce for industrial purposes for the agreed sum of £40,000, which was ten times the amount they paid The Honourable the Irish Society for the lands.

A deputation of ten families from Springtown Camp led by Mrs E McCarron requested a meeting with the housing sub-committee. The committee declined their request.

12 May 1966
The Rural Council stated that they would not make further offers to any of the residents who had refused an offer of a house. They proposed that these families now go to the bottom of the list.

1 December 1966
The remaining families refused to be housed miles out in the country, as most of their children were born in the camp. Derry Corporation gave warning that a 'notice to quit' would be served on the remaining residents of the camp.

2 February 1967
At Derry Court, ejectment notices were granted against the twelve remaining families at the camp, with decrees not being issued until 1 March 1967. The families appealed the decision. Bail was fixed at £25 in each case with one surety of £25.

8 February 1967
The remaining families refused to be housed miles away. A meeting was held in Dundonald House, Belfast. Present were: Ministry of Health and Social Services, Ministry of Home Affairs, Ministry of Development, Derry Corporation, County Council, Rural District Council and Northern Ireland Housing Trust.

The meeting expressed concern over the situation in Springtown Camp and there was major disagreement between the bodies present. It was suggested that the Housing Trust should house the remaining families inside the boundary and, in turn, the Rural Council could house the same number of Housing Trust tenants. The Housing Trust refused the suggestion, stating that they didn't want to be involved further with the problem of the camp.

5 March 1967
Wilfred Denis McNutt became the last baby born in Springtown Camp. He was baptised on this date in St Patrick's Church, Pennyburn.

30 March 1967
A meeting between the Rural Council and the Corporation's housing committee was held at the Rural Council offices at Altnagelvin, Derry, concerning the remaining tenants at Springtown Camp. The meeting achieved nothing.

July 1967
Corporation solicitors informed the committee that appeals by the families of the camp would not be heard until after the August holidays and that it was unlikely that possession of the huts would be achieved before the end of the year. Housing manager Murphy told the committee that the Northern Ireland Housing Trust would offer houses to four families at Creggan, the Rural Council would offer houses to four families at Lettershandoney and the Corporation would house two families. All the families had been informed of this.

Wednesday 11 October 1967
Kitty Lynch turned out the light and closed the door of her hut at 104 Springtown Camp for the last time. The story of Springtown Camp had ended.

After the Camp

3 November 1967
Mick Power worked his last day at the empty Springtown Camp.

31 December 1967
The man who had many a verbal battle with residents of the camp, Mr Dennis Arthur Murphy, Derry Corporation Housing Manager, resigned, just several weeks after Springtown Camp was closed.

Appendix B
Tenant Listings 1947–66

First List of Tenants in Springtown Camp, 1947–48

McCready, John and Annie	1	Green, Agnes	26
Burns, Charlotte, Victor and Frederick	2	Doherty, Thomas and Elizabeth	27
		O'Reilly, Patrick and Bridget	28
Thompson, Jean and James	2	O'Donnell, Annie	29
Armstrong, William and Catherine	3	Murray, Isobel	29
Sweeney, George and Catherine	4	Sweeney, James and Margaret	29a
Fleming, Joseph and Bridget	5	Sweeney, Mary and Evelyn	29a
Curley, Eileen	6	Smith, John and Martha	29b
Holden, Samuel and Sarah	7	Moore, Patrick and Susan	29c
Coyle, Dennis and Mary	8	Abraham, Albert and Sarah	29d
Lewis, Bernard and Isobel	9	Cunningham, Edward	30
McMenamin, Eileen	10	McCann, Lily, Joseph and Elizabeth	30
McMonagle, Charles and Kathleen	11		
Quigley, Thomas and Mary	12	Cullen, William and Susan	30a
Dalton, Eugene and Mary	13	Jones, Frederick and Sarah	30b
Sharpe, Margaret and Reginald	14	Carr, Eileen Grace	30c
McCloskey, John and Matilda	15	McGilloway, Thomas, Margaret and William	30d
Gilmore, Henry and Catherine	16		
O'Hara, James and Grace	17	Melarky, Joseph and Mary	31
McGinley, James and Nan	18	Gormley, Patrick and Mary	31a
Hegarty, James and Sarah	19	Brown, Daniel and Sarah	31b
McCafferty, Patrick and Kathleen	20	Doherty, James and Catherine	31c
Cullen, Hugh and Matilda	21	McCourt, James, Margaret, Henry and Mary	31d
Murray, William and Margaret	22		
McCourt, Thomas and Mary	23	Farren, Patrick and Elizabeth	32
Bradley, Francis and Catherine	24	Sweeney, John and Mary	32a
Diamond, Jeannie and Kathleen	25	Thompson, Robert and Pearl	33
McGlinchey, Michael and Mary	26	Eldeakin, James, Winifred and Thomas	33a

Doherty, Denis and Elizabeth	**33b**	Gallagher, James and Letitia	**64**
Cook, Susan	**33c**	McGee, Thomas and Mary	**65**
Sweeney, Daniel and Rosie	**33d**	Dougherty, Robert and Eileen	**66**
Campbell, Sarah	**33e**	McNair, Samuel and Rebecca	**67**
Campbell, James and Theresa	**33f**	Moore, John and Marguerite	**68**
Cassidy, James and Mary	**33g**	Maguire, Francis, Margaret and	
Flynn, Kathleen	**33h**	Margaret (Jnr)	**69**
Divin, James and Florence	**34**	McGowan, Anthony and Helen	**69a**
Smith, James and Molly	**35**	McDermott, David and Francis	**69b**
Nash, William and Mary Ann	**36**	Hegarty, William and Annie	**70**
Collett, Ernest and Elizabeth	**37**	Gallagher, James and Mary	**71**
Moore, Thomas and Bridget	**38**	Canning, Robert and Rebecca	**72**
McDaid, Pius and Agnes	**39**	Donaghy, Bernard, Sarah Jane,	
Doherty, George and Mary Ann	**40**	Alexander and Frank	**73**
Gallagher, Charles and Kathleen	**42**	Dean, Isobella	**74**
Donnelly, John and Mary	**43**	Gallagher, Cecilia	**74**
McLaughlin, Daniel and Mary	**44**	Fleming, William and Sophia	**74a**
Lynch, Thomas and Margaret	**45**	English, John and Frances	**74b**
McGinley, Bernard and Ellen	**46**	McGowan, George and Susan	**75**
Doherty, Bernard and Elizabeth	**47**	McCrudden, Frank and Mary	
Clifford, John, Margaret and		Anne	**76**
Mary	**48**	Feeney, Harry and Kathleen	**77**
Killen, Philip and Molly	**49**	Shields, John and Nora	**78**
Clark, George, Ada and Maurice	**50**	McElholm, Michael, Sarah and	
Quigley, William and Ethel	**51**	Mary Ann	**79**
Wilson, Michael and Isobella	**52**	McLaughlin, Eugene and	
Callaghan, Patrick and Jeannie	**53**	Catherine Agnes	**80**
Bridge, Edward and Rose Ann	**54**	Donnelly, Margaret	**81**
McCusker, Michael and Mary	**55**	Murray, John and Molly	**82**
McClean, James and Mary	**56**	King, Violet	**83**
Norby, Francis and Margaret	**57**	Cook, Sidney and Elizabeth	**84**
Duffy, Kathleen	**58**	McDermott, Minnie	**85**
Harkin, Patrick and Margaret	**59**	McGowan, James and Hannah	**86**
Walsh, William and Winifred	**60**	Porter, Samuel and Kathleen	**87**
Kearney, Margaret	**61**	Meehan, Patrick and Mary Ann	**88**
Doherty, James and Mary	**62**	Saunders, Johnny and Grace	**89**
McLaughlin, Agnes	**63**	McGlinchey, Andrew	**89**
Nelson, Gertrude	**63**	Smith, Melvyn and Elizabeth	**89a**
McCauley, John and Sarah	**63a**	Deery, James and Mary Ann	**89b**
Deery, William and Mary	**63b**	Ryan, Edward and Elizabeth	**89b**
Coyle, William and Mary Ellen	**63c**	Rankin, Daniel and Mary	**90**
O'Hagan, Edward J and		Armstrong, Robert and Sarah	**91**
Isobella	**63d**	McDevitt, John and Ellen	**92**

Saunders, William, John and William (Jnr)	93
O'Donnell, William and Mary	94
Bradley, Thomas L and Eileen	95
Brown, Patrick	95
Campbell, Joseph and Nora	96
Canning, Joseph and Frances	97
Gallagher, Ellen and Elizabeth	98
Park, John and Kathleen	98a
McCallion, William and Joan B	98b
McCloskey, Elizabeth	98c
O'Connor, James and Sarah	98d
Lliffe, Maurice and Mary Catherine	98e
McShane, Thomas and Isobel	98f
Burke, Patrick and Bridget	98g
Hegarty, Daniel and Theresa	98h
Shields, Manasses and Ellen	98i
Molloy, Thomas and Isabella	98j
Cullen, Hugh and Mary	98k
Nash, Alexander and Bridget	98l
Meenan, Patrick and Molly	98m
Johnston, Alexander and Elizabeth	98n
Lynn, Joseph and Catherine	98o
Tyldsley, Mary	99
Bryson, Margaret	99
Canny, Samuel and Kathleen	99a
Doherty, Kathleen	100
McLaughlin, Jack and Kathleen	101
McGuinness, Abraham and Eva	102
Crumlish, Charles and Susan	103
Thompson, Frederick and Margaret	104
Lynch, Edward and Kathleen	105
Adcock, Ralph and Dorothy	106
Robinson, Charles and Mary	107
King, John and Margaret	108
Stewart, George and Nellie	109
McElwee, John and Susan	110
McGowan, Samuel and Margaret	111
Smith, Mary	112
Henry, Frank and Mary J	113
Sweeney, John and Mary	114
McCready, Edward and Ellen	115
Lynch, Charles and Sarah	116
Montgomery, John and Mary A	117
Craig, Andrew and Mary	118
Harkin, Thomas and Mary	119
Brolly, Henry, Agnes and Mary	120
Burnside, Robert and Kathleen	121
Devine, Elizabeth	122
McClean, Matthew and Minnie	123
Devine, Patrick, Margaret and Patrick (Jnr)	124
Gamble, Robert and Martha	125
Colby, Ellen	126
Deery, Owen and Ellen	127
Scanlon, William, Margaret and James	128
McClelland, James and Annie	129
O'Reilly, James and Rose	131
Moore, John and Annie	132
Doherty, Joseph, Ellen and Patrick	133
McGinley, Patrick and Kathleen	133
Mitchell, Benjamin and Mary Ann	134
Wheeler, Frederick and Eileen	135
Clarke, Robert and Frances	136
Fox, Patrick and Frances	137
Sweeney, Eileen	138
Irwin, John and Annie	139
McCloskey, James and Annie	140
Shields, Edward	140
Brennan, John, Margaret, Daniel and Ita	141
Gallagher, George and Mary	142
McCarron, James, Frances and Charles	143
Delpinto, Raphael and Mary	144
Kelly, Edward and Mary B	145
Duffy, William and Ellen	146
Baldrick, Thomas and Kathleen	146a
Carlin, Hugh and Isobella	146b
Dolby, Earnest and Sarah Anne	147
Moore, Patrick and Rose Ann	147a
Coyle, Charles and Theresa	148
Moran, John and Kathleen	149
Ward, Henry and Ellen	150

O'Donnell, Francis and Grace	150a
Cromie, Robert and Annie	151
McConnell, William and Bridget	151a
McConnell, Ambrose and Philomena	151b
Quinn, James and Mary	152
Gormley, John and Dorothy	152a
Moore, Edward P, Mary and Edward P (Jnr)	153
Hemmett, Emily C	153
Griffin, John and Mary	154
Canning, Mary Ann	154
O'Donnell, William and Madge	154a
Hutton, James and Ellen	154b
Gallagher, Michael and Mary	154c
Tracey, Vincent and Millicent	154d
Brandon, James and Mary	154e
McCloskey, Edward and Mary Ann	155
Doherty, Frank and Margaret	156
Sweeney, Patrick and Margaret	157
Jennings, John P and Mary Rosa	158
Friel, William and Ellen	159
McGill, James and Bridget R	160
Boyle, James and Ellen	161
Duffy, Hugh and Catherine	162
Robinson, Samuel, Mary, Elizabeth and Sarah	163
Simms, Mary Josephine	164
Doherty, William and Rose	165
Burns, Betty and Ivy	165a
Toland, Patrick and Elizabeth	166
McGill, Frank and Martha	166a
Burns, James, Annie and Margaret	167
Fleming, Margaret J and Sarah	167a
Ferry, Margaret	167a
McIntyre, George and Margaret	168
Sharkey, Edward and Bridget	168a
McDermott, Charles and Frances	168b
Morrin, James and Kathleen	168c
O'Connor, Elizabeth and Harriett	168d
Deeney, James and Josephine	169
Walsh, Patrick and Georgina	170
McClelland, Alphonsus and Margaret M	171
Ramsey, Albert and Annie	172
Hillen, Charles, Mary, Susan and Susanna	173
Fox, John and Mary	174
Dean, George and Ellen	175
Curran, William and Kathleen	176
Shields, John and Louisa	178
Doherty, Charles and Mary	179
Quigley, Samuel and Bridget	180
Harkin, John and Sarah	181
Ferguson, William and Martha	182
Glenn, William and Elizabeth	183
McCafferty, Vincent and Nora	184
Curley, Charles and Ellen	185
Fleming, John and Patricia	186
Shields, Andrew and Mary	187
Mitchell, Gerald and Bridget	188
Ward, William and Kathleen	189
Young, Thomas and Lily	190
Mitchell, Robert	191
Quigley, Charles and Annie	192
Gallagher, Francis and Lily	193
Harrigan, Alphonsus and Margaret	194
Doolin, Robert and Ellen	195
Hyndman, Charles and Annie	196
Friel, Patrick and Catherine	197
McGonagle, Edward and Rose	198
Thompson, Joseph and Mary	199
Donaghy, John and Bridget	200
McWilliams, James and Sarah	201
Power, Michael and Dora	202
Burke, Frank and Bridget	203
Bryson, Thomas and Mary	204
Wilson, John and Sarah	205
Nash, Frank and Susan	206
Hamilton, Henry and Ellen	207
Whoriskey, John and Josephine	208
Campbell, Francis and Catherine	209
Ogle, Frank and Nellie	210
Killen, Alexander and Jeannie	211
McGeady, Mary	212

Mooney, Margaret	213	Kerrigan, Michael and Margaret	225
Probert, Albert and Bridget	214	Ward, Patrick J and Nora	226
Gormley, John and Elizabeth	215	Sheehan, Daniel and Sarah	227
Duddy, William and Mary	216	McMenamin, Frank	227
McDonald, James and Lana	217	Clingan, Rebecca	228
Brown, Hugh and Ellen	218	McLaughlin, Sarah	228
McMonagle, Hugh and Mary	219	McLoone, Mary and Mary (Jnr)	229
Duddy, Annie and Robert	220	Friel, James and Margaret	230
Spratt, Mary	221	Kelly, John and Rose	231
Lynch, Patrick and Bridget	222	McCormack, John and Edna	232
McCourt, James and Elizabeth	223	Boyle, Michael J and Bridget E	233
Thompson, Nicholas and Florence	224	Bradley, Daniel and Elizabeth	234

List of Families in Springtown Camp, 1953

Burns, Charles, Charlotte and Henry	2	Edgar, Willie and Mary	28
		Campbell, Patrick and Sarah	29
King, Violet	3	Saunders, William and Mary	29a
Sweeney, Annie	4	Sweeney, Margaret	29a
Fleming, Joseph and Bridget	5	Organ, James and Ellen	29b
Curley, Ellen	6	Moore, Patrick and Susan	29c
Holden, Sammy and Sarah	7	Moore, Thomas and Bridget	29d
Brolly, Margaret	8	Doherty, Elizabeth	30
Lewis, Bernard and Isobel	9	Cullen, William and Susan	30a
McMenamin, Eileen and Margaret	10	Harkin, John and Sarah	30b
McMonagle, Charles and Kathleen M	11	Montgomery, Mary	30c
		McCafferty, Patrick and Kathleen	30d
Quigley, Thomas and Mary	12	Buchanan, Sarah and Susan	31
Dalton, Eugene and Mary	13	Delapena, Susan	31
Hughes, Sarah	15	Gormley, Patrick, Mary and James	31a
Knipe, Mary	16		
Gilmore, Henry and Catherine	16	McGilloway, Thomas, William and Margaret	31b
O'Hara, James and Grace	17		
McGinley, Mary Ann	18	Higgins, Mary	31c
Moore, Daniel and Alice	19	McCourt, James and Margaret	31d
Angrove, Margaret	20	Farren, Patrick and Elizabeth	32
Cullen, Hugh and Matilda	21	Kavanagh, Gladys	32
McCourt, Mary	23	Sweeney, John, Ellen and Mary	32a
Bradley, Francis, Leo and Catherine	24	McLaughlin, Ellen	33
		Doherty, Dennis and Elizabeth	33b
Diamond, Jeannie and Kathleen	25	Moore, Patrick and Mary	33c
Tierney, Edward and Agnes	26	Sweeney, Danny and Rosie	33d

Colby, Ellen	**33e**	McNair, Samuel and Rebecca	67
Campbell, James	**33f**	Clarke, Robert and Frances	68
McLaughlin, Bridget	**33f**	O'Hagan, Charles and Margaret	69
Nelson, Gertrude	**33g**	McGowan, Anthony and Helen	**69a**
Doherty, John and Mary	**33h**	McDermott, David and Frances	**69b**
Devine, James and Florence	34	Hegarty, William and Annie	70
Smith, Seamus and Mary	35	McLaughlin, George and Marjorie	71
Nash, William and Mary Ann	36	Canning, Bernard, Robert and	
Collett, Ernest and Elizabeth	37	Rebecca	72
Doherty, Kathleen M	38	Muir, Robert	73
O'Reilly, Margaret	39	Deane, Isobel	74
O'Donnell, Daniel and Mary	40	Gallagher, Cecelia	74
Duffy, Mary Ann	40	George, Ellen	**74a**
McConomy, Robert and Jeannie	41	Green, Rebecca	**74a**
Gallagher, Charles and Kathleen	42	English, John and Frances	**74b**
Donnelly, John and Mary	43	Burke, Hannah	75
McLaughlin, Daniel and Mary	44	McLaughlin, Veronica	75
Lynch, Thomas and Margaret	45	Feeney, Harry and Kathleen	77
Coyle, Mary Ellen	46	Parsons, Catherine	78
Clifford, John and Margaret	48	Rodgers, Elizabeth	78
Killen, Phillip and Mary	49	McCafferty, John and Elizabeth	79
Harkin, Hugh and Mary	50	McLaughlin, Eugene and Agnes	80
Quigley, William and Ethel	51	Donnelly, Margaret	81
Wilson, Isabella	52	Gillespie, Gladys	82
Callaghan, Jeannie	53	Lynch, Patrick and Bridget	83
Bridge, Edward and Rose Anne	54	Cook, Sidney and Elizabeth	84
McCusker, Michael and Mary	55	McDermott, Mary	85
McClean, Mary	56	Porters, Samuel and Kathleen	87
Norby, Francis and Margaret	57	Meehan, Patrick and Mary Anne	88
Duffy, William	58	Saunders, William, John and Grace	89
McGinley, Patrick and Kathleen	59	McGlinchey, Matilda	89
Harkin, Mary Ann	60	Smith, Elizabeth and Melvin	**89a**
Wilson, Mary	60	Deery, James, Mary and Anne	**89b**
Walsh, Winifred	60	Rankin, Daniel and Mary	90
Kearney, Madge and Sarah	61	Armstrong, Robert and Sarah	91
McConway, Nellie	61	Bonnar, Frank and Susan	92
Griffin, John and Mary	63	Smith, Mary	93
Gormley, William and Mary	**63a**	O'Donnell, William and Mary	94
Deery, William and Mary	**63b**	Bradley, Thomas L and Eileen	95
Barr, Richard, Neil and Susan	**63b**	Brown, Patrick	95
O'Kane, Robert and Sarah	**63c**	Canning, Joseph and Frances	97
O'Hagan, John and Isobel	**63d**	Canning, Frank and Mary Anne	98
Shiels, Daniel and Bridget	64	Hasson, Daniel	**98b**

McCloskey, Elizabeth	98c	Gamble, Robert and Martha	125
O'Connor, John and Sarah	98d	Scanlon, William and Margaret	128
Lliffe, Maurice	98e	Unwin, Sarah	128
Doherty, Patrick and Annie F	98e	McClelland, James and Annie	129
Hegarty, Daniel and Theresa	98h	McShane, Thomas and Isobel	130
Fitzpatrick, Robert, Agnes and Hester	98i	O'Reilly, James, Ida and Rose	131
		Doherty, Joseph and Ellen	133
McCarron, Patrick and Evelyn C	98j	Burke, Patrick and Bridget	134
Nash, Alex and Bridget	98l	Harkin, Frank and Jeannie	135
Meenan, Mary T	98m	McGeady, Mary	136
Johnstone, Alex and Elizabeth	98n	McCallion, Margaret	136
Lynn, Joseph and Catherine	98o	Fox, Patrick and Frances	137
O'Kane, Margaret	98r	Melaugh, William James	137
Adcock, Ralph and Dorothy	99	Sweeney, Eileen	138
Canney, Samuel and Cathleen A	99a	Hasson, Alex and Margaret	139
Cassidy, James and Mary B	100	McCloskey, James and Annie	140
McLaughlin, John and Kathleen	101	Brennan, John and Margaret	141
McGuinness, Abraham and Eva M	102	Gallagher, Mary	142
Crumlish, Charles and Susan	103	McCarron, James, Frances and Charles	143
Thompson, Frederick, James and Margaret	104	Delpinto, Raphael and Mary Ann	144
		Kelly, Edward, Mary B	145
Lynch, Edward and Kathleen	105	Duffy, William and Ellen	146
King, John and Margaret	108	Baldrick, Thomas and Kathleen	146a
Stewart, George and Nellie	109	Carlin, Hugh, Isabella, Charles and Hugh (Jnr)	146b
McElwee, John and Susan	110		
Kelly, Mary	111	Campbell, Frank, Catherine and Isobel	148
McGowan, Samuel and Margaret	111		
Sweeney, John and Mary	114	Ward, John and Josephine M	150
McCready, Edward, Ellen, Susan and Patricia	115	O'Donnell, Francis and Grace	150a
Lynch, Charles, Sarah and Patrick	116	Doherty, Bridget	151
		McConnell, William and Bridget	151a
Ferry, John	117	McConnell, Ambrose and Philomena	151b
Killen, Kathleen	118		
Cooke, Susan	119	Quinn, James and Mary	152
Moore, Edward and Anna R	119	Duddy, Robert and Annie	152a
Brolly, Michael, Agnes and Anna	120	Killen, Jeannie	154
		McElholm, Michael and Mary Ann	154a
Parke, Johnny and Catherine	121		
McBrearty, John and Annie	122	Bradley, James and Mary	154b
Henry, Francis, Mary and Jane	123	Gallagher, Michael and Mary	154c
Spratt, William and Mary Ann	124	McCloskey, Mary A	155

McCarron, James and Frances	156	Ward, William and Kathleen	189
Sweeney, Patrick and Margaret	157	Young, Thomas and Elizabeth	190
Jennings, John and Mary Rose	158	Cassidy, Dorothy	192
Monteith, Patrick and Alice	160	Gallagher, Francis and Elizabeth	193
Robinson, Samuel and Mary	163	Canning, James and Annie	195
Brandon, James and Mary	164	Campbell, William and Margaret	196
Duddy, Elizabeth and Margaret	165a	Friel, Kathleen	197
Burns, Ivy	165a	McGonigle, Edward and Rose	198
Toland, Patrick and Elizabeth	166	McGinley, Bernard and Ellen	200
McGill, Francis and Martina	166a	McWilliams, James and Sarah	201
Burns, Hugh, Annie, James, Margaret and Philip	167	Jennings, James and Mary Elizabeth	202
Ferry, Bridget	167a	Callaghan, James and Bridget	204
Fleming, Sarah	167a	Hamilton, Henry, Ellen and Mary Ann	207
Long, George and Theresa	168	Whoriskey, John and Winifred	208
Mooney, Thomas and Annie	168a	Brown, Robert and Veronica	209
Morrin, James, Kathleen and Kathleen (Jnr)	168c	Sweeney, John and Mary	210
Connor, Harriett and Elizabeth	168d	Probert, Bridget	214
Deeney, James and Ellen	169	Duddy, William and Mary	216
Slater, Mary E	170	McDonald, James and Susan	217
McClelland, Alphonsus and Margaret	171	Brown, Hugh and Ellen	218
Leppard, James and Margaret	173	McMonagle, Hugh and Mary	219
Dean, George and Ellen	175	McCourt, James and Elizabeth	223
Curran, William and Kathleen	176	Thompson, Nicholas and Florence	224
Doherty, James and Mary	177	Kerrigan, Michael and Margaret	225
Shields, John and Louisa	178	Sheehan, Daniel and Sarah	227
Doherty, Annie R	182	Clingan, Rebecca	228
Curley, Charles and Ellen	185	McLaughlin, Sarah	228
Stanistreet, Albert and Margaret	185	McLoone, Mary and Mary (Jnr)	229
Shields, Mary	187	Friel, James and Margaret	230
Mitchell, Bridget and Gerald	188	Kelly, Rose	231
		Boyle, Michael and Bridget	233

By 1960 there were 132 huts remaining in Springtown Camp housing 160 families.

Lynch, Thomas and Margaret	3	Bradley, James and Mary	13
Fleming, Joseph and Bridget	5	Adcock, Ralph and Dorothy	15
Holden, Sammy, Sarah and Mary D	7	Gilmour, Henry and Catherine	16
Spratt, William, Mary and Ann	8	Knipe, Mary	16
Quigley, William and Ethel	10	O'Neill, Margaret	16

O'Hara, James and Grace	17	O'Donnell, Mary	40
McGinley, James, Mary and Ann	18	Duffy, Mary Ann	40
Cullen, Hugh, Matilda and Nancy	21	Morrison, Arthur	40
		Donnelly, John and Mary	43
McLaughlin, Charles and Bridget	23	McLaughlin, Daniel and Mary	44
Gallagher, John and Margaret	25	Harkin, Hugh and Mary	50
Moore, Mary	26	Hutton, Michael and Mary	50
Semple, Emily	26	Bridge, Edward and Rose Anne	54
Jackson, William and Elizabeth	27	Walsh, Winifred	60
Edgar, William and Mary	28	Conway, Ellen	61
Campbell, Patrick and Sarah	29	Duffy, William and Margaret	63
Saunders, William and Mary	29a	McBrearty, John and Annie	63a
Sweeney, Margaret	29a	O'Hagan, George and Mary	63b
Doherty, Leo and Ellen	29a	Green, Phillip and Clare	63c
Lynch, Charles and Sarah	29b	McKeever, Josephine	63c
Callaghan, James and Bridget	29c	O'Hagan, John, Isabel and William	63d
Moore, Thomas and Bridget	29d		
Collett, Ernest, Elizabeth and Morris	30	Doherty, Robert and Bridget	68
		Doherty, John and Mary	69b
O'Reilly, James and Margaret	30a	McDermott, David, Frances and Kathleen	69b
Deane, George and Ellen	30b		
Lewis, Isobel and Hugh	30c	McLaughlin, George and Marjorie	71
Quinn, James and Mary	30d	Parsons, Catherine	72
Toland, Patrick	30d	Brown, Veronica	72
Moore, Edward and Anna Rose	31	George, Ellen	74a
Gormley, Gerald, Patrick, Mary and James	31a	Green, Rebecca	74a
		English, John	74b
Slater, Mary	31b	Feeney, Henry and Kathleen	77
Curley, Charles, Elizabeth and Ellen	31c	Canavan, James, Margaret, Edward and Stephen	80
Holden, Ronald and Isabel	31c		
Jennings, John and Mary Rose	31d	Kelly, Margaret	84
Farren, Patrick and Elizabeth	32	McDermott, Mary	85
Trueman, Kathleen	32	Meehan, Mary Ann	88
McLaughlin, Ellen	33	Smith, Mary and John	89a
Campbell, William and Margaret	33a	Deery, James, Mary and Ann	89b
Divin, James and Florence	33c	Armstrong, Robert and Sarah	91
Sweeney, Daniel and Rose	33d	Porter, Samuel and Kathleen	92
Kiernan, Ann	33e	Canning, Joseph and Frances	97
Moore, James and Bridget	33e	Dunn, Martha and Stephen	98
Campbell, James and Ellen	33f	Moore, John and Annie	98b
McCarron, Evelyn	33g	McCloskey, Elizabeth	98c
Coyle, Robert and Mary Ellen	33h	Burke, Edward, Hannah and Patrick	98d
Lynch, Margaret	33h		

Cooke, Hugh and Margaret	98e	Campbell, Francis and Ellen	148
Doherty, Patrick, Annie F and Arthur	98e	Clarke, Robert and Frances	151
		McConnell, William and Bridget	151a
Hegarty, Daniel and Teresa	98h	Doherty, Mary and Margaret	151b
Fitzpatrick, Leo and Hester	98i	Killen, Jeannie and Frances	154a
Deery, James and Jean	98j	McCloskey, Edward and Mary	155
O'Kane, John and Margaret	98k	McAdams, Thomas and Jean	155
Rankin, Daniel and Mary	99a	McCarron, Frank, Margaret, Mary and Frances	156
McLaughlin, John and Kathleen	101		
Craig, John and Elizabeth	102	Robinson, Samuel and Mary	163
Gallagher, Daniel	102	Brandon, James and Mary	164
Crumlish, Charles and Susan	103	McCallion, Annie	164
Brolly, Henry and Mary	104	Duddy, Elizabeth	165a
Lynch, Edward, Kathleen and Mary	105	Burns, Hannah	165a
		O'Hagan, Charles and Margaret	166a
King, John and Margaret	108	Burns, Phillip, Margaret, James and Margaret (Jnr)	167
Stewart, George and Ellen	109		
Brolly, Michael and Anna	120	Harkin, Charles and Nancy	167
Parke, John and Catherine	121	Fleming, Sarah	167a
Scanlon, William, James and Jane	128	Long, Patrick and Patricia	168
		Mooney, Thomas and Annie	168a
Anderson, Joseph and Margaret	128	Morrin, William, Kathleen, Margaret and Kathleen (Jnr)	168c
Jennings, James, Mary Elizabeth	132		
Doherty, Joseph and Ellen	133	O'Connor, Harriet	168d
O'Hagan, James and Rose	134	McClelland, Alphonsus and Margaret	171
Wilkinson, William and Martha	135		
		Leppard, James, Margaret and Robert	173
McGeady, Mary	136		
Quigley, Robert and Kathleen	136	Curran, William and Kathleen	176
Fox, Patrick, Frances and Patrick (Jnr)	137	Mooney, Margaret	178
		Callaghan, James	178
O'Hagan, Charles and Bridget	138	Kelly, Edward and Mary B	185
McLaughlin, John, Agnes and Mary Ann	139	Shiels, Andrew and Mary	187
		Henry, Frank and Mary Jane	198
Sweeney, Margaret	140	McGinley, Bernard and Lena	200
Brennan, Margaret, Wilfred, Anna and Sheila	141	Sweeney, John and Mary	210
		McDonald, James and Susan	217
McNutt, John and Margaret	141	McMonagle, Hugh, Mary and Mary (Jnr)	219
Duffy, William, Eileen and Ellen	146		
McCullery, Kathleen	146	McCarron, Charles, Frances and James	225
Stanley, Elizabeth	146a		
Carlin, Hugh, Isabella and Hugh (Jnr)	146b	Friel, James and Margaret	227
		Boyle, Michael and Bridget	223

Families in Springtown Camp, 1966

Lynch, Thomas and Margaret	3	McLaughlin, George and Marjorie	105
Saunders, William James and Mary	10	Scanlon, James and Patrick	129
Morrison, Jane	18	Wilkinson, William, Martha, Mary and Brendan	135
Lynch, Charles and Sarah	29b		
McColgan, Hugh and Bridget	29c	McLaughlin, John, Agnes, Thomas and William	139
Kelly, Edward	32		
Kelly, James and Thomasina	33a	Morrin, Edward and Ellen	139
Kiernan, Ann	33e	McNutt, John and Margaret	141
McCallion, Dennis	33f	Duffy, William, Ellen, William (Jnr) and Kathleen	146
Parsons, Kathleen	74		
Kelly, Edward and Agnes	74	Walsh, Kathleen	151a
McCloskey, Elizabeth, Ronald and Patricia	98c	Robinson, Samuel and Elizabeth	165a
		Jackson, William and Elizabeth	167a
Morrin, William, John and Margaret	103	Henry, John and Phyllis	168
Lynch, Edward, Kathleen and George	104	Jennings, James and Mary Elizabeth	168a
Lynch, Mary, Frances and Sarah	104	Canavan, Edward, Margaret, Stephen and Martha	168c